A Handbook of
CHINESE
HEALING
HERBS

A Handbook of
CHINESE
HEALING
HERBS

Daniel Reid

BARNES
&NOBLE
BOOKS
NEW YORK

1999 Barnes & Noble Books

ISBN 0-7607-1907-1

Printed and bound in the United States of America

99 00 01 02 03   MC   9 8 7 6 5 4 3 2 1

BVG

CONTENTS

PREFACE

People these days frequently complain about the rising cost of health care, as though health were something money alone can buy. What they're really talking about is the rising cost of sickness, for sickness is what modern medicine caters to, not health. If people really cared for their health, which is not very costly, then sickness would be a rare aberration, not the common condition it has become throughout the world.

The reason it's so expensive to get sick today is that modern medicine too often neglects preventive health care, waiting instead until disease has become sufficiently entrenched in the human system to declare the patient "sick," then engaging the symptoms of the disease in a running battle of suppression. Modern medical care thus becomes an escalating war against increasingly severe symptoms, which continue to arise time and again throughout the body, while the root cause of the condition continues to fester unattended within. Many people are now convinced that the expensive chemicals, electronic gadgets, and radical surgical procedures employed by modern medicine to treat the symptoms of disease often do as much harm as good to the human system and sometimes create the conditions for even worse health problems later in life.

So what can we do to protect our health and nurse our minor ailments at home, before they become major diseases that require us to spend fortunes on modern drugs and surgery? We could begin by recognizing the fundamental tenet of traditional Chinese medicine that most health problems are self-inflicted and that the cause of most disease is the failure to take proper preventive measures. Next, we might recall that the best medicines and safest remedies still come, as they always have, from the mountains and valleys, fields and streams, forests and lakes that form our natural living environments.

Finally, we should take a hard, objective view at precisely what constitutes medicine. Many of the drugs introduced over the past fifty years by the modern medical industry produce unforeseen side effects; and many of them, such as antidepressants and sleeping pills, are highly addictive. By contrast, the traditional herbal remedies introduced in this book are founded on thousands of years of continuous research, development, and ongoing clinical experience, further validated today by scientific medical studies; these remedies are designed to "correct the root cause, not the superficial symptoms" of human disease.

Using Chinese herbal remedies at home is neither costly nor complicated, particularly when utilized for long-term preventive health care. When used to cure chronic or acute ailments, it's always best to consult a professional practitioner of traditional Chinese herbal medicine; even then you'll be preparing most of your remedies at home, in your own kitchen. The preparation of herbal remedies is more akin to cooking than it is to chemistry, and anyone who can boil an egg or make a pot of tea can easily learn how to prepare their own prescriptions at home.

This book was written to familiarize Western readers with the basic medical properties and therapeutic applications of some of the most important and effective herbs and herbal formulas used in traditional Chinese medicine from ancient times to the present day. The text combines traditional data, all of which were culled from original Chinese sources, with validating research from modern science. The latter was collected from various periodicals, journals, and herbal texts published in recent years by the growing number of Western herbal and medical scientists who are turning their talents to traditional medicine.

I wish to acknowledge the adept assistance provided by my wife, Chou Tung, who greatly facilitated the groundwork for this book by helping me sort and collate the mounds of traditional Chinese materials we collected for this project. As the Chinese would say, "She put her heart and liver into it," contributing not only her research but also valuable insights and practical points drawn from her own experience in the field.

Together we wish you a happy voyage of discovery as you set up your own "kitchen clinic" and start practicing the Way of Long Life *(chang shou dao)* with Chinese herbs.

A   Handbook of
CHINESE
HEALING
HERBS

INTRODUCTION

Traditional Chinese medicine (TCM) is the oldest and most comprehensive—and arguably the safest and most effective—system of human health care in the world. It has sustained the health and longevity of the world's longest ongoing civilization for over five thousand years, during which time its practitioners have carefully recorded the results of their meticulous research and clinical experience in medieval archives that span more than three thousand years of written history. Due to the ideogramic nature of the Chinese written language, which never changes with the vagaries of vernacular speech as alphabetic languages do, these ancient Chinese texts remain as clear and intelligible to contemporary practitioners today as they were to those who transcribed them through the ages.

Traditional Chinese medicine is like an ancient tree of knowledge that has survived the storms of history and continues to grow and bear fruit today. Deeply rooted in the Great Principle of Yin and Yang, the Five Elemental Energies, and other primordial principles of the Tao, it spreads its healing branches far and wide to cover "everything under heaven" in the broad field of human health care. Among the many branches that have sprouted from this venerable old tree, herbal medicine constitutes the biggest and most important one. It's also the most ancient: the Chinese credit the legendary emperor Shen Nung with discovering herbal medicine over five millennia ago. "Shen Nung tasted the myriad herbs," wrote the great Han dynasty historian Ssu-ma Chien two thousand years ago, "and so the art of medicine was born."

Chinese herbal medicine first evolved high up in the misty mountains of ancient China, as a by-product of Taoist hermits' perpetual search for the elusive Elixir of Life purported to confer physical immortality to hu-

3

mans. After thousands of years of trial-and-error experimentation with virtually every plant, animal, and mineral in nature's domain, the old Taoist sages finally learned that the only true "elixir" is an invisible force that lies hidden deep within the human system and that the only "immortality" any human can achieve is purely spiritual, not physical. But in the course of their search, the mountain hermits discovered that the plants they'd been fiddling with for so long did in fact have all sorts of practical therapeutic benefits for the physical, albeit mortal, human body, and that when correctly combined and properly prepared, they could confer health and long life to all human beings.

Modern Western medicine subscribes to the "single agent" theory of disease, whereby every disease is blamed on a specific external pathogen that invades the body from outside. Disease is thus attacked with knives, radiation, and powerful chemical agents designed to "kill" the alleged invader, and in the process these weapons often lay waste to the internal organs, impair immune response, and deplete vital energies, thereby sowing the seeds of even more severe ailments later.

Traditional Chinese medicine takes a different approach. It traces the root cause of all disease to critical imbalances and deficiencies among the various internal energies that govern and regulate the whole body. Whenever such states of imbalance or deficiency are left unchecked for too long, they eventually give rise to serious malfunctions in the body's biochemistry and internal organ systems, and that in turn impairs immunity, lowers resistance, and creates the conditions of vulnerability which *permit* germs, toxins, parasites, and other pathogens to gain a foothold in the body. By the time the obvious symptoms recognized by modern medicine appear, the disease has already reached a critical stage and is very difficult to cure. Moreover, symptoms of disease often manifest themselves in parts of the body far removed from the root cause, a phenomenon well known to traditional healers but usually lost on modern "specialists" trained to deal with only one part of the human body.

While modern Western medicine views disease as a malevolent external invasion by an enemy that must be killed, traditional Chinese medicine sees it more as a matter of "letting down your guard" and giving entry to the malevolent agents and energies that cause disease. Rather than treating the disease, as modern medicine does, the traditional Chinese physician treats the patient by correcting the critical imbalances in his or her energy system that opened the door to disease in the first place. "To restore equilibrium when energies are in excess or deficiency is the main object of the physician's endeavors," states a two-thousand-year-old Chinese medical text. This is known as "curing the root cause rather than treating the superficial symptoms." By virtue of their "natural affinity" *(gui jing)* for the specific organs and energies targeted by the physician, medicinal herbs reestablish optimum energy balance and restore organic harmony within the whole human system, thereby closing the windows of vulnerability (usually flung open by our own negligence), which allow ailments to enter and develop inside. States *The Yellow Emperor's Classic of Internal Medicine,* a two-thousand-year-old text that remains standard reading in TCM training today, "If it's too hot, cool it down; if it's too cold, warm it up; if it's too full, empty it; if it's too empty, fill it." *It* refers to the particular human energy system whose imbalance is responsible for the problem.

A typical example of modern Western medical practice is its response to acquired immune deficiency syndrome (AIDS). Western medicine claims that this disease is caused by the recently discovered human immunodeficiency virus (HIV), and it has responded to this challenge with total "germ warfare," using toxic drugs such as AZT to kill the invader, even in people who show no overt symptoms of AIDS, while the pharmaceutical industry rushes to develop vaccines that will supposedly protect the uninfected from ever contracting HIV, thereby conquering AIDS. By contrast, traditional Chinese medicine views AIDS as a condition of extreme vulnerability acquired by chronic long-term exposure to acute environmental pollution, both internal and external, further aggravated by poor diets and other personal habits that promote illness rather than health. In this scenario, HIV is just another one of many symptoms associated with immune system deficiency, not the cause of it. The traditional Chinese solution to AIDS is first to detoxify the major organs of the human system, particularly the liver and bloodstream, then to eliminate the personal habits, such as "junk food" diets, that impair human immune response and gradually rebuild immunity and vitality with proper nutrition, exercise, and supplemental herbs and formulas specifically designed to enhance human immune response.

"A stitch in time saves nine" has always been a fundamental tenet of traditional medicine, which regards the onset of any disease as a front-line failure in preventive health care, a view which places primary responsibility for health and disease on the patient's own personal lifestyle. Today, people tend to eat, drink, and behave in whatever manner pleases them, then run to the doctor for a "quick fix" whenever something goes wrong, as though their bodies were machines rather than living organisms. The net result of such mass negligence toward the basic facts of life is a global health crisis that is rapidly spinning out of control, and modern medicine has clearly failed to cope with this catastrophe.

The key to human health and longevity is and always has been preventive care, particularly the enhancement and maintenance of immune response. In today's polluted world and denatured habitats, preventive health care is even more important than it was in traditional times. As the American herbalist Dr. Daniel B. Mowrey points out in his book *The Scientific Validation of Herbal Medicine*, "We can only eliminate cancer and heart disease in this age by paying more attention to the health of the body and less to treating diseases; by devoting more effort to preventing, less to curing."

Any tradition with over five thousand years of continuous evolution behind it is bound to acquire a colorful patina of myth and legend liberally sprinkled with superstitious folklore, such as the Doctrine of Signatures, whereby, for example, ginseng root is regarded as a human panacea due to its resemblance to the human figure. This mythical veneer, coupled with the earthy symbolic terminology traditionally favored by the Chinese, is often cited by Western skeptics to deliberately discredit the entire field of herbal medicine. In fact, however, professional practitioners of TCM are no more guided by such hocus-pocus than professional Western physicians are guided by the superstitions of Western lore. Rather than investigating the basis upon which Chinese herbal medicine is founded, many Western doctors seem to spend more time worrying about losing their patients to this and other alternatives to Western drugs and surgery. Fortunately, the cutting edge of modern Western science is now beginning to validate many of the ancient premises of traditional Chinese medicine, while a new generation of enterprising Western herbalists is busy transplanting the ancient Chinese science of herbal healing into Western clinical practice, thereby providing Western patients with alternative therapies despite the disapproval of orthodox authorities and vested medical interests.

These Western medical authorities and the vested interests they represent constantly cite safety standards and scientific testing as excuses to obstruct the practice of Chinese herbal medicine in the West, blindly disregarding over three thousand years of cumulative clinical experience in China, all of it carefully recorded in ancient medical texts that are still in use today. The very fact that many ancient Chinese formulas have been in continuous use by millions of people for thousands of years, with consistently positive results, is clear testimony to their safety and reliability. This extensive record of clinical experience is arguably a more reliable basis for human therapeutics than the relatively brief and limited laboratory tests on which modern pharmaceutical standards are based.

One problem with Western scientific investigations of Chinese herbs is that they test only extracts and fractions of the plants, rather than the whole plants or plant parts. Concentrated isolates and refined fractions of medicinal plants are often toxic, and this finding is repeatedly used to discredit herbal medicine. In actual fact, whole plants work very differently in the human body than do the extracts and fractions investigated by Western science, and traditional Chinese medicine always employs whole herbs, precisely because they contain synergistic elements that naturally neutralize the negative effects of any toxic constituents the plant might contain. Whenever herbs that are known to contain toxic elements are used in complex formulas, they are always combined with other herbs that are known to specifically counteract the effects of those toxic elements.

Licorice root, for example, which is one of the oldest and most frequently employed herbs in the entire Chinese pharmacopeia, can be freely used for any period of time with absolutely no toxic side effects. Indeed, licorice is one of the greatest human detoxifiers in the Chinese pharmacopeia. However, the concentrated fractional extract of licorice root studied by most Western scientists (and used to make licorice candy in Europe) can in fact be quite toxic to humans in high doses, and this discovery is often cited to discredit the therapeutic benefits of the whole licorice root used in Chinese medicine. When Chinese herbalists use herbal concentrates, such as liquid extracts of ginseng, they always use concentrates of the whole plant or plant parts, which contain subtle synergistic elements that have yet to be isolated and identified by modern science.

Chinese herbal medicine has already become an important pillar in the New Medicine that is rapidly taking root and becoming the therapy of choice in many Eastern as well as a few medically enlightened Western countries, such as Russia. Combining the best of East and West by fusing modern Western medical technology with traditional Eastern therapies, the New Medicine is the wave of the future in human health care. The herbal branch of the New Medicine is also known as Green Medicine; the current revival of interest in herbal medicine is a reflection of the overall "greening" of consciousness occurring throughout the world today. People are finally beginning to realize that the fields and forests, rivers and lakes which we've been relentlessly polluting for so long may well contain the real remedies for cancer, AIDS, heart disease, and other scourges that continue to elude modern medical science. China, for example, recently disclosed the development of an effective remedy for the drug-resistant strains of malaria currently sweeping the tropical world; this "new" cure is extracted entirely from traditional Chinese herbs, not synthetic chemicals. In 1983, the public health ministry in Peking announced that a four-hundred-year-old prescription for hemorrhoids had been tested on forty thousand patients with a 96% cure rate and promptly declared this formula to be the officially designated cure for that ailment. Nature's cornucopia of herbal remedies is virtually boundless, and nowhere has this natural bounty been more studiously researched and practically utilized than in China.

However, if the world really wants to take advantage of the remarkable healing powers of medicinal plants, it must soon take steps to preserve the natural environments in which these precious plants thrive (and nowhere is the environment being degraded more rapidly today than in China itself). Healing plants grow in living soil and flowing water, utilizing the energies of sunlight and air; they cannot be cloned and reproduced in the laboratory without compromising their healing powers, which are drawn directly from the elements of nature. If we permit the earth to become barren, the entire field of herbal medicine will wither away with it, leaving us with no alternative to chemical and surgical medicine.

THE HERBS AND FORMULAS

There are over 2,000 items listed in Chinese herbal pharmacopeias, but only about 300 are used in general practice, of which less than one hundred are regarded as indispensable in formulating the most popular prescriptions. In order to provide more detailed information on the most important and therapeutically useful herbs, we have limited our selection for this book to 108 plants. The number 108 is highly auspicious in Taoism as well as Buddhism, and the *mala* (rosary) used in mantra and meditation practice in both traditions consists of 108 beads. So we present the 108 herbs described in this book as a sort of "rosary of remedies" for the reader's own health practices.

In traditional Chinese herbology, the term *herbal medicine* includes mineral and animal products as well as plants, but we've decided to limit our selection to medicinal plants only. Some minerals can become toxic in high doses or with prolonged use, and many animal products are becoming increasingly rare and expensive due to high demand and rapidly dwindling supply. However, a few of the formulas in chapter 4 do contain some mineral and animal ingredients that are not listed in the chapter on individual herbs. Vegetarians and others who do not wish to use animal products of any sort in their formulas will find suggestions for plant-derived substitutes listed in those entries.

Traditional Chinese pharmacopeias usually list medicinal herbs in categories based on their therapeutic effects, such as diaphoretics, digestives, tonics, and so forth, while most Western herbals are arranged either by botanical type or the category of ailment to be treated. While the Chinese method is useful to professional health practitioners trained in traditional Chinese medicine, it can be confusing to readers without previous background in TCM. Botanical categories do not necessarily reflect common therapeutic properties, and arrangement by ailment requires a lot of redundant listings because many herbs have multiple applications and would therefore have to be listed under many different ailments.

In this book, we decided to list the individual herbs in simple alphabetical order, according to the first letter in their common English names, if they have one, or else the first letter in their formal botanical Latin names. All relevant information regarding each herb's pharmacological properties and therapeutic uses is included within each entry, with data culled from both traditional Chinese and modern scientific sources.

The formulas listed in chapter 4 have all been selected from the vast collection of tried-and-true prescriptions that have been handed down throughout China's long history from master herbalist to aspiring apprentice. Most of the great classics have long been recorded in various Chinese medical texts, but many of these ancient formulas were subsequently amended and improved by later practitioners, and they continue to evolve today as contemporary healers adapt them to contemporary conditions. As much as possible, we provide a complete "pedigree" for each formula, tracing its history from the original creator to its present form, including some changes we have made ourselves, based on our own practical experience in the field. The formulas are arranged according to their basic functional categories, such as Digestive System, Respiratory System, Male and Female Reproductive Systems, Tonics, and so on. We also introduce some traditional Chinese ways of using medicinal herbs at home that are not yet very familiar to the Western world, such as herbal porridges, herbal poultices, and herbal pillows that work while you sleep.

In order to find the specific herbs and formulas recommended for specific symptoms and ailments, simply consult the Index of Symptoms and Ailments, which lists the applicable herbs and formulas by number. Technical terms used to describe herbal therapeutics, such as antiphlogistic and carminative, are listed and defined in the Glossary of Therapeutic Terms. In addition, there are brief chapters on basic Chinese medical terminology and traditional methods of preparing herbal remedies at home, plus appendices on herbal suppliers, herbal schools, and additional recommended reading in the field.

We hope that readers find interesting food for thought and effective prescriptions for health within these pages, and that each of you discovers herein at least one herb or formula that fits your own personal requirements as perfectly as a key fits a lock. If that key helps you unlock the gate to your own health and longevity, then this book will have served the purpose for which it was written.

1

TRADITIONAL CHINESE MEDICINE

Basic Terms and Concepts

Chinese herbal medicine is governed by the same universal principles of balance and harmony that run throughout the traditional Chinese arts and sciences. Simply known as the Way (Tao), Chinese philosophy draws its inspiration and insight directly from the perennial patterns of nature, which is why the Tao transcends all cultural boundaries and consistently withstands the tests of time. While a complete discussion of the theoretical roots of traditional Chinese medicine lies beyond the scope of this book, a brief review of the most basic terms and concepts will help the reader to establish the proper philosophical perspective and make more scientific sense of the information provided in each herbal entry.

YIN AND YANG

The Great Principle of Yin and Yang is the first and foremost law of the manifest universe. It delineates and defines the opposite yet complementary poles that lie at the heart of all dynamic forces, initiate all growth and transformation, and maintain the balance and harmony of the vital energies on which human health and longevity depend. Yin and yang are not different types of energy but, rather, complementary poles of the same basic energies of the universe, such as the hot and cold of heat energy, the bright and dark of light energy, and the positive and negative of electromagnetic energy. The vital organ-energies of the human body also function as complementary couples of yin and yang: the yin heart is functionally linked with the yang small intestine; yin liver is paired with yang gallbladder; yin kidneys are coupled with yang bladder; and so forth.

In Chinese herbal medicine, all medicinal herbs are categorized according to their degree of influence on the balance of yin and yang in the various vital energies of the human system. Yang herbs heat up the system, accelerate metabolism, and stimulate the vital organs. They are graded either hot or warm, depending on their therapeutic degree. Yin herbs cool the system, slow down the internal energies, and sedate the vital organs. They are tagged cold or cool, according to strength. Herbs whose therapeutic effects are equally balanced between yin and yang and do not steer the system in either direction are called neutral.

Yin and yang are also involved in traditional Chinese diagnosis, the object of which is to determine and locate the basic energy imbalance responsible for the ailment. Acute constipation, for example, is regarded as a hot yang condition and is therefore treated with cooling yin herbs such as rhubarb and aloe. Anemia and chronic fatigue are diagnosed as cold yin ailments, for which warming yang herbs such as ginseng and angelica are prescribed. Diagnosis and therapy are thus closely coordinated for maximum efficacy in practice by the common parameters of yin and yang, which reveal how the macrocosmic forces of the universe operate within the microcosm of the human system.

THE FIVE ELEMENTAL ENERGIES

"The Five Elemental Energies of Wood, Fire, Earth, Metal, and Water encompass all the myriad phenomena of nature. It is a paradigm that applies equally to humans," states *The Yellow Emperor's Classic of Internal Medicine*. As functional manifestations of yin and yang, the Five Elemental Energies are the fundamental forces of nature whose constant transformations and interactions "make the world go 'round." As another ancient Chinese text puts it, "The Five Elemental Energies combine and recombine in innumerable ways to produce manifest existence. All things contain all Five Elemental Energies in various proportions."

The Five Elemental Energies transform, manifest, and maintain their own natural equilibrium through an automatic system of checks and balances based on the creative and control cycles, or mother-son and victor-vanquished relationships. These elementary energy cycles, which remain in constant flux, modulate the dynamics of the polar force fields in which energies move, manifest, and transform. By administering herbs and formulas whose governing elemental energies have specific natural affinity for the ailing organ and its associated energy channel, the herbalist utilizes the creative and control cycles of the Five Elemental Energies to stimulate or sedate, increase or decrease, generate or subjugate, and otherwise balance and harmonize the vital energies involved in regulating human health.

The creative cycle is one of generation and stimulation: Wood generates Fire; Fire generates Earth; Earth generates Metal; Metal generates Water; Water generates Wood. The control cycle dominates and sedates: Metal sedates Wood; Wood sedates Earth; Earth sedates Water; Water sedates Fire; Fire sedates Metal. These complementary energy cycles are schematically summarized in Figure 1.

Each pair of functionally coupled yin/yang organs, such as heart and small intestine, kidney and bladder, is governed by one of the Five Elemental Energies. Thus the heart (yin) and small intestine (yang) are ruled by Fire energy, the kidneys (yin) and bladder (yang) by Water energy, and so forth (see Figure 2). If, for example, the Water energy of the kidney is deficient, it loses control of the Fire energy of the heart due to imbalance in the control cycle. In this case, the Fire energy of the heart might flare up and burn out of control, giving rise to such symptoms as high blood pressure, heart palpitations, and rapid pulse. In Western practice, these symp-

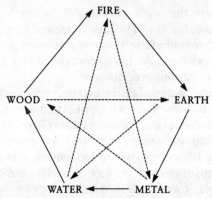

Fig. 1: The creative and control cycles governing the relationships among the Five Elemental Energies

toms would most likely be diagnosed and treated as a "heart problem," but TCM sees the root cause as a critical deficiency in kidney energy. So instead of treating the heart, the traditional Chinese physician would go directly to the root cause and treat the kidneys by prescribing herbs to nourish and increase the Water energy of the kidneys. When the kidneys' Water energy is restored to normal, it automatically regains control over the heart's Fire energy, and all abnormal heart symptoms disappear. In this case, the Western allopathic approach of administering drugs to lower blood pressure and regulate pulse would have provided temporary symptomatic relief to the heart without doing anything to cure the root cause in the kidneys. Instead, the kidneys would have continued to deteriorate due to neglect, further aggravated by the toxic side effects of the drugs, causing increasingly severe heart symptoms that required even stronger drugs to control, in a deadly cycle.

Another manifestation of the Five Elemental Energies in nature is the Five Flavors, and this is the aspect by which the basic therapeutic properties of medicinal herbs are identified. Camphor, for example, falls into the pungent category of flavors, which is a manifestation of Metal energy. Metal governs the lungs and large intestine, and camphor thus has a natural affinity for these organs and can be used to correct respiratory and lower bowel problems. Sweet herbs have the properties of Earth energy and can therefore be used for ailments of the stomach and spleen/pancreas, the corresponding Earth organs. Most medicinal herbs contain more than one energy/flavor and can thus be used to treat more than one organ-energy system. When combined together in complex formulas, the elemental energies of the constituent herbs mix and metabolize in complex ways in the human system, which is why extensive clinical experience is so important in Chinese herbal medicine.

There are many other fundamental qualities and relationships in nature that reflect the Five Elemental Energies and are governed by their creative and control cycles, but for the purposes of our discussion here, the following set of associated aspects will suffice:

ELEMENTAL			VITAL ORGAN	
Energy	*Flavor*	*Color*	*Yin*	*Yang*
Fire	Bitter	Red	Heart	Small Intestine
Earth	Sweet	Yellow	Spleen/Pancreas	Stomach
Metal	Pungent	White	Lungs	Large Intestine
Water	Salty	Black	Kidneys	Bladder
Wood	Sour	Green	Liver	Gallbladder
Fire II	Bitter	Red	Pericardium	Triple Burner

Fig. 2. The Five Elemental Energies and their related organs, flavors, and colors.

THE SIX EVILS

The diagnostic and therapeutic terminology used in traditional Chinese medicine includes a number of terms that most Westerners associate more with weather than medicine. As the *Encyclopedia of Chinese Medicine* explains, "When the six environmental energies of Wind, Cold, Heat, Dampness, Dryness, and Fire grow extreme or occur out of season, they become causes of disease and are known as the Six Evils."

The Six Evils are regarded as the primary external causes of disease. By contrast, Western medicine still clings to the notion that germs are the main cause, a theory first proposed by Louis Pasteur. Pasteur discovered that most diseases are associated with the presence of particular germs and therefore concluded that germs are the primary cause of disease. However, his theory fails to account for the fact that some people do not contract diseases even after repeated and prolonged exposure to the same germs that cause others to fall ill after just one brief exposure.

According to the Chinese view, exposure to the Six Evils of extreme environmental conditions knocks the human energy system off balance, thereby impairing resistance and immunity and opening the door to attack by all sorts of debilitating external factors, including germs. People who take preventive measures to avoid or counteract exposure to aberrant external energies maintain balance and harmony among the vital energies that regulate their internal defense systems, and thus they usually remain invulnerable to the very same germs that appear to make others sick. From this point of view, it is not the germ that actually "causes" the disease: it is unguarded exposure to aberrant environmental energies that sets the stage for disease by knocking a hole in one's natural defenses and permitting germs and other noxious elements to gain entry.

In traditional times, the Six Evils were associated mainly with various extremes of weather and unseasonal climatic conditions, such as intense heat spells, excessive humidity, sudden cold, wild winds, and so forth. Today, modern technology and urban life-styles have introduced even more virulent forms of the Six Evils into our living environments, including air-conditioning, central heating, fluorescent lights, microwave radiation, artificial electromagnetic fields, polluted air and water, and so forth. These factors constitute an intensive, nonstop assault on the balance and integrity of human energies, the first casualty of which is invariably the immune system. Conventional modern life-styles cause even more cumulative damage to human resistance and immunity than do natural forces, paving the way for all sorts of pathogens and poisons to enter and corrupt the human body.

Wind: Wind is the first of the Six Evils. It is the prevailing environmental energy of spring, when it usually comes as a mild, refreshing breeze. In other seasons, however, wind can become the carrier of aberrant energies associated with those seasons. Summer has its hot winds, winter its cold winds (which blow open the gates to influenza), and autumn its dry winds. Symptoms of wind injury include fever and chills, profuse sweating, coughs, and sinus congestion. Wind also carries dust, germs, smoke, and other pollutants and pathogens. Due to its swift and sudden nature, wind is regarded as the Chief of the Six Evils.

In addition to external wind, Chinese medicine also recognizes internal wind arising from extreme imbalances in the vital energies of the internal organs. For example, inflammation of the liver can give rise to excess liver wind, which ascends to the head and causes such symptoms as headache, blurry vision, insomnia, and dizziness.

Modern industrial sources of wind evil include air-conditioning (dry cold wind) and central heating (dry hot wind), as well as radiation and smog.

Cold: Cold evil is associated with winter and Water. Sudden exposure to cold when resistance is low can cause chills and fever, cessation of sweating, and bodily pains. If it settles in the abdomen, it causes diarrhea, cramps, and flatulence. Internal cold arises from deficient yang energy in the vital organs and can cause cold hands and feet, diarrhea, and loss of sexual vitality. The most prevalent modern form of external cold evil is air-conditioning, while the primary modern sources of internal cold are excessive consumption of ice-cold beverages and cold yin foods, and synthetic drugs that suppress various vital functions, such as barbiturates and antibiotics.

Heat: Heat injury results from exposure to excessively hot air temperatures for prolonged periods and usually occurs in summer. Symptoms include headache, chronic thirst, hot spells, profuse sweating, and irritability. In other seasons, heat can combine with other environmental energies and give rise to damp heat, dry heat, or wind heat. Today, central heating is the main artificial source of heat evil and usually takes form as dry heat.

Dampness: Damp evil is traditionally associated with the humidity of late summer, when it takes form as summer rains, humid weather, morning mists, damp ground, and mildew. The human system is particularly vulnerable to damp injury during sleep, and its symptoms include fatigue, lethargy, cold sweat, rheumatic pains, and bloating. Internal dampness arises mainly from excessive consumption of alcohol, coffee, tea, sugary soft drinks, ice-cold fruits, and sweets, all of which damage the internal organs and suppress vital functions, particularly in the pancreas, spleen, and adrenal glands. Today, the most pervasive source of internal damp evil is diet, especially junk foods made with refined white sugar and starch, which are major contributing factors in diabetes, blood toxemia, and immune deficiency.

Dryness: Dry evil is associated with autumn, results from insufficient moisture in the air, and is particularly injurious to the lungs. It combines readily with other aberrant energies to form dry cold, dry heat, and dry wind, all of which can cause various respiratory disorders. Since the lungs (yin) are paired with the large intestine (yang), dry injury can also cause hard stools and constipation. Insufficient bodily fluids give rise to internal dryness, causing such symptoms as constant thirst, dry throat, chapped lips, dry skin, and nausea. Smoking and air pollution are the most damaging modern forms of internal dry evil, while air-conditioning and central heating are major artificial sources of cold dryness and hot dryness.

Fire: Fire injury results from prolonged unguarded exposure to extremes of any one or more of the other five seasonal energies. Thus Fire evil refers to any extremely abnormal environmental energy that causes injury beyond the usual symptoms associated with the original condition and starts causing permanent damage to the vital organs. For example, when prolonged exposure to the internal dry evil of smoking or air pollution goes beyond the usual symptoms of coughs and dry throat and starts causing permanent problems such as emphysema or cancer, then it is regarded as having become Fire evil. Symptoms of internal Fire are caused by overstimulation or abuse of the internal organs, such as ulcers from the stomach Fire of overconsumption of rich foods, cirrhosis from the liver Fire of alcohol abuse, cancer from the lung Fire of smoking, and so on.

The antidote to evil energy is pure energy, and medicinal herbs can be used both curatively and preventively to suffuse the human system and all its vital organs with pure energy, which drives evil energies out of the system and establishes a strong defense against their return. *The Yellow Emperor's Classic of Internal Medicine* states, "Where evil energy gathers, weakness occurs. When pure energy collects internally, evil energy cannot cause damage to the organs. When pure energy flourishes, evil energy flees. When evil energy is driven out of the system, pure energy grows."

THE EIGHT INDICATORS

During the course of long-term cures, especially for chronic conditions, symptoms often move, transform, disappear, reappear elsewhere, and undergo sudden changes. The Eight Indicators are somatic signs that clearly reflect the shifting symptomatic state of the patient's condition. Herbal therapy usually continues for periods of at least a few weeks or months up to several years, and during this time the patient must visit the therapist periodically for what is known in Chinese medicine as differential diagnosis, whereby the course of the patient's treatment is carefully monitored for any symptomatic changes as reflected by the Eight Indicators. Herbal prescriptions are then adjusted to suit the patient's new symptomatic status. The Eight Indicators thus enable the therapist to select precisely the right combinations of herbs appropriate for each progressive stage of the cure, so that the herbs work in concert with the body's own internal healing mechanisms.

Yin and Yang: These two are known as the Commanders of the Eight Indicators and are the most important signposts in the diagnosis and treatment of disease. In fact, the other six are simply more specific aspects of yin and yang symptomology. All diseases and their symptoms are first diagnosed in terms of the yin and yang polarity of the various vital organs and energies affected by the ailment. For example, high temperature, constipation, profuse sweating, and hypertension are all common indicators of a basically yang disease, whereas chills, diarrhea, pallid complexion, chronic fatigue, weakness, and aversion to cold indicate a basically yin condition. Yang symptoms are treated with cooling yin herbs, while yin symptoms are counteracted with warming yang herbs.

Internal (yin) and External (yang): These signs inform the therapist where the disease is located and in which direction the symptoms are moving, as well as how severe the condition has become. If symptoms are moving inward toward the organs, glands, and bones, it indicates that the disease is growing worse. When a patient's condition is improving, symptoms will generally move outward toward the surface for elimination, which is a clear sign that the chosen therapy is working. During the course of treatment, symptoms can shift rapidly between the surface and interior, and herbal formulas must be adjusted accordingly in order to assist rather than interfere with the body's own natural healing processes.

Cold (yin) and Hot (yang): Cold and hot indicate the basic nature of the disease as reflected by symptomatic changes in the aberrant energies associated with it, such as high or low body temperature, flushed or pale complexion, light or dark urine, hard or soft stools, and so on. These indicators not only transform swiftly but can also take opposite directions in different parts of the body. For example, bloodshot eyes and sore throat indicate that the patient's condition is currently hot on top, while accompanying abdominal bloating and diarrhea mean that it is cold below. Herbal formulas must be periodically adjusted in order to correct imbalances caused by aberrant energies.

Empty (yin) and Full (yang): These indicate the degree to which an ailment has depleted (empty) or overstimulated (full) the vital organs and energies affected by the ailment. They also reflect the level of the patient's resistance and the current balance in the battle between pure and evil energies in the body. When herbs that boost immunity and resistance are prescribed in time, pure energy flourishes and grows full, while the evil energy of disease becomes increasingly empty as it is driven out of the system. When immunity and resistance become severely impaired by prolonged neglect or abuse, the body acquires a chronic immune deficiency, a condition in which pure energy drains away and becomes progressively more empty, while the myriad evil energies that cause disease flourish and grow full.

Except for yin and yang, which are general indicators of overall conditions, the other six signs usually manifest in combinations of varying complexity. If a hot symptom appears on the surface, it is called external hot; if a full symptom manifests internally, it is internal cold; and so forth. For general diagnostic purposes, however, the Eight Indicators in their basic singular forms usually suffice to keep track of symptomatic changes during the course of treatment.

THE TWELVE VITAL ORGANS AND MERIDIANS

Traditional Chinese medicine views the vital organs in a different light than conventional Western medicine, focusing more on their functional relationships than their physical forms and treating their malfunctions more on the level of energy than physiology. Each organ is governed by a specific vital energy associated with one of the Five Elemental Energies of nature, and each organ-energy runs through its own special channel, or meridian, all of which are connected through a network that feeds energy to the entire body. The functional relationships among the vital organs and their energies are determined by the creative and control cycles of the Five Elemental Energies. For example, heart-energy (Fire) is stimulated by liver-energy (Wood) through the creative mother-son relationship of Wood to Fire, but it is sedated by kidney-energy (Water) via the control victor-vanquished relationship of Water to Fire. Experienced physicians can detect and "read" all twelve organ-energy pulses by applying subtle finger pressure to vital points on the patient's wrist, but there are more obvious external signs, such as complexion, eyes, tongue, hair, and so on, which clearly reflect the condition of the internal organ-energies.

Following is a brief review of the twelve vital organs and their related energies according to the traditional Chinese view.

Fire Energy, Yin Organ (Heart): Known as the King of the Vital Organs, the heart commands the entire body and all of its parts by controlling circulation and distribution of blood and nourishment. The heart also houses the spirit and controls emotions. Among the first symptoms of deficient heart-energy are loss of emotional control and mental instability.

Heart conditions are reflected externally by the color and texture of tongue fur and by facial complexion. A ruddy flushed face, for example, indicates overactive heart-energy. The heart meridian runs from the inside tip of the little finger up along the inside of the arm and into the armpit.

Fire Energy, Yang Organ (Small Intestine): As the body's Minister of Reception, the small intestine receives partially digested food from the stomach and completes the digestive process, after which it assimilates the pure nutrients and sends the impure wastes down to the colon for excretion. Linked to the heart by Fire energy, the small intestine controls the baser emotions that spill over from the higher-minded heart during periods of emotional turmoil, giving rise to the familiar "butterfly" feeling in the gut. Its energy meridians start at the tips of the little fingers, travel up the outside of the arms, shoulders, and neck, into the head, where they influence the regulatory functions of the pituitary gland.

Wood Energy, Yin Organ (Liver): The liver is the Chief of Staff and holds responsibility for filtering, purifying, nourishing, and storing blood. It also breaks down complex proteins, fats, and carbohydrates and synthesizes the various types of proteins required for growth and repair of bodily tissues. Liver-energy controls the peripheral nervous system, which in turn regulates the activity of muscles and tendons and thus determines physical coordination. Ambition, drive, and creativity are governed by the Wood energy of the liver, which can give rise to intense anger and frustration when obstructed.

Liver function is reflected externally by the condition of fingernails and toenails, and also by the eyes and vision. Yellow eyes and blurry vision, for example, are well-known indicators of liver jaundice. The liver meridian starts at the base of the big toenail, runs up the inside of the leg into the torso, and terminates just below the rib cage.

Wood Energy, Yang Organ (Gallbladder): The Honorable Minister of the Central Clearing Department, the gallbladder secretes the potent bile fluids required to digest and metabolize fats and oils. Its energy governs muscular strength and flexibility, as well as the mental qualities of daring and decisiveness; the Chinese word for "daring" is *dadan,* or "big gall."

The gallbladder meridian travels from the base of the fourth toenail up along the outside of the leg and rib cage, under the arm and across the back of the shoulders and neck, up over the top of the skull to the forehead, and back down the side of the head around the ears. Common tension headaches are often caused by obstructions in the gallbladder meridians, especially at the shoulders and neck.

Earth Energy, Yin Organ (Spleen and Pancreas): In Chinese medicine, the spleen and pancreas are considered to be governed by the same energy. Called Minister of the Granary, the spleen and pancreas control extraction and assimilation of nutrients by secreting the digestive enzymes required by the small intestine. They also regulate the quality and quantity of blood in circulation and directly influence muscle tone.

Imbalances in spleen-energy and pancreas-energy are reflected externally by the color and tone of the lips and manifest emotionally with temper tantrums and moodiness. The spleen meridian starts at the inside tip of the big toe, runs up the inside of the leg, continues along the side of the torso and up to the top of the rib cage.

Earth Energy, Yang Organ (Stomach): The stomach is called the Minister of the Mill and the Sea of Nourishment. It predigests bulk foods and fluids before sending them down to the small intestine for complete digestion and assimilation of nutrients. It also extracts the Five Elemental Energies from ingested foods and fluids and delivers them via the meridian system directly to the lungs, where they combine with the energy extracted from air to form what is known as True Human Energy.

Metal Energy, Yin Organ (Lungs): The lungs, or Prime Minister, control breath and assist the King heart with circulation of blood and energy. Breath regulates respiration, supports metabolism, and controls pulse. Lung deficiency is reflected by pallid skin and poor complexion because the skin, which also "breathes" through the pores, is an external extension of the lungs. The nose is the lungs' external aperture and the gate of breath: a clogged or runny nose usually indicates some sort of lung malfunction. Since breathing regulates the autonomic nervous system, it forms a bridge linking body and mind, which is why breath control is cultivated in all yoga and meditation systems.

Anxiety inhibits lung-energy and causes shallow, rapid breathing patterns; conversely, shallow breathing renders a person more vulnerable to anxiety. The lung meridian goes from the tip of the thumb, up along the inside of the arm into the chest.

Metal Energy, Yin Organ (Large Intestine): As Minister of Transportation, the large intestine manages the transformation of digestive wastes from liquid into solid form and transports them onward to the rectum for excretion. It helps regulate the balance and purity of body fluids by recovering water from digestive wastes and by assisting the lungs in controlling perspiration through the skin. Its functions are directly influenced by the lungs via expansion and contraction of the diaphragm. Deep breathing therefore aids peristalsis and regulates abdominal pressure.

The large intestine meridian starts at the tip of the index finger, runs up along the outside of the arm and side of the neck, then across the cheek to the base of each nostril.

Water Energy, Yin Organ (Kidneys): Called the Minister of Power, kidney-energy is so important that it's also known as the Root of Life. The kidney organ-energy system includes the adrenal glands, which sit like hats on top of the kidneys and regulate a wide range of vital functions, including immunity and sexual potency. It also includes the testicles in men and ovaries in women, which are known as the external kidneys. The kidneys themselves filter fluid wastes from the blood and excrete them through the bladder as urine.

Kidney-energy controls growth and development of bones and marrow, which produce red and white blood cells. Kidney deficiency is thus a prime cause of anemia and immune deficiency. Kidney conditions are reflected externally by the tone of hair on the head and body, and kidney malfunctions often manifest as tinnitus (ringing in the ears). The kidneys house courage and willpower, which is why deficient kidney-energy often results in feelings of fear and paranoia. The kidney meridians travel from the soles of the feet, up the insides of the legs, then up along the center of the torso to the top of the chest.

Water Energy, Yang Organ (Bladder): This organ is called Minister of the Reservoir, and it manages the storage and excretion of urine, which is the bladder's only physiological function. Bladder-energy, however, is closely connected with the balance and functional integrity of the entire autonomic nervous system. That's because the bladder meridians, which begin in the feet and run up the back of the legs, split at the base of the spine to form four parallel channels (two on each side of the spine) that run all the way up the back to the neck, where they rejoin into two channels that continue up over the skull to the forehead and eye sockets. Chronic stress causes chronic tension in the spinal channels of the bladder meridian, triggering an exhausting hyperactivity of the sympathetic, or action, branch of the autonomic nervous system. Chinese massage and acupuncture therapy focus a lot of attention on the four spinal branches of the bladder meridian due to their powerful influence over a wide range of vital functions via their proximity to the spinal cord.

Fire Energy, Yin Organ II (Pericardium): The pericardium, or heart sac, also known as the King's Bodyguard, is not recognized as a vital organ in Western medicine, but Chinese medicine regards it as a second Fire energy, yin organ whose sole role is to protect the all-important heart from physical damage as well as from aberrant emotional energies arising from other organs, such as anger from the liver, fear from the kidneys, and so forth. Without the pericardium's protection, heart-energy would become very vulnerable to injury from the waves of aberrant energies constantly generated in other organs by emotional turmoil and stress.

The pericardium also helps regulate the flow of blood in the major veins and arteries of the heart. Emotionally, the pericardium refines the coarse raw energy of animal sexuality with the higher tenderness and love that reside in the human heart, thereby refining sexual lust with human love.

The pericardium meridian runs from the tips of the middle fingers, across the palms and wrists, up along the inner forearms and biceps into the chest.

Fire Energy, Yang Organ II (Triple Burner): Also unrecognized as a vital organ in Western medicine, the Triple Burner, or Minister of Dikes and Dredges, is not a physical organ but, rather, a functional energy system involved in the regulation of other organs and the movement of energies. It has three parts: the Upper Burner goes from the tongue down to the entrance of the stomach, regulates intake of air, food, and fluids, and harmonizes heart- and lung-energies; the Middle Burner runs from the stomach's entrance down to the exit at the pyloric valve, controls digestion, and harmonizes the energies of the stomach, spleen, and pancreas; the Lower Burner starts at the pyloric valve and terminates at the anus. It regulates extraction and assimilation of nutrients and excretion of liquid and solid wastes, and it harmonizes the functions of liver, kidneys, bladder, and bowels, as well as sexual and reproductive functions.

The Triple Burner meridian starts at the top of the fourth finger, goes across the back of the hand and up the outside of the arm, across the top of the shoulder, up the neck and around the ear, terminating at the temple.

2

THE KITCHEN CLINIC
Preparing Chinese Herbs at Home

Entering a traditional Chinese herbal pharmacy today is like walking into a living antique: entire walls of wooden drawers worn to a smooth patina, each one elegantly engraved with the ancient Chinese ideograms denoting what's inside; a long hardwood counter for preparing prescriptions; simple hand-held balance scales and the ubiquitous abacus for weights and calculations; old iron choppers and stone grinders; a few scrolls of calligraphy and landscape painting on the walls; and an exotic potpourri of heady aromas wafting up from bundles of twisted twigs and gnarled roots, shriveled leaves and shrunken flowers, dried scorpions and petrified sea horses, stretched lizards, preserved snakes, and some things that defy description. A visit to a traditional Chinese herbalist is always interesting, often entertaining, and never boring.

The pharmacist's role is to weigh, blend, and dispense the herbal formulas prescribed by the physician and brought in by the patient. The patient then takes the herbs home and prepares them in the kitchen, employing one of the traditional methods discussed below. If the pharmacy is large and sufficiently well staffed, they may be willing to prepare the decoction, pills, capsules, paste, liquor, or whatever the prescription stipulates, for an additional service charge. However, it's more interesting to do it yourself at home, and this is also the best way to quickly gain your own "clinical experience." If you don't know any qualified practitioners of traditional Chinese medicine but would like to try some Chinese herbal remedies, just go to any Chinese pharmacy and ask for an introduction. Some pharmacies have a licensed herbal physician on the premises to perform diagnosis and formulate prescriptions on a walk-in basis, and virtually all herbal pharmacists are themselves qualified to recommend remedies for common ailments and chronic degenerative disorders.

In traditional Chinese homes, the kitchen has always doubled as an herbal clinic—a place where both food and medicine are prepared, sometimes together and sometimes separately, for the health and longevity of the entire family. The preparation of popular herbal potions has always been common knowledge in traditional Chinese societies. In the kitchen clinic, one quickly learns which herbs work best for certain conditions, which foods to combine or avoid combining with particular herbs, how to properly prepare simple formulas, when to take them, and other practical points. In this way, you gradually gain a working knowledge that allows you to handle many common health problems at home, and preventive health care soon becomes a way of life.

The only things you need in order to convert your own kitchen into an herbal clinic are the following: stovetop-safe Pyrex glass or ceramic cooking vessels with lids; a scale; measuring cup; airtight storage containers; a sieve; cheesecloth; a stove, preferably gas; pure water, either bottled, filtered, or distilled; "00"-size gelatin capsules; honey; and, if you want to prepare tonic herbal liquors, distilled spirits such as vodka, rum, or brandy.

The most popular methods of preparing Chinese herbs and formulas at home are briefly described below. These methods can be used for single herbs and simple combinations, as well as complex formulas.

Unless otherwise stated, the dosages given for the herbs and formulas in this book are sufficient for 1 day's use. A typical course of treatment with Chinese herbs continues for 7–10 days, unless otherwise specified by the physician or herbalist. If you don't get positive results after 1 week, try another herb or formula recommended for the same symptoms.

METHODS OF PREPARING CHINESE HERBS

DECOCTION *(tang)*

Known as "broth" in Chinese, decoction is the oldest and most traditional way of preparing medicinal herbs for use at home, although pills, capsules, and concentrates are becoming increasingly popular for their convenience. The main advantages of decoction are thorough extraction of the herbs' complete medicinal potential, rapid absorption, and swift onset of therapeutic effects, all of which are desirable qualities in acute conditions. The only real disadvantage is that it's somewhat time consuming for those who live in the fast lane.

Measure out and place the herb(s) inside a clean Pyrex glass pot (of the stovetop-safe variety) or ceramic cooking vessel (never use metal), then add 3–4 cups of pure water. If you've had a formula blended for you at a pharmacy, each day's dose will be individually wrapped, one packet per day prescribed (e.g., ten packets for a 10-day course), so all you need to do is empty one packet into the vessel with the water to prepare 1 day's dose.

Bring the mixture to a boil, lower the heat to a simmer, cover, and let it continue boiling slowly until the broth is reduced to $1/3$–$1/2$ of its original volume, or about 1–2 cups. Strain it through a cloth-lined sieve and reserve the broth. Add two more cups of fresh water to the dregs, boil again, reduce to 1 cup, strain, and add this to the first portion, discarding the dregs. Divide the broth into two or three equal portions, according to the prescription, and drink it warm, between meals, on an empty stomach for rapid assimilation. It's a good idea to keep the second and third doses in the refrigerator, then warm them up on the stove (*not* in a microwave) prior to ingestion.

Steam Decoction: Another version of this method is to use what's known as a ginseng cooker, which consists of a small ceramic bowl with a lid, into which the herb or herb mixture is placed along with only 2–3 ounces of pure water. This vessel is then covered tightly and set on a rack inside a larger pot (metal can be used for the external vessel) with water in it, and is steamed for several hours; additional water is added to the steamer as needed. This method is best when preparing single or simple combinations of potent tonic herbs, such as old ginseng, but it is not suitable for complex formulas. It yields a very pure, potent, fast-acting extract known as medicinal dew *(yao lu).*

POWDERS *(san)*

Most herbal pharmacies and supply houses will grind individual herbs and blended formulas into a fine powder if you request this when ordering. Alternatively, you can use an electric coffee grinder or food processor to powder most herbs in your own kitchen. Powdered herbs act more slowly and gently than decoctions, and due to gradual absorption, their effects are less intense but last longer. These traits are most suitable for chronic conditions requiring long-term therapy.

The simplest way to use powders is to spoon the required dose directly into your mouth and chase it down with warm water or warm wine; Japanese sake is very good for this purpose. If the taste or texture of powdered herbs bothers your palate, you can use the powder to make infusions, capsules, pastes, or pills.

Infusions (cha): Place the specified dose of powder (usually about 3–5 grams) in a cup and add boiling water, letting it steep 3–5 minutes. Drink this "herbal tea," preferably on an empty stomach, two or three times per day.

Capsules (jiao niang): The simple gelatin capsule is probably the single most useful modern invention for traditional herbal medicine. It permits easy administration of bitter and pungent herbs whose taste makes decoctions and infusions hard to swallow. It also facilitates long-term storage of prepared powder formulas, insures precise dosage, and provides a convenient way of taking herbal remedies "on the run" and "on the road."

Ask the pharmacist to grind the herbs to a superfine powder and encapsulate it in "00"-size gelatin capsules, which hold about 1 gram each, or do this yourself at home. Take two capsules three times daily, or three capsules twice a day, preferably with warm water or wine on an empty stomach. If the herbs upset your empty stomach, take the capsules about half an hour after meals. To make an infusion, empty the contents of three capsules into a cup and add boiling water.

Pastes (gao): Place the finely powdered herbs inside a large glass or ceramic bowl and stir in just enough honey to form a thick paste that has a consistency similar to peanut butter or bread dough. Eat 1 full teaspoon two or three times daily, or as prescribed, preferably on an empty stomach, and then drink a cup of warm water or wine. Keep the paste in the refrigerator.

Pills (wan): Prepare a honey paste with the powdered herbs and then use your thumb and index finger to roll small pills. The size varies from buckshot pellets to large beans, depending on the formula. Place the pills on a baking sheet and set in the oven at the lowest possible temperature for 10–15 minutes, or just until the honey forms a glaze. Let the pills cool thoroughly before storing them in an airtight container; refrigeration is not required. Depending on the formula and size of pill, one dose usually consists of about five to fifteen pills, to be taken two or three times daily on an empty stomach (unless otherwise specified) with warm water or wine.

Pills can also be made with other bases, including flour paste, plain water, beeswax, and fermented dough, but these are more complicated and should only be prepared by trained herbalists. For home use, honey is the simplest and most reliable base.

OINTMENTS *(yio)*

Herbal ointments are made by blending finely powdered herbs into an oil base for external use. Tiger Balm is probably the most widely recognized Chinese herbal ointment in the world, but there are many others. Popular bases include yellow petroleum jelly, beeswax, lard, lanolin, black sesame oil, and almond oil. Heat the base until warm, then add the powdered herbs and stir well.

Store in small jars with airtight lids. Refrigeration is not required.

HERBAL LIQUORS *(yao jiou)*

Steeping medicinal herbs in strong distilled spirits for three months to a year yields a potent herbal liquor that fully extracts the essences and energies of the ingredients and passes them swiftly into the bloodstream for rapid results. This is an ancient and effective method for drawing out the full potency of herbal formulas, particularly tonics, and it remains a popular way of using tonics throughout the Far East today. It's also a very economical way of using the more expensive tonic herbs, such as very old ginseng and tender young deer horn.

Proportions vary according to the properties of the herb used as well as personal taste. Generally about 60–120 grams of herbs are used per liter of distilled spirits. For long-term use, it's more efficient to prepare larger batches, such as the six-plus-three-bottle formulas given in this book, which yield nine bottles. Any distilled liquors can be used, but we recommend vodka, rum, or brandy as the best choices.

Buy the bulk herbs chopped or broken into pieces, but not powdered, and place them all inside a large, clean vessel of glass or ceramic. Pour six 1-liter bottles of vodka or other spirits over the herbs and make an airtight seal, then set the jug aside to steep for at least 3 months, shaking it well once in a while. The longer you age this herbal liquor, the stronger it gets and the better it tastes.

After 3 or more months, open the vessel and pour *half* the brew through a cloth filter and funnel the filtered brew into clean liquor bottles. Add three more bottles of fresh spirits to the herbs in the vessel, reseal it, and steep it for another 3–6 months, after which you can strain the entire batch and discard the spent herbs. Total yield is about nine bottles, which should be stored in individual liquor bottles with tight corks or caps. Add a bit of raw sugar or honey, or rock crystallized sugar, to each bottle to enhance the flavor and facilitate rapid absorption and metabolism. The bottles can be stored indefinitely, unrefrigerated, without losing their potency, as long as they are properly sealed.

Single-herb liquors can also be prepared by the bottle simply by putting 75–100 grams of the herb (such as ginseng, angelica, wolfberry, or deer horn) into a bottle of vodka, rum, or brandy, then sealing it and letting it steep for 3–6 months. Some people like to keep half a dozen different varieties of herbal liquor "on tap" at home at all times.

A standard dose of herbal liquor ranges from 1–2 fluid ounces, depending on your individual constitution, the season, and the particular purpose for which you are using it. Use a bit more in winter and cold climates, and less during summer and in tropical climates. Take a larger amount for more immediate and dramatic effects, less for gradual tonification during long-term use.

For maximum benefits and rapid assimilation, it's best to take herbal liquors on an empty stomach, twice a day. Our favorite times are about 1 hour before dinner, when it sharpens the appetite, and an hour before going to bed at night, when it warms the body and promotes sound sleep. On very cold winter mornings, taking a dose as soon as you get out of bed may "warm up your motor." If you find the taste too strong, simply add an equal measure of plain warm water. If you are sensitive to alcohol, pour some boiling water onto a dose and let it steep for a few minutes; this will evaporate most of the alcohol without losing any of the herbal essence.

HERBAL PORRIDGES *(yao jou)*

This is a traditional and typically practical Chinese way of blending food and medicine, though it is not well known in the West. Herbal porridges are usually prepared in a base of brown rice, Job's Tears, barley, or millet and served for breakfast, though they can be eaten any time of day or night as a convenient herbal snack. They turn food into medicine and transform medicine into palatable food.

To make an herbal porridge, first wash the whole

grain(s) well in running water, drain, then soak them for an hour or two in pure water (see individual recipe for the quantity of water required). Add a pinch of sea salt and bring to a boil. Lower the heat, add the herbs, and simmer for an hour or two, adding water as needed to maintain a porridge consistency. Boil the grain until it is thoroughly cooked and the porridge is thick. It should be eaten hot, either plain, sweetened with honey, or seasoned with a small amount of Chinese sesame oil, sea salt, and chopped scallions. You can keep the porridge warm on the stove and snack on it throughout the day, but leftovers should not be kept for the next day.

HERBAL POULTICES *(fu yao)*

Poultices are made by mixing powdered herbs with water to form a thick paste for external appiication. The paste is spread thickly onto a square of cellophane or wax paper, which is placed over the injured area and taped securely to the skin. Keep it taped in place for 12–24 hours and replace as needed for up to a week of daily therapy. Chinese herbal poultices relieve pain and repair physical damage to joints, muscles, tendons, ligaments, and bones; they have tremendous potential applications in athletic injuries and modern sports medicine. Fresh herbal poultices made at home immediately prior to application are much stronger and more effective than the factory-prepared patches available at herb shops. However, people with hypersensitive skin must be careful when using fresh poultices because the potent vapors can irritate sensitive skin as it enters the tissues below, leaving a rash.

HERBAL PILLOWS *(yao jen)*

Most people spend about one-third of their lives lying asleep in bed, and herbal pillows permit this time to be effectively used for herbal therapy. The dried herbs are stuffed into a small cotton pillowcase, which is then sewn closed. The heat from your head warms up the herbs inside the pillow, releasing their aromatic vapors and essential energies, which rise up through the cloth and enter your system with every breath. It's best to use a small, well-stuffed pillow in order to prevent the herbs from bunching together; this also saves money on herbs. Depending on the sort of herbs inside, an herbal pillow can be used for 6 months up to a year or two before replacing the herbs. You'll know the herbs are spent when the pillow is no longer aromatic in the morning.

A Few Tips

Herbal medicine is just one branch on the great tree of Chinese health care, and it yields far more fruit when practiced in concert with the other major branches, such as diet and nutrition, detoxification and purification, exercise, and meditation. Using Chinese herbal medicine alone, isolated from its traditional context, is like cutting a branch from an old tree and trying to graft it to a different species: the results are rarely as fruitful as the original organic system. Readers sincerely interested in using Chinese medicinal herbs as a means to take their lives into their own hands and pave their own way to health and longevity should consider including the following suggestions in their practice.

INTERNAL CLEANSING

Purifying the bloodstream, detoxifying the tissues, and cleansing the internal organs of metabolic wastes and digestive debris accumulated from decades of wrong food, medicine, and habits is by far the most important first step on the path to renewed health and rejuvenation. Toxic tissues, impure blood, clogged colons, and swollen livers release a constant stream of poisons that pollutes the entire system, largely negating the benefits of herbal therapy. It is like pouring pure water into a contaminated vessel.

The only way to eliminate these toxins is by fasting at least once or twice a year, for 3–7 days each time. Thorough cleansing of all bodily tissues may take years to accomplish, but the benefits of fasting become immediately apparent the very first time you try it and are

cumulative. Each fast greatly enhances the results derived from subsequent herbal therapies.

During the fast, you can use either pure water or
freshly extracted fruit juice diluted by half with pure
water. It is most important to use a high-grade psyllium-
husk preparation four or five times daily throughout the
duration of the fast in order to sweep the bowels clean
of all toxic debris. If you also do daily colonic irriga-
tions, either at home or a clinic, you will at least triple
the quantity of toxic waste eliminated from your system
during any fast. The appendix "Herbal Suppliers" lists
a few reliable sources of psyllium, bentonite, cleansing
herbs, and other internal cleansing supplements.

DIET AND NUTRITION
After ridding your system of toxins, it's totally self-de-
feating to return to the eating habits that poisoned you
in the first place. Study the science of proper food combining (trophology), learn how to use vitamins, minerals, and other nutritional supplements, and put this
knowledge into practice in your daily life. Use common
sense instead of blind gluttony at the dining table, and
above all, eliminate all factory-prepared junk and fast
foods.

Whenever commencing a course of Chinese herbal
therapy, it's extremely important to follow the dietary
guidelines dispensed along with your prescriptions. Be
particularly careful when using strongly flavored foods,
such as ginger, garlic, chilies, and onions. The Five Flavors are direct manifestations of the Five Elemental
Energies in food, and the strength of a food's flavor is a
measure of its energy. Strongly flavored foods thus have
strong pharmacodynamic properties when ingested; depending on how they interact with the energies of various herbs, these properties either conflict or synergize
favorably with whatever herbal formulas you're using.
For this reason, compliance with dietary advice is very
important in Chinese herbal therapy.

WESTERN DRUGS
If you want to try Chinese herbal remedies for problems
that have plagued you for years, it's very important to

first terminate whatever synthetic Western chemicals you are already using for these conditions, but this should only be done under the supervision of your physician or other qualified health professional. If your physician is prejudiced against alternative therapies and won't even discuss herbal medicine, find another physician.

Chinese herbs work in conjunction with the body's own natural healing mechanisms and other vital functions, whereas most Western drugs override and suppress natural mechanisms. With rare exceptions, modern allopathic drugs are incompatible with traditional herbal remedies because they disrupt the very energies and vital functions with which medicinal herbs work in concert.

EXERCISE

Herbal medicines operate on an energy level as well as essence. The biochemical essence of an herb travels in the bloodstream, while its essential energy moves in the meridian network. Exercises that promote smooth circulation of blood as well as energy, such as T'ai Chi, *chee-gung,* yoga, and meditation, greatly enhance the distribution and utilization of the herbs' therapeutic energies and biochemical essences; in this way maximum benefit is obtained.

SEXUAL DISCIPLINE

According to traditional Chinese medical views, excess loss of semen is one of the primary causes of premature aging, loss of vitality, and immune deficiency in men. This is why Chinese herbals list so many herbs and formulas to control nocturnal emission and premature ejaculation. When a man is already weak and ailing and undertakes a course of herbal therapy, it becomes even more important for him to minimize his loss of semen in order to preserve his vital energies for internal healing. On the other hand, disciplined sexual intercourse, which involves frequent and prolonged "contact without leakage" (i.e., intercourse without male ejaculation) is often recommended as a quick and effective way of building up internal energy in men, and thus the cooperation of his partner becomes important. The two-thousand-year-old treatise on sex entitled *Su Nu Ching* ("Classic of the Plain Girl") says:

> By treasuring his semen, cultivating his spirit, and taking medicinal herbs, a man can certainly attain long life. However, if he is ignorant of the Tao of sex, taking herbs will do him no good. . . . It is because man has lost knowledge of the Tao of sex that he now suffers such early death.

Such advice is given throughout Taoist literature and medical treatises, and many modern studies have validated this view. Though most Western men regard genital orgasm as an inviolable rite (and right) of sexual intercourse, we suggest that they at least read some of the excellent books now available in English on Chinese sexual yoga (see the appendix "Recommended Reading") and put some of these principles into practice on a trial basis. These ancient Chinese texts also suggest some excellent practices for women, both "dual" (with a partner) and "solo" (alone), to enhance female sexual energy and transform it into pure vitality for health and longevity.

PROFESSIONAL ADVICE

Last but certainly not least, it's always helpful to solicit the advice of a health professional who is properly qualified in traditional Chinese medicine. This eliminates almost all doctors who are trained exclusively in conventional Western medicine, but today you don't necessarily have to travel to the Far East or the nearest Chinatown to find well-qualified guidance in Chinese herbal therapy. There are numerous Western health professionals in the United States, Europe, and Australia today who have mastered the principles and practices of Chinese medicine and can guide you on the path of herbal therapy.

The herbs and formulas presented in this book can

be safely used at home without outside professional advice, as long as the accompanying information is followed precisely. However, some friendly professional guidance can help you to avoid wasting time and money on "trial runs" and to derive even greater benefits from the materials introduced herein.

3

CHINESE MATERIA MEDICA

108 Medicinal Herbs

The 108 medicinal herbs described in this chapter are arranged in alphabetical order by their common English names, if they have one, or else by their formal Latin names. The romanized Chinese names appear in italics, along with their original Chinese ideograms and any other names by which the herbs are commonly known in English or Chinese.

Each herb is briefly described in terms of its basic botanical features, biochemical constituents, special traits, native distribution, and other identifying characteristics. The parts used in medicine and the herb's essential nature in traditional terms of energy, flavor, and organ affinity are noted next, followed by a list of its main therapeutic effects in contemporary Western medical terminology. Readers who are unfamiliar with these terms will find them defined in the Glossary of Therapeutic Terms (see page 294).

For most of the herbs, we have also included a brief note on its therapeutic effects in terms of traditional Chinese medicine (TCM). This information is provided for readers who wish to further familiarize themselves with the basic principles of traditional Chinese therapeutics; it can also be used as a guide for those who decide to embark on the path of traditional Chinese health care under the supervision of a professional practitioner of TCM.

The major symptoms and ailments for which each

herb is used are listed under "Indications," using contemporary Western medical terms, followed in most cases with a brief note on basic TCM indicators.

Under "Dosage," the preferred method of preparing the herb is given, followed by information on the quantity (in metric grams) for 1 day's use, division of doses, and administration. Sometimes additional suggestions for preparing and administering the herb, and combining it with others, are also given here.

Any conditions or situations prohibiting use of the herb are listed under "Contraindications," and any herbs, foods, or other compounds and elements that conflict pharmacologically with the herb and should therefore be avoided during therapy are listed under "Incompatibles."

All but a few of the entries conclude with the section "Remarks," which includes traditional Chinese lore and medical information about the herb, the latest modern scientific discoveries regarding its medical properties, clinical studies on the herb's efficacy, and other relevant items of interest.

List of Herbs

1. *Achyranthes bidentata*   *(niou hsi)*
2. Akebia   *(mu tung)*
3. *Aloe vera*   *(lu hui)*
4. Amber   *(hu buo)*
5. *Anemarrhena asphodeloides*   *(jih mu)*
6. Angelica   *(dang gui)*
7. *Angelica anomala*   *(bai jih)*
8. *Angelica pubescens,* purple   *(chiang huo)*
9. *Angelica pubescens,* yellow   *(du huo)*
10. *Asarum sieboldi*   *(hsi hsin)*
11. Astragalus   *(huang chi)*
12. Balloon flower   *(jie geng)*
13. Belvedere cypress   *(di fu dze)*
14. Black pepper   *(hu jiao)*
15. *Bletilla striata*   *(bai ji)*

16.	Blue morning glory	*(chien niu)*
17.	Broomrape	*(rou tsung rung)*
18.	Burdock	*(niu bang dze)*
19.	Cardamom	*(yi jih ren)*
20.	Cattail	*(pu huang)*
21.	Chinese cornbind	*(ho shou wu)*
22.	Chinese jujube	*(da dzao)*
23.	Chinese wolfberry	*(gou ji dze)*
24.	Chinese yam	*(shan yao)*
25.	Chrysanthemum	*(ju hua)*
26.	*Cimicifuga foetida*	*(sheng ma)*
27.	Cinnamon	*(rou gui)*
28.	*Cnidium monnieri*	*(she chuang dze)*
29.	*Codonopsis dangshen*	*(dang shen)*
30.	Coltsfoot	*(kuan dung hua)*
31.	*Corydalis ambigua*	*(yen hu suo)*
32.	Costus	*(mu hsiang)*
33.	Cowherd	*(wang bu liu hsing)*
34.	Creeping lilyturf	*(mai men dung)*
35.	*Curculigo ensifolia*	*(hsien yu)*
36.	*Cynomorium coccineum*	*(suo yang)*
37.	Dandelion	*(pu gung ying)*
38.	*Dendrobium nobile*	*(shih hu)*
39.	Dodder	*(tu seh dze)*
40.	Dogwood tree	*(shan ju yu)*
41.	*Dryopteris crassirhizoma*	*(guan jung)*
42.	Eagle wood	*(chen hsiang)*
43.	*Eclipta prostrata*	*(han lien tsao)*
44.	*Eleutherococcus gracilistylus*	*(wu jia pi)*
45.	*Elsholtzia splendens*	*(hsiang ru)*
46.	*Eriocaulon sieboldianum*	*(gu jing tsao)*
47.	Eucommia	*(du jung)*
48.	Fennel	*(hui hsiang)*
49.	Foxnut	*(chien shih)*
50.	Garlic	*(da suan)*
51.	*Gastrodia elata*	*(tien ma)*
52.	Gentian	*(lung dan tsao)*

53.	Ginger, dried	*(gan jiang)*
54.	Ginkgo kernels	*(ying hsing)*
55.	Ginkgo root	*(bai guo gen)*
56.	Ginseng	*(ren shen)*
57.	Gotu kola	*(di chien tsao)*
58.	Grains-of-paradise	*(sha ren)*
59.	*Gynura pinnatifida*	*(san chi)*
60.	Hare's ear	*(chai hu)*
61.	Horny goat weed	*(yin yang huo)*
62.	Indian madder	*(chien tsao)*
63.	Japanese catnip	*(jing jie)*
64.	Japanese honeysuckle	*(jin yin hua)*
65.	Japanese wax privet	*(nu jen dze)*
66.	Job's tears	*(yi yi ren)*
67.	Joint fir	*(ma huang)*
68.	*Justicia gendarussa*	*(chin jiao)*
69.	Kudzu vine	*(geh gen)*
70.	*Ledebouriella seseloides*	*(fang feng)*
71.	Leonurus	*(yi mu tsao)*
72.	Licorice	*(gan tsao)*
73.	*Ligusticum wallichii*	*(chuan hsiung)*
74.	Lotus seeds	*(lien dze)*
75.	Mastic tree	*(ru hsiang)*
76.	Mint	*(bo he)*
77.	Mishmi bitter	*(huang lien)*
78.	Morinda root	*(ba ji tien)*
79.	Multiflora rose	*(bao chiang wei)*
80.	Nutmeg	*(rou dou kou)*
81.	*Pinella ternata*	*(ban hsia)*
82.	Plantain	*(che chien dze)*
83.	*Polygala tenuifolia*	*(yuan jih)*
84.	*Polygonatum cirrhifolium*	*(huang jing)*
85.	*Psoralea corylifolia*	*(bu gu jih)*
86.	Raspberry	*(fu pen dze)*
87.	*Rehmannia glutinosa*	*(di huang)*
88.	Sandalwood	*(tan hsiang)*
89.	Schisandra	*(wu wei dze)*

90.	Shiny asparagus	*(tien men dung)*
91.	Sickle senna	*(jue ming dze)*
92.	Solomon's seal	*(yu ju)*
93.	Szechuan pepper	*(chuan jiao)*
94.	Teasel	*(hsu duan)*
95.	Thistle type	*(tsang shu)*
96.	*Thuja orientalis*	*(bo dze ren)*
97.	Tibetan saffron	*(dzang hung hua)*
98.	Tiger thistle	*(da ji hua)*
99.	Tree peony	*(mu dan pi)*
100.	*Tribulus terrestris*	*(ji li dze)*
101.	Trifoliate orange	*(jih shih)*
102.	Tuckahoe	*(fu ling)*
103.	Weeping golden bell	*(lien chiao)*
104.	White peony	*(bai shao)*
105.	Wild Chinese jujube	*(suan dzao ren)*
106.	Wild Chinese violet	*(dze hua di ding)*
107.	Winter worm–summer grass	*(dung chiung-hsia tsao)*
108.	Yellow starwort	*(hsuan fu hua)*

1. ACHYRANTHES BIDENTATA

牛膝 *niou hsi (niu xi)*

This is a perennial herb with slender stalks and opposite elliptical leaves. The greenish purple stems have large joints that resemble the knee of an ox, hence the Chinese name *niou hsi,* "ox-knee." The best-quality roots are straight and flexible, streaked lengthwise with fine wrinkles, brownish yellow in color, and contain saponins. One ancient source says that the staminate plant, which has large purple joints, is medicinally superior to the pistillate plant, which has small green joints. The shoots of all varieties of this plant are edible.

The herb is native to China, Japan, India, Southeast Asia, Indonesia, and Sri Lanka.

MEDICINAL PART: root

NATURE:
Energy:	neutral
Flavor:	bitter, sour
Affinity:	liver, kidneys

THERAPEUTIC EFFECTS: diuretic; emmenagogue; tonic; promotes circulation and dissolves clots; relieves pain in knees and lower back; clears bruising (TCM: tonifies liver- and kidney-energy; nourishes sinews and bones)

INDICATIONS: menstrual disorders; stiffness and pain in lower back, waist, and knees (lumbago); bleeding gums, nosebleeds, and blood in sputum; urethritis; traumatic injuries to bones and joints; poor circulation (TCM: empty kidney-yin)

DOSAGE: decoction: 5–10 grams daily, in two doses, on an empty stomach

CONTRAINDICATIONS: nocturnal emission; painful bloating in legs and knees (TCM: empty spleen-energy)

INCOMPATIBLES: tortoise shell; *Cynanchum japonicum;* mutton

REMARKS: Chinese herbals particularly recommend this herb as a diuretic remedy for bladder and urinary tract problems, and as an effective emmenagogue for menstrual disorders. For sciatica and lumbago due to deficiency in kidney-energy, use with an equal portion of eucommia. As a remedy for blood and circulatory problems, combine with *Rehmannia glutinosa*.

2. AKEBIA, *Akebia quinata*

木通 *mu tung (mu tong)*

OTHER NAMES: *tung tsao* (perforated grass)

A climbing vine with a jointed, woody stem that varies in thickness from 1–7 centimeters, the plant is distinguished by small tubular holes in the marrow, large enough for air to be blown through, hence the Chinese name *mu tung*, "perforated wood." The wood is yellow and arranged in vascular plates. The medicinal part is sold in sliced transverse sections of the ligneous (woody) stem, about 1 centimeter in diameter, and contains 30% potassium salts, which accounts for its diuretic action. The fruit is edible and has a white pulp with black kernels and a pleasant sweet taste.

The plant is native to eastern China and Japan.

MEDICINAL PART: stem

NATURE: Energy: cold
         Flavor: bitter
         Affinity: heart, lungs, bladder, small
                   intestine

THERAPEUTIC EFFECTS: diuretic; antiphlogistic; analgesic; galactagogue; facilitates labor in childbirth

INDICATIONS: pain and oppression in the chest; angina; chronic thirst; abscesses on tongue and mouth; scanty, painful urination; painful swelling in legs and feet; insufficient lactation; restlessness and insomnia; dry sore throat; sinus congestion; laryngitis

DOSAGE: decoction: 4–9 grams, in two doses, on an empty stomach

CONTRAINDICATIONS: chronic profuse sweating

INCOMPATIBLES: none

REMARKS: A popular traditional remedy for insufficient lactation in nursing mothers is to simmer 10–15 grams of this herb together with pork knuckles for 3 hours, adding water as needed, then drinking the herbal broth throughout the day.

3. ALOE VERA

 lu hui

OTHER NAMES: Barbados aloe; Curaçao aloe; *Aloe barbadensis; Aloe vulgaris; hsiang dan* (elephant's gall)

Aloe is a succulent stemless plant with erect juicy leaves 30–60 centimeters long, grayish green color, with spiny edges. The active herb is derived from the condensed juice of the fresh leaves and comes in irregularly shaped chunks about 2 centimeters thick, with a waxy texture and varying in color from orange-brown to black. It is highly aromatic and has a sharply bitter taste, hence the Chinese name meaning "elephant's gall." The juice contains about 20% aloin compounds, which are split in the small intestine to yield emodin.

Aloe vera is native to Africa, India, West Indies, and the Mediterranean, but it is also widely cultivated now in Southeast Asia.

MEDICINAL PART: condensed juice of fresh leaves

NATURE: Energy: very cold
         Flavor: very bitter
         Affinity: liver, stomach, large intestine

THERAPEUTIC EFFECTS: laxative; purgative; stomachic; emmenagogue; antiseptic; refrigerant; helps regulate blood pressure by clearing debris from veins and arteries (TCM: sedative to liver-energy)

INDICATIONS: Internal: chronic constipation and related skin problems; gastritis, ulcers, indigestion, abdominal pains, and heartburn; high or low blood pressure; headache, dizziness, and irritability due to liver inflammations; intestinal parasites (TCM: ascending liver-fire; excess heat in large intestine)

External: premature balding; scrapes, burns, sunburns, skin blemishes, and frostbite; athlete's foot; insect bites; acne; hemorrhoids

DOSAGE: Condensed juice purchased from Chinese pharmacy should be taken in the following dosages for internal use, mixed with a few ounces of water:

stomachic	0.1–0.2 gram
laxative	0.3–0.6 gram
purgative	0.8–1.0 gram

If fresh aloe plants are available, freshly extracted juice is more potent and acts more swiftly. For internal use, adults should use the juice from about 15 grams of fresh aloe leaf, while children under twelve should use no more than 5 grams. Wash the leaf well under running water and scrape away the spiny edges. Cut it into small chunks and grind it to a fluid pulp in a mortar or electric blender. Line a clean bowl with a piece of cheesecloth, pour the pulp onto the cloth, wrap the cloth tightly around the pulp, and squeeze all the juice from the pulp through the cloth into the bowl. Keep the juice refrigerated in a glass jar and take it in two to three doses, on an empty stomach, any time of day or night. You can take it straight or diluted with a few ounces of pure water, plain or with a little honey. Smaller doses provide relief for the stomach ailments listed above, while larger doses can be used for chronic constipation. Aloe can be used for prolonged periods without losing its efficacy.

For external use, simply rub the freshly extracted

juice, undiluted, directly onto the affected area of the skin. The juice will remain fresh and potent in the refrigerator for 4–5 days, after which it should be discarded. Freshly cut aloe leaves will retain their potency for up to a week in the refrigerator if well wrapped in cellophane.

CONTRAINDICATIONS: children with empty-cold constitutions (very pale, frail, prone to respiratory disorders) should not use aloe; adults should not exceed the daily dosages suggested above

INCOMPATIBLES: none

REMARKS: According to recent scientific research in Japan, fresh aloe juice contains elements that slow the growth and spread of cancerous cells. Although aloe is not regarded as a cure for cancer, it has definitely been shown to have potent preventive properties against its development when taken on a regular, long-term basis.

Since aloe does not lose its therapeutic efficacy with prolonged use, it is a very reliable remedy for chronic constipation.

For eczema, psoriasis, and similar skin afflictions, Chinese herbals recommend an external wash composed of a decoction of aloe and licorice, which should be used to cleanse the affected areas three times daily for 3–7 days.

4. AMBER, *Pinites succinifer*

琥 珀 *hu buo (hu bo)*

OTHER NAME: "tiger's soul"

The Chinese name meaning tiger's soul is based on the old legend that when a tiger dies, its spirit enters the earth and is transformed into this substance. It is said to be the resin of an extinct species of pine that has "lain in the earth for a thousand years." Ancient Greek and Chinese, as well as modern observers, all agree on this point. Pieces containing the preserved bodies of ants, bees, and other insects are particularly valued, and the finest specimens are often fashioned into ornaments for the wealthy. It ranges in color from a milky yellow to a dark, transparent golden brown. Amber should always be purchased from reliable sources, because imposters made from colophony and copal are often sold as the real thing and are difficult for the untrained eye to distinguish.

Major sources of amber include India, Africa, Burma, Yunnan and other areas of southern China, and Korea.

MEDICINAL PART: petrified resin

NATURE: Energy: neutral
          Flavor: sweet
          Affinity: kidneys

THERAPEUTIC EFFECTS: alterative; tonic; diuretic; sedative; nervine; dissolves clots in bloodstream; helps eliminate cataracts (TCM: sedates kidney-energy and cools excess fire in bladder)

INDICATIONS: blood in urine; dark cloudy urine; scant urination; amenorrhea; nocturnal emission; nervous convulsive disorders; hysteria; cataracts (TCM: internal heat in kidney and bladder)

DOSAGE: powder (plain, capsules, infusion, or honey pills): 0.9–2 grams

CONTRAINDICATIONS: none

INCOMPATIBLES: none

REMARKS: Throughout the ancient Asian world, amber was considered to contain special supernatural powers and healing energies that protected those who wore it on their bodies. It remains a very popular material for making *malas,* the bead rosaries used throughout Asia for meditation and mantra practice. The mystical lore associated with the herb inevitably became entangled with its reputed medicinal properties, but all magic and mysticism aside, amber possesses therapeutic properties, particularly for disorders of the nervous system.

5. ANEMARRHENA ASPHODELOIDES

知母 jih mu (zhi mu)

This is a liliaceous plant with a thick rhizome covered with erect yellowish or reddish hairs. The flowers are purplish on the inside, yellowish on the outside, and resemble those of the garlic plant. The herb is sold in flat, irregular, shriveled pieces about 10 centimeters long and 20 millimeters thick. It has a bitter taste but a pleasant odor. The herb contains the saponin asphonin, which has antipyretic properties, and a large amount of mucilage.

The herb grows plentifully in the mountains north of Peking and in most of the northern Chinese provinces.

MEDICINAL PARTS: rhizomes, stems

NATURE: Energy: cold
Flavor: bitter
Affinity: kidneys, lungs, stomach

THERAPEUTIC EFFECTS: antipyretic; demulcent; emollient to bowels; diuretic; reduces swelling (TCM: nourishes kidney-yin; clears internal heat)

INDICATIONS: nocturnal emission, night sweats, impotence, insufficient erection due to adrenal deficiency; diarrhea; constipation; thirst, insomnia, and irritability due to excess internal heat; pneumonia and bronchitis (TCM: empty kidney-yin; empty yin)

DOSAGE: decoction: 6–12 grams, in two doses, on an empty stomach

powder: plain, capsules, or pills; 5–10 grams, in two doses, on an empty stomach, with warm water or wine

CONTRAINDICATIONS: TCM: empty-cold conditions in spleen and stomach; diarrhea that has become completely watery; prolonged use may cause chronic loose bowels

INCOMPATIBLES: iron preparations; iron utensils

6. ANGELICA*, *Angelica sinensis*

當歸 *dang gui*

OTHER NAMES: honeywort; *shan chin* (mountain celery); *Angelica polymorpha*

This fragrant perennial herb produces brown, fleshy rootstocks that branch into masses of large, pliant, densely packed rootlets, somewhat like gentian. It is highly aromatic, with a bittersweet taste that resembles celery, hence the Chinese nickname. It has always been highly reputed in China and Japan, ranking close to licorice in frequency of use in formulas, and is particularly valued for its efficacy in every type of female menstrual disorder.

The herb is grown most abundantly in the provinces of central and western China, and also in Japan.

MEDICINAL PART: root

NATURE: Energy: warm
         Flavor: bitter, sweet, slightly pungent
         Affinity: liver, spleen

THERAPEUTIC EFFECTS: emmenagogue; tonic; analgesic; sedative; alterative; stimulates appetite; improves muscle tone; stimulates immune system (TCM: tonifies blood)

---

*Among the four Chinese herbs tagged in Western Latin terminology under the genus *Angelica,* only *Angelica sinensis,* which is one of the most widely used herbs in Chinese medicine, is known by the common English name Angelica, or Angelica Root. The other three were designated in the Angelica category rather arbitrarily, and are not traditionally used in Western herbology, so they have no common English names.

INDICATIONS: irregular, insufficient, profuse, painful, and otherwise abnormal menstruation; premenstrual syndrome (PMS); headache; pain from traumatic injury or surgical wounds; paralysis; poor appetite; cancer (TCM: empty blood)

DOSAGE: Decoction: for painful and/or irregular menstruation, add one whole, uncut angelica root to 2 cups pure water and decoct to 1 cup of broth. Divide into two doses and take on an empty stomach in the morning and at bedtime.

For heavy bleeding from hemorrhages in uterus, decoct 10 grams of angelica with 10 grams of Japanese catnip, using 1 cup of rice wine or sherry and 2 cups pure water. Take in two doses, on an empty stomach, morning and bedtime.

CONTRAINDICATIONS: diarrhea

INCOMPATIBLES: fresh ginger, herbs of *Acorus* species, seaweed

REMARKS: This has long been regarded as one of the primary herbs for all sorts of female disorders related to blood, menstruation, and pregnancy, and it's therefore known as the Great Tonic for All Female Deficiencies. Modern scientific research validates these traditional claims. The herb has been shown to contain estrogenic compounds called phytoestrogens, which account for its menstrual-regulating properties. It also helps control fungal infections such as *Candida albicans,* which is the main causative agent in vaginal yeast infections.

The herb has also been proven to enhance immunity by stimulating the production and activity of white blood cells, such as B-lymphocytes and T-lymphocytes, and by increasing production of interferon and leukocytes as well. These properties account for the herb's anticancer activity.

Angelica is regarded as one of the most balanced yin tonics, just as ginseng is the perfect yang tonic. Combining the two therefore provides complete and balanced tonification of both yin and yang energies.

7. ANGELICA ANOMALA

白芷 *bai jih (bai zhi)*

OTHER NAMES: *fang-hsiang* (floral fragrance)

This is a perennial alpine herb that grows to 2 meters tall, with hollow, purplish green stems and a compressed, ovoid fruit with four membranous edges. The medicinal root varies in size, with a brownish yellow exterior, whitish interior, and transversal wrinkles and ridges that are dotted with resinous spots. It is very aromatic, and in ancient China it was worn together with other fragrant herbs in a sachet tucked into one's robes. It is highly regarded as a remedy for female reproductive system disorders.

The herb is native to western and central China, as well as Japan.

MEDICINAL PART: root

NATURE: Energy: warm
Flavor: pungent, bitter
Affinity: lungs, stomach

THERAPEUTIC EFFECTS: analgesic; sedative; antidote; aromatic; promotes circulation; reduces swelling (TCM: relieves discomforts of wind injury)

INDICATIONS: frontal headaches; dizziness; sore and watery eyes; toothache; itchy skin rashes; nasal congestion; leukorrhea; snakebites (TCM: external-wind injuries)

DOSAGE: powder: plain, pills, capsules, or infusion; 3 grams, once daily, on an empty stomach; if any of the above conditions are accompanied by abnormal sweating, such as profuse, cold, and nocturnal sweat, raise dose to 6 grams and take with some warm wine

CONTRAINDICATIONS: TCM: empty-blood symptoms

INCOMPATIBLES: *Inula chinensis* (English elecampane)

8. ANGELICA PUBESCENS (PURPLE)

羌活 *chiang huo*

This is a variety of the species *Angelica pubescens*, listed as #9 below. It is much darker in color, ranging from dark purple to green, has denser foliage, and is far more aromatic. The roots are jointed with internodes about 2 centimeters apart and arranged in wedges of brittle woody tissue, with red cortical fibers between the interior and epidermis.

The herb comes from the same general areas in China as its close cousin *du huo,* but usually farther to the west. The name *chiang* is derived from the name of the main minority tribe living along the Tibetan-Szechuan border region.

MEDICINAL PART: root

NATURE: Energy: warm
              Flavor: pungent, bitter
              Affinity: kidneys, bladder

THERAPEUTIC EFFECTS: diaphoretic; analgesic; anti-rheumatic (TCM: releases internal heat and expels toxins from surface)

INDICATIONS: dizziness and bloodshot eyes; loss of speech due to stroke; arthritic and rheumatic pains that move from joint to joint throughout the whole body (TCM: internal damp-heat symptoms)

DOSAGE: decoction: 3–6 grams, in two doses, on an empty stomach. For shifting rheumatic pains throughout the body, decoct 7 grams each of both varieties of *Angelica pubescens (du huo, chiang huo)* with 7 grams of *Pinus sinensis* twigs in 3 cups of rice wine, reducing broth by half. Divide into two portions, and take only one portion per day on an empty stomach.

CONTRAINDICATIONS: none

INCOMPATIBLES: none

9. ANGELICA PUBESCENS (YELLOW)

獨活 *du huo*

OTHER NAME: *Angelica grosserrata*

An unbelliferous plant with trifoliate leaves and a slender stalk, the herb comes in long, twisted rootlets, deeply striated lengthwise and crosswise. The color is yellowish brown outside, dirty white inside.

The plant is native to Szechuan and other western provinces of China, as well as Tibet.

MEDICINAL PARTS: root

NATURE: Energy: slightly warm
Flavor: pungent, bitter
Affinity: kidneys, bladder

THERAPEUTIC EFFECTS: diaphoretic; analgesic; antirheumatic (TCM: releases internal heat)

INDICATIONS: headache, dizziness, blurry vision, and toothache caused by exposure to wind; arthritis, rheumatism, and numbness in extremities caused by exposure to dampness; pain in lower back and knees (TCM: external-wind injury; external-damp injury)

DOSAGE: decoction: 3–6 grams, in two doses, on an empty stomach

CONTRAINDICATIONS: none

INCOMPATIBLES: none

10. ASARUM SIEBOLDI

細辛 *hsi hsin (xi xin)*

OTHER NAME: *Asarum heterotropoides*

The leaf stalks of this perennial herb are a distinctive violet color, and the fleshy rhizome produces very fine, fibrous rootlets with an acrid taste and strong aroma, containing about 3% essential oil. It is particularly effective as an analgesic remedy for all types of aches and pains in the head.

The plant is found principally in Manchuria, Korea, Japan, and the northernmost provinces of China.

MEDICINAL PARTS: rootlets; whole plant can also be used

NATURE: Energy: warm
Flavor: pungent
Affinity: liver, kidneys, heart, lungs

THERAPEUTIC EFFECTS: analgesic; diaphoretic; expectorant; sedative; galactagogue; relieves chronic thirst (TCM: nourishes kidney-essence; tonifies liver-energy; clears internal heat)

INDICATIONS: congestion in eustachian tubes and upper sinus cavities; fevers and chills; headaches and toothaches; arthritis (TCM: internal-cold symptoms; empty kidney-yin)

DOSAGE: decoction: 3–4 grams, in two doses, on an empty stomach

CONTRAINDICATIONS: none

INCOMPATIBLES: astragalus; dogwood tree; potassium nitrate; magnesium silicate

REMARKS: For earaches, traditional sources suggest making pea-sized pills by mixing the powdered herb with vinegar, then placing a pill inside each ear and letting it slowly dissolve. The same sources recommend placing some of the powdered herb for gradual absorption into the navel to eliminate abscesses inside the mouth.

For contagious colds, bronchitis, pneumonia, and other lung infections in elderly and physically weak patients, Chinese herbals suggest a decoction of 3 grams of this herb combined with 4 grams of joint fir *(Ephedra)* and 5 grams aconite.

For halitosis (bad breath), decoct 3 grams of the herb in 1 cup water and use the warm broth to gargle and rinse the mouth, spitting it out afterward.

11. ASTRAGALUS, *Astragalus hoantchy* 黄耆 *huang chi (huang qi)*

OTHER NAME: *Astragalus membranaceus*

This popular tonic herb grows to a height of about 1 meter, with rigid stalks that sprout eight to twelve pairs of leaflets. The medicinal root is covered with a tough, fibrous, yellowish brown skin and is sold in flexible slices 15–20 centimeters long. The marrow is yellowish white and has a sweet taste that resembles licorice. It contains glycosides, saponins, and essential fatty acids.

The herb is grown mostly in northern China, Japan, and Korea, each region producing its own distinctive variety. All types can be used in formulas calling for astragalus, but the most medicinally potent and somewhat more expensive variety comes from northern China.

MEDICINAL PART: root

NATURE:	Energy:	slightly warm
	Flavor:	sweet, slightly sour
	Affinity:	spleen, lungs

THERAPEUTIC EFFECTS: immunotonic; cardiotonic; diuretic; controls profuse perspiration; lowers blood pressure; lowers blood sugar; improves circulation in flesh and skin (TCM: tonifies primordial energy; nourishes essence)

INDICATIONS: immune deficiency; cancer; chronic fatigue; high blood pressure; prolapse of internal organs; diabetes; cold and weak limbs; colds and flu; bronchitis; hepatitis; adrenal deficiency (TCM: deficient energy; external-empty symptoms, such as abnormal profuse sweating)

DOSAGE: decoction: 8–12 grams, in two doses, on an empty stomach.

liquor: steep 80–100 grams of the sliced root in 1 liter of spirits for 2–3 months; take 1 ounce, twice daily, on an empty stomach, straight or diluted with 1–2 ounces pure water; for better results, also add 40–50 grams ginseng

CONTRAINDICATIONS: none

INCOMPATIBLES: *Chinemys reevesii* (tortoise shell); opiates

REMARKS: According to Chinese herbology, this herb enhances immunity by protecting the body from invasion by the Six Evils of aberrant or extreme environmental energies, such as wind and cold, and by increasing circulation of *wei-chee* (protective energy) around the surface of the body. It also stimulates production and circulation of immunological factors in the blood.

Modern research validates the traditional immunotonic claims for astragalus. An article published in *Cancer* magazine by the American Cancer Society reported that a fluid extract of this herb restored normal immune response in 90% of cancer patients studied. Other studies on cancer patients lend further support to this evidence. One way astragalus boosts immunity is by increasing the production and activity of white blood cells specifically involved in fighting disease. Clinical studies have also shown that cancer patients who take astragalus while undergoing chemotherapy, which severely inhibits natural immune responses, recover faster and live significantly longer than those who do not use this herb. Astragalus does not contain components that directly attack cancer cells; instead, it strengthens the body's own immune defenses against the development of cancer.

Modern Chinese research has shown that astragalus helps the body resist virus infections, particularly in the lungs, by increasing production of interferon, an immune factor that inhibits viral growth.

Because of this herb's powerful enhancement of immune response, it is currently under study as a treatment for AIDS. AIDS patients show an unusually high count of T-suppressor cells, which impair immunity by suppressing activity of T-cells, one of the body's primary immune factors. Astragalus has been shown to significantly reduce the number of T-suppressor cells in cases of human immune deficiency.

The herb's immunotonic properties are even further enhanced when combined with ginseng, *Codonopsis,* schisandra, angelica, and/or licorice. It can also be blended with the North American immunotonic herb echinacea.

12. BALLOON FLOWER

Platycodon grandiflorum

桔梗 *jie geng*

OTHER NAMES: *Platycodon chinensis; Campanula grandiflora*

A perennial herb that grows on a slender stem to a height of 60–100 centimeters with violet-blue flowers that blossom from ballooning buds, the young plant, long used as a cooking herb in China, is considered to have vermicidal properties. The root is yellowish white and about the size of a small finger. Due to its resemblance to ginseng, it is one of the roots sometimes fraudulently substituted for the latter. It has a bittersweet taste and contains saponins.

The plant is native to China and Japan.

MEDICINAL PART: root

NATURE: Energy: neutral
             Flavor: bitter, pungent
             Affinity: lungs

THERAPEUTIC EFFECTS: expectorant; bronchodilator (TCM: nourishes blood; clears phlegm)

INDICATIONS: bronchitis; tonsillitis; heavy coughs with phlegm; sore throat; abscesses in mouth and throat; lung infections; chest pains; abdominal pains with loose bowels

DOSAGE: decoction: 3–5 grams, in two doses, on an empty stomach

CONTRAINDICATIONS: none

INCOMPATIBLES: gentian; *Bletilla striata;* pork

REMARKS: This herb is particularly effective in dissolving accumulations of hard, heavy phlegm in the throat, bronchial tubes, and lungs, then expelling them by stimulating a strong flow of secretions from the mucous membranes in the throat. This makes the herb a good choice as an expectorant for heavy smokers.

For persistent hiccoughs (hiccups), Chinese herbals suggest a decoction of 15 grams *Codonopsis* with 5 grams balloon flower. Drink warm in one dose.

13. BELVEDERE CYPRESS

Kochia scoparia

地膚子 *di fu dze (di fu zi)*

OTHER NAMES: *sao jou tsao* (broom grass); *Chenopodium scoparia*

This plant is native to the fields and marshes of Central Asia but is also cultivated in gardens, the tender young leaves often being used as food. The mature plant, whose stem turns reddish in autumn, has long been used for making brooms, hence the Chinese nickname. The green round seeds are medicinal and contain saponins.

MEDICINAL PART: seed

NATURE: Energy: cold
             Flavor: sweet, bitter
             Affinity: kidneys

THERAPEUTIC EFFECTS: tonic; diuretic; astringent; antiphlogistic; purifies blood (TCM: tonifies primordial essence and energy)

INDICATIONS: impotence; urinary incontinence; inflammation and infection of the urinary tract (urethritis); hemorrhoids (TCM: deficient kidney-energy)

DOSAGE: decoction of seeds: 6–10 grams, in three doses, on an empty stomach

CONTRAINDICATIONS: none

INCOMPATIBLES: cuttlefish

REMARKS: Other parts of this plant also find use in herbal medicine. The shoots and stems are traditionally prescribed for dysentery, diarrhea, and other digestive tract disorders but are not used much in Chinese medicine today.

The leaves can be boiled in water to make a cooling external wash for the relief of heat rash, itching, allergic reactions, and similar skin disorders. Chinese herbals also say that this solution can be used as an eyewash to help correct night blindness.

14. BLACK PEPPER, *Piper nigrum*

胡椒 *hu jiao*

A woody vine with aerial roots and herbaceous branches, black pepper is native to the Indonesian archipelago, which has traditionally been the major source of the herb. It is also indigenous to the island of Hainan in the far south of China. The fruits, or "corns," occur in drupes of globular berries, about 6 millimeters in diameter, grayish black in color, and are highly aromatic. Though both black and white peppercorns are used as kitchen condiments in China, the native capsicum and *Zanthoxylum* (Szechuan pepper) varieties are far more commonly used due to abundant supply and low cost.

MEDICINAL PART: dried unripe fruit

NATURE: Energy: hot
           Flavor: pungent
           Affinity: spleen, stomach

THERAPEUTIC EFFECTS: stomachic; carminative; eliminative; stimulates gastric mucosa; antidote to fish, shellfish, and meat poisoning (TCM: eliminates gastric stagnation due to damp-cold in digestive tract)

INDICATIONS: sluggish digestion; abdominal pain due to stagnation; watery vomiting; food poisoning (fish and meat); obesity; sinus congestion (TCM: damp-cold in spleen and stomach; cold in bowels)

DOSAGE: decoction: 1.5–3 grams, in two doses, 30–40 minutes after meals.

powder: if decoctions of black pepper are too strong for your system, simply add ground pepper to food in the kitchen and on the dining table, which provides gentler, more gradual therapeutic actions

CONTRAINDICATIONS: hot inflammatory condition in the digestive tract

INCOMPATIBLES: none

REMARKS: Black pepper provides powerful stimulation to the functions of the entire digestive tract, from stomach to large intestine. It is therefore a good remedy for sluggish digestion, which is often a major contributing factor in obesity, fatigue, and low metabolism.

As a hot yang herb, it can be liberally applied to fresh, raw vegetable salads as a way of balancing the cold yin energies that such salads introduce into the digestive system.

15. BLETILLA STRIATA
白芨 *bai ji*

OTHER NAMES: *lan hua* (orchid); *Bletilla hyacinthina*

This is a perennial orchid with violet blossoms, 20–30 centimeters tall, long cultivated in China for decorative as well as medicinal purposes. The bulbs are highly mucilaginous, and when dried, they become hard, flat, oval disks, umbilicated on one side, the interior translucent and whitish, with a gummy bitter taste.

The herb is cultivated in China and Southeast Asia.

MEDICINAL PART: bulb (tuber)

NATURE: Energy: slightly cold
            Flavor: bitter, sweet, sour
            Affinity: lungs, liver, stomach

THERAPEUTIC EFFECTS: hemostatic; astringent; emollient; antiphlogistic; reduces swelling; promotes healing and regeneration of wounded tissues; eliminates stagnant blood from organs (TCM: tonifies lung-energy)

INDICATIONS: internal: blood in sputum and vomit; nosebleeds; hemorrhages in stomach and lungs; tuberculosis

external: broken bones and other traumatic injuries; burns; festering abscesses; swelling and inflammation; facial blemishes; cracked skin on feet, hands, and elbows; skin sores; burns; acne

DOSAGE: internal: decoction: 3–6 grams, in two doses, on an empty stomach

powder: 1–3 grams, in two doses, on an empty stomach

external: make an ointment using the powdered herb and black sesame oil, and apply externally, two or three times daily, to burns, sores, blemishes, cracked skin, and other skin disorders

CONTRAINDICATIONS: none

INCOMPATIBLES: aconite, almonds

REMARKS: Traditional sources suggest adding powdered amethyst (silica with trace manganese oxide; *dze shih ying*) to the above ointment in order to further enhance its healing powers.

16. BLUE MORNING GLORY

Pharbitis hederacea

牽牛 *chien niu (qian niu)*

OTHER NAMES: *hei chou* (black taurus); *Pharbitis nil; Ipomoea hederacea*

This climbing vine is frequently cultivated for its beautiful blue flower, and in China the capsules of the unripe fruit are gathered and roasted with honey to be eaten as a sweet. The medicinal seeds come in black and white varieties, the mother plant of the latter usually referred to as *Pharbitis nil* in Western herbology. Both varieties are used in medicine, but the black type is generally regarded as delivering swifter results. The seeds are trigonal in form, about 6 millimeters by 4 millimeters, with a smooth surface and deep violet color. They are bitter and slightly toxic.

The plant is native to the tropical regions of China, India, and parts of Southeast Asia but is also widely cultivated elsewhere.

MEDICINAL PART: seed

NATURE: Energy: cold
              Flavor: bitter
              Affinity: kidneys, lungs, large intestine

THERAPEUTIC EFFECTS: diuretic; cathartic; anthelmintic; antiphlogistic; expectorant (TCM: purges downward)

INDICATIONS: Water retention and related shortness of breath; constipation; intestinal parasites; swelling of tissues (TCM: internal stagnation due to excess water-energy)

DOSAGE: decoction: 1–3 grams, in two doses, on an empty stomach

CONTRAINDICATIONS: pregnancy; lactation; diarrhea and other conditions that cause dehydration through rapid loss of fluids

INCOMPATIBLES: none

REMARKS: The herb is mildly poisonous due to the presence of a toxin that has abortive properties, which is why it should be strictly avoided by pregnant women, even though they often suffer from the very conditions for which it is usually prescribed. The herb also has very drying properties and should therefore be used only for as long as needed to relieve symptoms; if symptoms persist, discontinue and try a different herb or formula.

Blue morning glory's therapeutic benefits are somewhat enhanced when used in combination with costus and ginger. Simply add 1–2 grams of each to the above decoction.

17. BROOMRAPE, *Cistanche salsa*

肉苁蓉 *rou tsung rung (rou cong rong)*

OTHER NAMES: *Boschniakia glabra; Orobanche ammophyla*

Several plants of the Orobanchaceae family are represented by the term *tsung rung,* all of them interchangeably employed in herbal medicine. They are annual parasitic herbs with scaly stalks and scaly roots that resemble flesh, hence the Chinese prefix *rou* (flesh). The cylindrical stalk grows from a tuberous root, and both parts are eaten, either raw or stewed with meat. Ancient Chinese legend says that the plant originally sprang from semen dropped on the ground by wild stallions. The fleshy stem is prepared for medicine by cleaning it and then soaking it in wine, after which the central fibers are removed. It is then salted and dried in the sun.

The herb is native to northern China, Mongolia, and Siberia.

MEDICINAL PART: fleshy stem

NATURE: Energy: warm
Flavor: sweet, sour, salty
Affinity: kidneys, large intestine

THERAPEUTIC EFFECTS: aphrodisiac; tonic; demulcent; emollient; laxative (TCM: tonifies kidney-yang; nourishes kidney-yin)

INDICATIONS: impotence; infertility (male and female); premature ejaculation; spermatorrhea; lumbago; constipation; numbness and pain in knees (TCM: empty kidney-yang; internal-dry in large intestine)

DOSAGE: decoction: 6–12 grams, in two or three doses, on an empty stomach

powder: 2–3 grams, three times daily, on an empty stomach

CONTRAINDICATIONS: none

INCOMPATIBLES: iron compounds and utensils

REMARKS: This herb has long been renowned in China as a potent sexual tonic for both men and women. Yang Kui-gei (Precious Concubine), the pampered and notoriously seductive consort to the elegant Tang dynasty emperor Ming Huang (eighth century CE), is said to have used this herb daily as a sexual tonic.

Most women use it primarily to promote healthy ovulation and enhance fertility, while men enjoy it mainly to strengthen their sexual organs and increase sexual vitality. It is particularly recommended as a cure and preventive for excess loss of semen due to involuntary ejaculation, a condition that Chinese physicians regard as a grave threat to male health and longevity. Therefore ancient Chinese almanacs sometimes refer to it as the Magic Medicine of Eternal Youth and Immortality.

18. BURDOCK, *Arctium lappa*

牛蒡子 *niu bang dze (niu bang zi)*

OTHER NAMES: lappa; thorny burr; beggar's buttons; *da li dze* (great power seeds)

This plant grows up to 1.5 meters tall and is commonly found in open fields and along country roads. It is a biennial herb, with a sturdy stem, heart-shaped leaves, and purple flowers. The root is thick and has a brownish gray skin, with pithy white flesh inside. The seeds are oblong, about 7 millimeters by 3 millimeters, gray with black spots. The root contains 40%–70% inulin, and the seeds contain essential oil, fatty oil, and arctiin. They are used together in medicine and have similar properties, though each has its own special applications as well, a few of which are discussed below.

The herb is native to northern China but also grows abundantly in Europe and North America.

MEDICINAL PARTS: seed; root

NATURE: Energy: cold
Flavor: seeds, pungent; root, bitter
Affinity: lungs, stomach

THERAPEUTIC EFFECTS: antiphlogistic; antitussive; diuretic; expectorant; laxative; alterative; relieves lymph congestion; antidote to toxins in bones (TCM: expels wind-dampness and wind-heat; clears internal heat)

INDICATIONS: lumbago; pneumonia and bronchitis; lung congestion; urethritis and syphilis; abscesses, boils, cankers; chicken pox in children; measles and smallpox; bladder stones (TCM: wind-heat injury; internal wind-damp; energy stagnation in waist and knees)

DOSAGE: decoction of seeds and/or roots: 3–10 grams, in three doses, on an empty stomach

CONTRAINDICATIONS: none

INCOMPATIBLES: none

REMARKS: Burdock is widely used by herbalists throughout the world. Cleansing, soothing, and purifying to the entire system, it can be combined with various other alterative and detoxifying herbs to focus on specific systems, such as blood, lymph, urinary tract, respiratory tract, and so on.

Traditional Chinese herbals suggest many different uses for various parts of the plant. For dandruff, pulverize the leaves, then simmer with a little water until it's reduced to a thick paste; rub the paste well into the scalp and leave it on overnight; next morning wash it out with a decoction of *Gleditschia sinensis (dzao-jia);* continue for up to a week, or until dandruff clears.

To facilitate recovery from stroke, pulverize the root with some water, using a mortar, food processor, or blender, then extract the pure juice by squeezing the pureed root through a cloth or fine sieve. Mix with some honey and take 1 teaspoon twice daily on an empty stomach.

The great Ming dynasty herbalist Lee Shih-chen suggests that when using decoctions of burdock to treat children for chicken pox, results will be much swifter if the child's mother takes some of the root and seeds into her mouth and masticates it to a pulp with saliva, then rubs the pulp onto the crown point *(bai hui)* of the child's head, securing it in place with a small bandage. Change the dressing once a day until the ailment is cured.

19. CARDAMOM, *Alpina oxyphylla*

益智仁 *yi jih ren (yi zhi ren)*

OTHER NAMES: *Elettaria cardamomum; Amomum amarum*

A sturdy perennial herb that grows to a height of 2.5 meters, with a floral stalk rising straight up from the root, cardamom is an aromatic herb and cooking condiment native to India, Malaysia, and parts of southern China. The medicinal seeds are contained in a small fruit that grows as a capsule on the stalk. They are irregular in shape, about 5 millimeters by 3 millimeters, grayish brown in color, with a warm taste somewhat like myrrh, and contain 2%–8% volatile oil.

MEDICINAL PART: seed

NATURE: Energy: warm
Flavor: pungent
Affinity: spleen, kidneys

THERAPEUTIC EFFECTS: stomachic; carminative; astringent; stimulant; controls excess urination and loose bowels (TCM: tonifies kidney-yang; nourishes bone and sinew; warms kidney and spleen)

INDICATIONS: spermatorrhea; urinary incontinence; diarrhea; abdominal pains; premature ejaculation; impotence; vomiting (TCM: cold-spleen and cold-kidney symptoms; deficient kidney-yang; vomiting and diarrhea due to internal cold)

DOSAGE: decoction: 3–10 grams, in two doses, on an empty stomach
    powder: plain, infusion, or capsules; 3–9 grams, in three doses, on an empty stomach

CONTRAINDICATION: stomach ulcers

INCOMPATIBLES: none

20. CATTAIL, *Typha latifolia*

蒲黄, *pu huang*

OTHER NAMES: Bulrush; *hsiang pu* (fragrant rush); *Typha orientalis*

A reed type of plant that grows in dense stands along the banks of ponds and streams; the long reddish leaves, which grow up to 2.5 meters long, are used to make mats and fans in China. The young shoots are gathered in spring and either pickled or steamed as food. The heart of the young plant, which grows in mud at the bottom of ponds, is also used as food, usually steeped raw in vinegar. The pollen of the flowers is a fine golden dust, from which the herb takes its Chinese name *pu huang*, "golden rush," and is sometimes mixed with honey to be eaten as a sweet. When collecting the medicinal pollen, it becomes mixed with the stamens and hairy sepals of the flowering spike and must therefore be sifted before it is used as medicine.

The plant grows plentifully in the northern regions of China, Europe, and North America.

MEDICINAL PART: pollen

NATURE: Energy: neutral
           Flavor: sweet
           Affinity: liver, pericardium

THERAPEUTIC EFFECTS: diuretic; hemostatic; astringent; promotes circulation; dissolves clots (TCM: balances energy-and-blood circulation)

INDICATIONS: menorrhagia; dysmenorrhea; abdominal pain after childbirth; chronic liver inflammation and accompanying pain in rib cage; spermatorrhea; pain and pressure in chest; internal hemorrhages due to traumatic injuries (TCM: functional disharmony in energy-and-blood circulation)

DOSAGE: decoction: 4–9 grams, in two doses, on an empty stomach

CONTRAINDICATIONS: use only as long as required to relieve symptoms

INCOMPATIBLES: none

REMARKS: The dregs remaining after the pollen has been sifted from the stamens and sepals can be browned in an oven or hot skillet and then used as an internal or external astringent in dysentery and other forms of bowel hemorrhage.

21. CHINESE CORNBIND

Polygonum multiflorum

何首烏 *ho shou wu*

OTHER NAMES: *jiao teng* ("tangled vine")

This perennial herb grows to heights of 7–10 meters, with large heart-shaped leaves and a tuber-ous root to which the Chinese have long attributed mysterious properties of re-juvenation. In ancient times it is said to have been used by a king surnamed Ho,  whose head *(shou)* of white hair turned black *(wu)* again after using it, hence the Chinese name *ho shou wu*. The herb is sold in flat, irregular pieces, ligneous and cre-nated, with a reddish brown color. It contains no toxins.

The plant is native to southwestern China, Taiwan, Japan, and Vietnam.

MEDICINAL PARTS: roots, stems, leaves

NATURE:
Energy:	warm
Flavor:	bitter, sour
Affinity:	liver, kidneys

THERAPEUTIC EFFECTS: demulcent to bowels; anti-rheumatic; strengthens sinew and bone; promotes male and female fertility; darkens gray hair; builds bone mar-row (TCM: nourishes semen and blood; tonifies liver- and kidney-energy; expels wind-dampness)

INDICATIONS: dizziness; insomnia; spermatorrhea; ab-dominal pain after childbirth; weak "rubbery" feeling in knees and lower back; anemia; constipation due to dry bowels; premature gray hair; abscesses; colitis (TCM: deficient kidney-yin and liver-yin; empty blood)

DOSAGE: decoction: 9–15 grams, in two doses, on an empty stomach

liquor: steep 50–80 grams in 1 liter of spirits for 1–2 months, take 1 ounce on an empty stomach, two times daily (morning and bedtime); can be used for long-term therapy as a tonic rejuvenator

CONTRAINDICATIONS: none

INCOMPATIBLES: any sort of blood product (pig blood, chicken blood, and so on); scaleless fish; white turnip; onions; garlic; iron compounds and utensils

REMARKS: Contemporary clinical evidence shows that this herb is also an effective remedy for high blood pressure and arteriosclerosis.

22. CHINESE JUJUBE, *Ziziphus vulgaris* 大枣 *da dzao (da zao)*

OTHER NAMES: Chinese date; *gan dzao* (sweet jujube)

This is the common culti- vated variety of Chinese ju- jube, which has been grown throughout China since an- cient times and remains one of the most widely em- ployed herbs in the Chinese pharmacopeia. It grows on a spiny deciduous shrub about 10 meters high, with 2-centimeter-long oblong fruits that turn dark reddish brown when ripe. The variety grown in northern China is often referred to as *bei dzao* (northern jujube), and the southern type, *nan dzao* (southern jujube).

The herb is widely cultivated in China, Japan, Korea, Europe, India, Afghanistan, and parts of Southeast Asia. The Japanese variety, which is smaller than others, does not have much therapeutic value and is used mainly in food products. The Korean product is generally regarded as the best on the market today, but due to limited supplies, Chinese and European varieties comprise the bulk of the trade.

MEDICINAL PART: fruit

NATURE: Energy: neutral
           Flavor: sweet
           Affinity: spleen

THERAPEUTIC EFFECTS: tonic; nutrient; sedative; antitussive; emollient to lungs; promotes secretions of vital fluids; retards aging (TCM: tonifies spleen- and stomach-energy; nourishes blood; warming)

INDICATIONS: fatigue; insomnia; hypertension; physical exhaustion; malnutrition (TCM: empty spleen and stomach symptoms; internal-cold symptoms; deficient energy)

DOSAGE: decoction: six to twelve fruits, crushed (use pliers to crush the kernels inside as well), in two doses, on an empty stomach

CONTRAINDICATIONS: gastritis, bloating, and other stomach disorders

INCOMPATIBLES: aconite, onions, fish; herbs of the Menispermaceae family

REMARKS: When using jujube, it's very important to crush the kernels inside in order to release their active constituents; ordinary pliers do the job very well. In TCM, the 3-year-old kernels are regarded as particularly efficacious for abdominal pains and as an external application to wounds.

Jujubes are frequently included in formulas for warming tonic herbal liquors; in addition to lending their own warming tonic properties to the brew, they also act to prolong, enhance, and harmonize the effects of the other ingredients. They have a unique capacity to draw out the powers and balance the energies of whatever other herbs they're combined with.

Jujubes are said to "clear the nine openings," the apertures that connect the human system to the external environment, such as eyes, ears, nose, throat, anus, and so on. The herb facilitates the flow of energies through these apertures, as well as throughout the entire human system, removing any obstructions to the smooth flow of vital energies. Jujubes are therefore good energy supplements. When included in tonic formulas, they insure that the herbal essences are all well circulated in the bloodstream and their energies properly distributed in the meridians.

23. CHINESE WOLFBERRY

Lycium chinense

枸杞子 *gou ji dze (gou ji zi)*

OTHER NAMES: *yang ru* (goat milk); *Lycium barbatum*

This plant occurs as a common shrub throughout the northern and western regions of China, growing to a height of about 1 meter, with delicate edible leaves and small purple flowers. The fruit is a small, oval, reddish orange berry about 2 centimeters long, with a sweet but rather coarse taste. Inferior grades are often soaked in red coloring to improve their appearance for sale, so be sure to specify the natural, undyed herb when shopping for it.

Today most wolfberry comes from China and Japan.

MEDICINAL PART: fruit

NATURE: Energy: neutral
         Flavor: sweet
         Affinity: liver, kidneys

THERAPEUTIC EFFECTS: tonic; nutrient; emollient to lungs; relieves chronic thirst; corrects blurry vision (TCM: nourishes kidney-yin; tonifies liver-energy)

INDICATIONS: spermatorrhea; weak knees; lumbago; dizziness; headache; blurry or weak vision; fatigue; thirst (TCM: deficient liver-yin; deficient kidney-yin)

DOSAGE: decoction: 6–12 grams, in two doses, on an empty stomach; the berries can be eaten along with the broth

liquor: steep 80 grams in 1 liter of spirits for 2 months; add some honey; take 1 ounce, twice daily, on an empty stomach; berries need not be strained out.

cooking: 15–20 grams can be added to stewed meat, chicken, and seafood dishes; eat the berries along with the rest of the stew

CONTRAINDICATIONS: weak digestion; fever; arthritis

INCOMPATIBLES: be sure not to use any sort of iron, aluminum, or other metal utensils when preparing wolfberry

REMARKS: Wolfberry has been a popular health tonic since ancient times in China, and it appears in many longevity formulas. Among its many benefits, it is especially good medicine for eye problems and improves vision. The elderly and infirm frequently use it to strengthen weak legs and knees. The herb has nutritional as well as medicinal value, and its sweet flavor lends itself very well to cooking. Soaked for a day or two in some honey and rum, wolfberries make a tasty tonic snack, but they're quite potent taken "straight," so don't eat too many at one time.

For strong tonification of kidney-energy and sexual vitality, combine with *Rehmannia glutinosa*. For balanced heart and kidney (Fire and Water) tonification, combine with ginseng.

24. CHINESE YAM, *Dioscorea opposita*

山藥 *shan yao*

OTHER NAMES: *Dioscorea japonica; D. batatas*

This beanlike plant has long tuberous roots and spade-shaped leaves, with stems that twine consistently to the right or left, depending on the species, of which at least six hundred have been identified worldwide. Many varieties are edible and nutritious, but the Chinese yam described here is cultivated exclusively for the pharmacy, as reflected in the Chinese name *shan yao* (mountain medicine). The tough outer skin is entirely removed, and the dried white flesh of the tubers is sliced into long thin slabs. The flesh contains starch, mucilage, the enzyme amylase, fat, sugar, and the amino acids arginine, leucine, and tyrosine.

The plant is cultivated for medicine primarily in China and Japan.

MEDICINAL PART: tuber

NATURE: Energy: neutral
                     Flavor: sweet
                     Affinity: spleen, lungs

THERAPEUTIC EFFECTS: stomachic; digestive, antidiarrhetic; moistens skin and hair; stimulates endocrine secretions; immunotonic; strengthens kidney functions; stimulates appetite (TCM: tonifies spleen- and lungenergy; tonifies yin-energy; nourishes semen-essence)

INDICATIONS: spermatorrhea, nocturnal emissions, and related fatigue and neurasthenia; chronic fatigue; leukorrhea; loss of appetite; immune deficiency; abscesses, boils, carbuncles, and other skin sores and infections; cold or weak limbs (TCM: empty spleen and stomach; deficient yin-energy)

DOSAGE: decoction: 10–25 grams, in two doses, on an empty stomach.

poultice: for external application to festering skin sores such as those listed above, also for bruises and hard swellings, mix the powdered herb with a little water to form a poultice paste and apply to affected area once daily, leaving it in place at least 8–12 hours

CONTRAINDICATIONS: constipation; high blood pressure

INCOMPATIBLES: pork; onion

REMARKS: This is one of several herbs currently under intensive medical research in China as a tonic restorative for immune deficiency. The herb helps restore impaired immune functions, stimulates secretions of vital immune factors, and enhances overall immune response throughout the system.

In order to better bring out its benefits as a sexual tonic for impotence and lumbago in men and infertility or frigidity in women, combine with young deer horn shavings *(Cervus nippon, lu rung)*.

A convenient and tasty way to use this herb for long-term tonification is to add it as an ingredient to an herbal porridge with Chinese jujube, such as herbal porridge #4, on page 268.

25. CHRYSANTHEMUM

Chrysanthemum morifolium

菊花 *ju hua*

OTHER NAME: *Chrysanthemum sinense*

A perennial herb of the Compositae family, this particular variety grows wild in many parts of China, particularly in the north; it has also been culti-vated in Chinese gardens as a favorite winter flower ever since ancient times. The wild plant, which seldom exceeds half a meter in height, bears small flower heads in late autumn, with yellow florets and rose-colored rays. Cultivated varieties come in different colors and sizes, and although some sources make a few minor distinctions among the medicinal properties of the different types, their therapeutic actions are all largely identical. The flowers, which are dried for sale, have a pale yellow color and bittersweet flavor.

The herb is cultivated for medicinal use primarily in China and Japan.

MEDICINAL PART: flower

NATURE: Energy: cool
             Flavor: sweet, bitter
             Affinity: lungs, liver

THERAPEUTIC EFFECTS: antipyretic; refrigerant; lowers blood pressure; improves vision (TCM: clears internal heat; nourishes blood)

INDICATIONS: headache, dizziness, eye aches, and blurry vision due to kidney and liver dysfunctions; high blood pressure; numbness in extremities (TCM: wind-heat injury; internal heat)

DOSAGE: infusion: in a large teapot or similar non-metallic vessel, put 8–10 grams of dried flowers and add about 1 liter of boiling water; steep 15–30 minutes, then pour into a separate pot; drink frequently throughout the day, either warm, room temperature, or slightly chilled; the herb can be steeped up to three times; to further improve the flavor and enhance the therapeutic benefits, you can add 4–5 grams of either licorice or Chinese wolfberry (but not both) to the pot

wine: steep 20–30 grams in 1 liter of rice wine (Japanese sake is best for this purpose) or ordinary dry sherry, for 1–2 weeks only; take 1 ounce, two or three times daily, on an empty stomach, mainly for digestive, circulatory, and nervous disorders

pillow: make a small pillow with the dried flowers and use for respiratory ailments, headaches, and inflamed eyes; be sure to thoroughly dry the flowers in the sun for 2 days before making the pillow, and check the contents frequently for mildew, redrying in the sun as required

CONTRAINDICATIONS: none

INCOMPATIBLES: none

REMARKS: Infusions of chrysanthemum are particularly good for swelling, inflammation, and itching in the eyes, both internally and as an external wash. In cases of conjunctivitis, daily eyewashes with this herb relieve discomfort and hasten the healing effects of other medicines.

26. CIMICIFUGA FOETIDA

升麻 *sheng ma*

OTHER NAMES: *Actea spicata; Cimicifuga japonica*

A tall perennial herb with small white flowers and clusters of black fruit follicles, this plant comes in several varieties throughout China, the main source being the mountain ravines of Szechuan. All sorts of wondrous properties are ascribed to this herb in Chinese medical texts, but so far modern pharmaceutical science has failed to verify most of them. The medicinal root contains tannin and a resin called cimicifugin.

The plant is found in China, Siberia, and Europe, while a related species, *Cimicifuga racemosa*, was a popular medicinal herb in North America during the nineteenth century.

MEDICINAL PART: root

NATURE: Energy: cool
          Flavor: sweet, pungent, slightly bitter
          Affinity: kidney

THERAPEUTIC EFFECTS: diaphoretic; antipyretic; analgesic; antidote (TCM: stimulates yang-energy; clears internal heat)

INDICATIONS: headache; fever and chills; red and painful eyes; mouth and lip abscesses; bronchial infections with heavy cough; spermatorrhea; cold feet; diarrhea; prolapse of anus; thyroid disorders (TCM: deficient yang-energy; internal heat)

DOSAGE: decoction: 6–9 grams, in two doses, on an empty stomach (the decoction can also be used as a gargle in bronchial infections, tonsillitis, and other sore throat conditions)

powder: plain or capsules; 2–3 grams, two or three times daily

CONTRAINDICATIONS: TCM: deficient yin-energy

INCOMPATIBLES: none

27. CINNAMON, *Cinnamomum cassia*
肉桂 *rou qui*

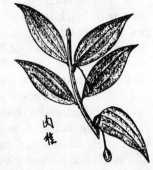

OTHER NAMES: cassia; *mu gui* (wood cinnamon); *cinnamomum aromaticum*

Grown in the southern regions of China since ancient times, the cassia or cinnamon tree grows to a height of 10 meters and is cultivated primarily for its reddish brown, strongly aromatic bark, which comes in rolled tubes. Sometimes an essential oil containing 80% cinnamic aldehyde is extracted from the bark, and both the oil and the bark are used in cooking as well as medicine.

The tree is native to southern China, Vietnam, Laos, and Sumatra. A variety called *an gui* or *an nan gui* from Vietnam is regarded to be the best.

MEDICINAL PART: unscraped bark of large mature trees

NATURE: Energy: very hot
Flavor: pungent, sweet
Affinity: liver, spleen, kidneys

THERAPEUTIC EFFECTS: stomachic; analgesic; stimulant; astringent; diaphoretic; improves vision; enhances circulation (TCM: tonifies yang-energy; warming)

INDICATIONS: loss of appetite; fatigue; abdominal pain; lack of energy after long illness or surgery; dysmenorrhea; red and swollen eyes; cold extremities (TCM: deficient kidney-yang; deficient spleen-yang; internal cold in abdomen; deficient blood and energy)

DOSAGE: decoction: 2–5 grams, in two doses, on an empty stomach; for greater therapeutic benefits, add 2 grams of licorice and three slices of ginseng to this decoction; the ginseng can be chewed afterward to extract its full potential

CONTRAINDICATIONS: none

INCOMPATIBLES: onions; kaolin

REMARKS: Cinnamon is known in TCM as an excellent synergist for many other herbs, particularly yang tonics. It is used to enhance the warming and tonic properties of herbal liquors, and also to improve their flavor.

As one of the most warming herbs in the Chinese pharmacopeia, cinnamon is an excellent choice for warming up cold hands and feet and cold internal organs. Its heating and diaphoretic properties can be used in combination with *Ephedra* during the early stages of colds and flu to induce perspiration and drive internal heat out through the pores of the skin.

Modern research has also shown that the volatile oil extracted from cinnamon has significant antiviral activity.

28. CNIDIUM MONNIERI

蛇床子 *she chuang dze (she chuang zi)*

OTHER NAME: *Selinum monnieri*

A fragrant annual herb with an erect stem and bi-pinnate leaves, the plant grows about 50–70 centimeters tall and is found almost everywhere in China. The medicinal seeds are grayish yellow in color and look like grains of millet. They contain 1.3% essential oil, including borneol, pinene, camphene, and terpineol.

In addition to China, the herb is found in Vietnam, Laos, Siberia, and eastern Europe.

MEDICINAL PART: seed

NATURE:
Energy:	warm	
Flavor:	pungent, bitter	
Affinity:	kidneys	

THERAPEUTIC EFFECTS: tonic; antirheumatic; antiseptic; aphrodisiac; astringent; stimulant (TCM: tonifies kidney-yang; stimulates yang-energy; expels wind-damp)

INDICATIONS: impotence; female infertility; vaginal itching and yeast infections; damp itchy scrotum; abscesses; ringworm (TCM: deficient kidney-yang; wind-damp symptoms; infertility due to internal cold in uterus)

DOSAGE: decoction: 5–10 grams, in two doses, on an empty stomach

powder: plain, capsules, or pills; 3–9 grams, in two or three doses, on an empty stomach

external wash: decoct 10 grams and use the broth as an antiseptic wash for vaginal itching, yeast infections, itchy rash on scrotum, abscesses, and other itchy, damp skin infections; can also be used as an astringent wash for hemorrhoids

CONTRAINDICATIONS: males with chronic spermatorrhea and premature ejaculation should avoid using this herb, because it will increase the amount of semen lost during ejaculation and thus cause further enervation and weakness; in such cases, herbs that specifically control involuntary ejaculation should be used first, in conjunction with Taoist sexual yoga, in order to gain voluntary control of ejaculation, then start using herbs such as this to boost semen production, promote fertility, and elevate sexual potency.

INCOMPATIBLES: tree peony, croton, *Fritillaria verticillata*

REMARKS: This is one of the best Chinese herbs to use as an antiseptic and astringent external wash for all sorts of damp, itchy skin conditions and infections, particularly on the scrotum and vagina. It's effective against many strains of yeast that commonly infect the female genital region, and it can be applied for this purpose to wash the inside of the vagina as well as the external area.

29. CODONOPSIS DANGSHEN

黨參 *dang shen*

OTHER NAMES: bastard ginseng; *Campanumaea pilosula*

This is one of several plants of the Campanulaceae family whose roots resemble ginseng and are sometimes fraudulently substituted for true ginseng. It is a perennial herb that grows about 1 meter high, with long oval leaves and a yellowish brown, deeply wrinkled root about 25 centimeters long. The Chinese pharmacopeia classifies this herb with true ginseng *(ren shen),* hence the name includes the generic term for ginseng *(shen),* and indeed its therapeutic properties are quite similar, although not as strong. *Dang* refers to the name of the region in ancient China from which this herb originally came *(Shang dang),* and thus it was originally listed as *Shang dang ren sheng,* which was later contracted to *dang shen.* The interior of the root is brittle and has a light-colored central pith. Its taste is sweet and malty, and it contains saponin.

The herb comes primarily from its original sources in northern China.

MEDICINAL PART: root

NATURE: Energy: warm
Flavor: sweet
Affinity: spleen, lungs

THERAPEUTIC EFFECTS: stomachic; cardiotonic; builds immunity and raises resistance; lowers blood pressure; raises blood sugar (TCM: tonifies spleen- and lung-energy; nourishes blood and energy)

INDICATIONS: chronic fatigue; hypertension; loss of appetite; indigestion due to hyperacidity; loose bowels; pale complexion; exhaustion after surgery or childbirth;

body bloating and facial swelling due to edema; immune deficiency; hypoglycemia (low blood sugar) (TCM: deficient blood and energy; deficient spleen-energy)

DOSAGE: decoction: 10–15 grams, in two doses, on an empty stomach; for digestive ailments, spleen dysfunction, and chronic fatigue, add 6–8 grams of Chinese jujube (crush the flesh and kernels with pliers first)

CONTRAINDICATIONS: none

INCOMPATIBLES: none

REMARKS: Since this herb acts similarly to ginseng, it can be substituted for the latter when ginseng is too costly or in short supply. It is often used instead of ginseng for mild chronic conditions that do not require high-potency herbs. Recent research has also established *dang shen* as an effective preventive against many forms of heart disease. Since it lends itself well to cooking, it can be used daily in the kitchen as an ingredient in stews, soups, and porridges, or simply boiled in chicken broth, as a general nutrient tonic for the whole family and a specific preventive against heart disease.

For maximum therapeutic results in cases of physical exhaustion, recuperation from surgery or childbirth, and weak digestion, Chinese herbals recommend the following blend of food and medicine: roast 30 grams of brown rice in a hot, dry skillet or oven just until its color starts to darken and its aroma is released; combine with 30 grams *Codonopsis,* add 5 cups pure water, bring to boil, and decoct to 2 cups. Drink the broth warm in three daily doses, on an empty stomach. Nursing mothers can use this nourishing herbal broth both as a fortifying energy tonic to recover their strength, and also as a galactagogue to increase the quantity and quality of their milk.

According to the traditional Chinese view, the reason that this herb is such a reliable energy tonic is because of its affinity for the spleen and lungs, which are the two major organ-energy systems responsible for the extraction of energy from food and air through digestion and respiration. By enhancing supplies of energy derived from food and air, this herb provides the body with the essential ingredients it requires to produce True Human Energy *(jeng chee),* the basic fuel of life.

30. COLTSFOOT, *Tussilago farfara*
款冬花 *kuan dung hua*

OTHER NAMES: cough wort; horse hoof

This perennial herb has a soft cottony down on the stem and the underside of the leaves, and large yellow flowers that look like daisies. The leaves, which are 12–20 centimeters long and shaped like a colt's foot, do not unfold until the flowers have withered. The floral buds are pungent and contain saponins, inulin, stearin, and choline.

Coltsfoot is native to northern China, Europe, Africa, and Siberia, but it has long been naturalized in North America, where the leaves rather than the flowers comprise the main medicinal part.

MEDICINAL PARTS: flowers and floral buds; leaves

NATURE: Energy: warm
         Flavor: pungent
         Affinity: lungs

THERAPEUTIC EFFECTS: antitussive; expectorant; antiphlogistic; demulcent to lungs (TCM: tonifies lung-energy)

INDICATIONS: coughs, including "smoker's cough"; asthma; shortness of breath due to lung congestion; acute or chronic lung infections (TCM: empty lung-energy)

DOSAGE: decoction of flowers and buds: 5–12 grams, in two doses, on an empty stomach.

decoction of leaves: 5–10 grams, in two doses, on an

empty stomach; used primarily for pulmonary congestion with cough

CONTRAINDICATIONS: none

INCOMPATIBLES: *Gleditschia chinensis,* mirabilite, *Scrophularia,* astragalus, forsythia, ephedra, *Celosia argentea*

REMARKS: In China, the leaves and flowers are coarsely chopped and smoked for the treatment of chronic coughs. Habitual cigarette smokers occasionally substitute this herb for tobacco when their lungs get too congested. China even produces a popular brand of cigarettes using coltsfoot in place of tobacco and markets it as a remedy for smoker's cough.

31. CORYDALIS AMBIGUA

延胡索 *yen hu suo*

An herbaceous perennial herb with a soft erect stem about 20 centimeters high, this plant, according to Ming dynasty master herbalist Lee Shih-chen, originally came from "the land of the northeastern Barbarians," which refers to Siberia, Kamchatka, and the Amur region. The medicinal root is sold as small, flat, hard tubers, about 15–20 centimeters thick and 20 millimeters in diameter, with a wrinkled, reddish yellow exterior and a light yellow, semitranslucent interior. It has a bitter taste and contains numerous potent alkaloids, including corydaline, corybulbine, isocorybulbine, corycavidine, corydine, and others.

The plant grows in Siberia, Manchuria, northern China, and Japan.

MEDICINAL PART: root

NATURE: Energy: warm
            Flavor: bitter, pungent
            Affinity: kidneys

THERAPEUTIC EFFECTS: analgesic, antispasmodic, sedative, emmenagogue, deobstruent; promotes circulation of blood (TCM: regulates energy)

INDICATIONS: bodily aches and pains; menstrual disorders; uterine congestion after childbirth; bruises and clots due to broken bones and other traumatic injuries (TCM: energy and blood stagnation; ascending energy)

DOSAGE: decoction: 4–10 grams, in three doses, on an empty stomach

CONTRAINDICATIONS: none

INCOMPATIBLES: iron, aluminum, and other metal compounds and utensils

32. COSTUS, *Saussurea lappa*

木香 *mu hsiang (mu xiang)*

OTHER NAMES: *Aplotaxis lappa; Aucklandia costus;* kusta

A perennial herb with a sturdy stem, large, heart-shaped leaves, and purple florets, the plant grows to a height of 2 meters. The herb used to be shipped to China in enormous quantities from the Indian ports of Bombay and Calcutta, where it was delivered after harvest from Kashmir. The medicinal root is sold in chipped fragments about 4 centimeters long by 1 centimeter wide, light brown on the outside and white on the inside, resembling old pieces of broken bone. It has a fragrant aroma somewhat similar to musk and a bitter, mucilaginous taste. It was formerly used in southern China to make incense and protect clothing from infestation by moths and other insects. The root contains the alkaloid saussurine and essential oil.

The herb is native to northern India, Persia, and Syria, and also grows in Yunnan, Honan, and a few other parts of China.

MEDICINAL PART: root

NATURE: Energy: warm
         Flavor: pungent; bitter
         Affinity: spleen, large intestine

THERAPEUTIC EFFECTS: stomachic; analgesic; carminative; antiseptic; calms fetus; antidote; deodorant (TCM: regulates energy; tonifies large intestine–energy)

INDICATIONS: pressure, pain, and gas in abdomen; diarrhea and dysentery; angina and other oppressive chest pains; nausea; asthma; body odor (TCM: cold injury; bodily pains due to energy imbalance)

DOSAGE: decoction: 1.5–8 grams, in three doses, on an empty stomach

fresh root: the extracted juice of the fresh root, if available, is a particularly effective asthma remedy; 15–20 grams of fresh root per day, in three doses, on an empty stomach; dilute the juice with some pure water before ingesting

CONTRAINDICATIONS: use this herb only as long as required for symptoms; excessive use can inhibit and disrupt human energies

INCOMPATIBLES: none

33. COWHERD, *Saponaria vaccaria*

王不留行 *wang bu liu hsing*
(*wang bu lio xing*)

OTHER NAMES: soapwort; *jin gung hua* (forbidden palace flower)

An annual herb that grows to a height of 30–60 centimeters, it has an erect stem, opposite oblong leaves, and pink bell-shaped flowers with a cylindrical calyx enclosing the seed capsule. It grows in open fields and has a smooth, slippery surface that can easily cause a fall if stepped on. Therefore, a prince in ancient times forbade the plant to be grown within the palace grounds; thus the two Chinese names meaning "unpopular at court" and "forbidden palace flower." The medicinal seeds are round, reddish brown, and look like mustard seeds. They are bitter and contain saponin.

The plant is native to various regions in western Asia and southern Europe but is now cultivated in China as well.

MEDICINAL PART: seed

NATURE: Energy: neutral
          Flavor: bitter, sweet
          Affinity: liver, stomach

THERAPEUTIC EFFECTS: styptic; astringent; analgesic; laxative; galactagogue; emmenagogue; expectorant (TCM: stimulates meridians)

INDICATIONS: stroke; numbness in extremities; bleeding cuts and abrasions; abscesses; chronic cough; insufficient lactation; headaches

DOSAGE: external use: the powdered herb can be applied directly to wounds, abscesses, and so on, in order to stop bleeding and promote rapid healing

internal use: decoction: 5–7 grams, in two doses, before or after food; due to the herb's extreme bitterness, it is usually combined with other herbs, depending on the ailment to be treated

CONTRAINDICATIONS: pregnancy

INCOMPATIBLES: none

REMARKS: This herb is used for its astringent properties in a patent formula called Prostate Gland Pills, for swelling and inflammation of the prostate. The formula is quite effective, but during treatment the herb causes some men to temporarily lose the capacity to sustain erection, a side effect that disappears when the herb is withdrawn. In fact, this effect helps support the therapy, because men are supposed to refrain from sexual intercourse anyway during treatment for prostate problems.

34. CREEPING LILYTURF

Liriope spicata

麦門冬 *mai men dung*

OTHER NAME: *Ophiopogon spicatus*

This is a perennial herb with a short, thick rootstock and long stiff leaves, about 30 centimeters long by 5 millimeters wide, which resemble the leaves of the garlic plant. It bears violet flowers in the autumn and blue berries in the winter. The tuberous roots are medicinal and appear as shriveled, pale yellow, flexible tubers about 4 centimeters long, with a sweet taste and pleasant fragrance. It is nontoxic, and the fresh herb can be eaten as food.

The plant grows plentifully in China and Japan.

MEDICINAL PART: root tuber

NATURE:
  Energy: slightly cold
  Flavor: sweet, slightly bitter
  Affinity: heart, stomach, lungs

THERAPEUTIC EFFECTS: nutrient; antitussive; antiphlogistic; stomachic; emollient; galactagogue; diuretic; cardiotonic; promotes secretions of vital fluids (TCM: nourishes yin-energy; tonifies stomach-energy; tonifies heart-energy; clears internal heat)

INDICATIONS: weak cardiac function; poor circulation; recuperation from surgery, illness, or childbirth; shortness of breath; insufficient lactation; chronic dry cough; blood in sputum; hypoglycemia (TCM: deficient lung-yin; internal heat in lungs; deficient heart-energy; deficient vital fluids)

DOSAGE: decoction: 6–12 grams, in two doses, on an empty stomach
  cooking: this herb lends itself very well to culinary

uses, and its therapeutic powers are enhanced when combined and consumed with food; 10–15 grams can be added to various stews, soups, and herbal porridges

CONTRAINDICATIONS: People with generally weak constitutions, poor digestion, and chronic diarrhea should avoid single use of this herb. When the herb is cooked and eaten together with food, however, these contraindications do not apply. (TCM: internal cold in stomach)

INCOMPATIBLES: coltsfoot; *Sophora angustifolia; Celosia argentea;* edible tree lichens (tree ears)

REMARKS: This herb is particularly useful for recuperation after surgery, childbirth, or serious illness, especially after a bout of pneumonia or other severe lung infection. By strengthening the lungs and enhancing respiration, it increases the supply of oxygen and energy extracted from air through breathing.

35. CURCULIGO ENSIFOLIA
仙茅 hsien yu (hsien mao)

OTHER NAMES: *Curculigo orchiodes; Hypoxis aurea; po luo men shen* (Brahmin ginseng)

This is a biennial herb that grows up to 50 centimeters high, with long wide leaves, 30 centimeters by 20 centimeters, and yellow flowers. The Chinese names meaning "immortal reed" and "Brahmin ginseng" are derived from the facts that the herb was originally imported to China from India and has restorative properties similar to ginseng. The tuberous roots have a coarse, dark brown outer skin and yellowish white interior and are about the size of a little finger, much like ginseng. The herb is mildly toxic and contains 4% tannin.

The plant grows in India, Malaysia, Southeast Asia, and southern China.

MEDICINAL PART: root

NATURE:
Energy:	warm
Flavor:	pungent
Affinity:	kidneys

THERAPEUTIC EFFECTS: tonic; stimulant; aphrodisiac; digestive; strengthens urinary tract (TCM: warms kidney-yang; tonifies sinew and bone)

INDICATIONS: impotence; urinary incontinence; fatigue; cold chest pains; numbness in extremities; premature senility; tinnitus (TCM: cold-full in uterus; cold sperm [male sterility])

DOSAGE: decoction: 5–9 grams, in two doses, on an empty stomach
   powder: plain, capsules, pills, or paste; 6–9 grams, in two or three doses, on an empty stomach

CONTRAINDICATIONS: (TCM: empty yin with flaring fire symptoms)

INCOMPATIBLES: iron, aluminum, and other metal compounds and utensils

REMARKS: The "empty yin with flaring fire" symptoms referred to above is a male degenerative condition in which kidney Water (yin) becomes severely depleted (empty) due to excessive loss of semen, while the kidney Fire (yang) of sexual desire flares out of control as kidney Water grows progressively weaker and thus loses its natural restraining influence over kidney Fire, permitting sexual desire to flare out of control. Not only does this condition cause excessive loss of semen through voluntary sexual activity, it also causes involuntary loss through spermatorrhea and nocturnal emission. In Chinese medicine, involuntary ejaculation is seen as a warning signal from the body that a man's sexual potency is on the brink of complete depletion, not as a harmless way of expelling excess semen, as in the conventional Western view. Empty yin with flaring fire can drive men into self-destructive cycles of increasing sexual indulgence with diminishing sexual potency, a sort of uncontrollable "sexual addiction" that has become very common in modern urban life-styles. Aphrodisiacs should be strictly avoided until kidney Water (that is, sexual glands and fluids) have been fully replenished with plenty of rest, good nutrition, restorative yin tonics, and disciplined conservation of semen.

Ming dynasty herbalist Lee Shih-chen provides the following special recipe for impotence and related tinnitus (ringing in the ears): combine 15 grams of this herb with 15 grams each of the fruits and roots of *Rosa laevigana* (Cherokee rose), stuff the herbs inside the cavity of a fresh range-fed chicken, and stew in a combination of wine and water for 2–3 hours.

36. CYNOMORIUM COCCINEUM

鎖陽 *suo yang*

OTHER NAME: squaw root

Similar in size and shape to broomrape, with which it is sometimes confused, this herb first came to China from the Mongol steppes. Most Western botanists categorize it as a *Balanophora,* while others group it with *Orobanche* (along with broomrape). It has a fleshy, reddish brown root, scaled and wrinkled, with a strong semblance to a phallus. It is said that lecherous Mongol women used it for masturbation, and that the root grows erect when it comes into contact with the female sexual organ. Remarkably, a related species in North America is known as squaw root for precisely the same reason. Like broomrape, the herb is said to have sprouted from spots where wild stallions dropped semen onto the ground. Due to these virile associations, the root has long been regarded as an aphrodisiac for women and a stimulator of semen production in men.

The herb grows mostly in Mongolia but also in parts of northern and western China.

MEDICINAL PARTS: root, stem

NATURE: Energy: warm
         Flavor: sweet
         Affinity: kidneys, large intestine

THERAPEUTIC EFFECTS: aphrodisiac; tonic; promotes semen production; demulcent (TCM: tonifies kidney-yin and kidney-yang; nourishes marrow)

INDICATIONS: impotence; spermatorrhea; nocturnal emissions; premature ejaculation; weakness in lower back and knees; dry skin and mouth; thirst; constipation due to dry bowels and old age (TCM: deficient kidney-energy; internal-dry symptoms)

DOSAGE: decoction: 5–12 grams, in two doses, on an empty stomach

powder: pills or paste; 4–9 grams, in two or three doses, on an empty stomach

CONTRAINDICATIONS: none

INCOMPATIBLES: none

REMARKS: The obvious phallic imagery and sexual lore associated with this herb might incline skeptics to discount its reputation as an aphrodisiac as a typical example of the Doctrine of Signatures, rather than herbal science. In fact, however, the herb's sexually fortifying properties have been long established by clinical experience in China.

For swifter results when using the herb as a remedy for impotence and premature ejaculation, Chinese herbals suggest a decoction of the following herbs, taken in three daily doses, on an empty stomach:

Cynomorium	15 grams
Codonopsis	12 grams
Chinese yam	12 grams
Raspberry	9 grams

37. DANDELION, *Taraxacum officinale*
蒲公英 *pu gung ying*

OTHER NAMES: blow ball; lion's tooth; *Leontodon taraxacum; huang hua di ding* (yellow flower earth nail)

This perennial herb belongs to the sunflower family and grows in fields and gardens throughout the world. The plant has shiny green, tooth-edged leaves and a single yellow flower that blooms from April to November. The root and stem yield a milky fluid

when cut. The leaves can be added to soups and salads, and in China the tender young shoots are used as a cooking herb. In Western herbology, only the root is used, but in TCM the entire plant is employed as medicine.

The plant grows freely in the temperate zones throughout the world.

MEDICINAL PART: whole plant

NATURE: Energy: cold
            Flavor: bitter, sweet
            Affinity: liver, stomach

THERAPEUTIC EFFECTS: antidote; cholagogue; galactagogue; stomachic; deobstruent; antipyretic; reduces swelling and dissolves clots; purifies blood (TCM: clears internal heat)

INDICATIONS: food poisoning; pain and swelling in breasts; breast tumors; congestion and inflammation of liver and gallbladder; kidney and gallbladder stones; tuberculosis and clots in lungs; snakebite (TCM: internal heat)

DOSAGE: if you wish to pick your own plants for medicinal use, pull the entire plant, including roots, from the soil, remove dirt, dry them well in the sun and wind, and store for use in decoctions, as follows:

for liver and gallbladder disorders and related tension, nausea, and irritability: 6–8 plants, in two doses, on an empty stomach, for 10 days–2 weeks

for insufficient lactation: 10 plants, in three doses, on an empty stomach

for breast tumors and related pain and swelling: 20 plants, in three doses, on an empty stomach

external use: the juice of the whole fresh plants can be applied as antidote in poisonous snakebites

CONTRAINDICATIONS: none

INCOMPATIBLES: none

REMARKS: Dandelion is a medicinal herb that lends itself very well to use as food. The leaves—which contain 7,000 units of vitamin A per ounce (compared to only

1,275 for carrots), as well as vitamins B, C, and many minerals—make a tasty and nutritious contribution to salads and soups. In order to eliminate the bitter taste, you can either soak the leaves in salt water for 30 minutes, or blanch them briefly in boiling water. During World War II in Germany, dandelion root was dried and ground as a substitute for coffee, and this has remained a popular habit in European health circles.

In TCM, the herb is reputed as a particularly effective remedy for disorders of the female reproductive organs, especially the breasts, and for all sorts of hepatic dysfunctions. This is due to the herb's potent decongestive, deobstruent, and detoxicant properties, which work equally effectively on blood, bile, phlegm, tumors, and organ tissues. It's an excellent choice for detoxifying the blood, liver, and kidneys whenever you feel a toxic "hangover" from excess consumption of alcohol, drugs, junk food, and other metabolic poisons.

38. DENDROBIUM NOBILE

石斛 *shih hu*

OTHER NAMES: *huang tsao* (yellow grass); *Epidendrum monile*

This is a perennial epiphyte of the Orchidaceae family that grows on stones in alpine areas, hence the prefix *shih* (stone). It has straight, solid, cylindrical stems that are jointed and golden yellow in color. The plant blooms in clusters of two to four flowers, either white or purple, and has two pairs of pollen sacs.

The herb is native to western China, Laos, and the Himalayan region.

MEDICINAL PARTS: root, stem

NATURE:
	Energy:	cold
	Flavor:	slightly sweet, slightly salty
	Affinity:	kidneys, stomach, large intestine

THERAPEUTIC EFFECTS: tonic; stimulant; stomachic; secretagogue; salivant; promotes peristalsis (TCM: tonifies kidney energy; nourishes semen-essence)

INDICATIONS: nervous exhaustion; adrenal deficiency; night sweats; nocturnal emissions; weakness in lower back and knees (male); dehydration (TCM: deficient kidney-energy)

DOSAGE: decoction: 6–12 grams, in two doses, on an empty stomach; this herb requires some extra boiling time to extract its potential, so add 1 extra cup of water

CONTRAINDICATIONS: none

INCOMPATIBLES: *Croton tiglium*

39. DODDER, *Cuscuta japonica*

菟絲子 *tu seh dze (tu si zi)*

OTHER NAMES: *yu nu* (jade woman); *yeh hu sse* (wild fox silk); *Cuscuta chinensis*

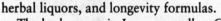

An annual parasitic herb with a reddish brown filament stem and few leaves, dodder occurs in numerous varieties throughout China. The medicinal seeds are brown, about 1 millimeter in diameter, with little taste or smell; they contain the glycoside cuscutin. They have long been a popular ingredient in sexual tonics, especially herbal liquors, and longevity formulas.

The herb grows in Japan as well as China.

MEDICINAL PART: seed

NATURE: Energy: neutral
Flavor: sweet, pungent
Affinity: kidneys, liver

THERAPEUTIC EFFECTS: tonic; nutrient; stimulant; retards aging; improves vision; strengthens urinary tract; strengthens bone and sinew (TCM: tonifies kidney- and liver-energy; nourishes semen-essence)

INDICATIONS: impotence; premature ejaculation; nocturnal emissions; urinary incontinence; lumbago; leukorrhea; premature senility (TCM: deficient liver-energy; empty kidney-energy; empty-cold symptoms)

DOSAGE: decoction: 7–12 grams, in 2 doses, on an empty stomach

CONTRAINDICATIONS: If you have any sores, abscesses, or other open wounds that have not fully healed, you should not use this herb for more than one month at a time; prolonged use retards the healing of such wounds. In such cases, discontinue for 2–3 weeks while sores heal, then resume use.

INCOMPATIBLES: none

REMARKS: This herb is reputed to confer longevity when used for prolonged periods, particularly in combination with Chinese yam. The herb is nontoxic and can therefore be used continuously for long-term periods, except for the contraindication noted above.

40. DOGWOOD TREE

Cornus officinalis

山茱萸 *shan ju yu (shan zhu yu)*

OTHER NAME: *rou dzao* (fleshy jujube)

A large, thorny, deciduous shrub that grows to a height of 10 meters, this plant is found in the mountainous regions of China. It bears white flowers that resemble those of the apricot, and a red fruit, the kernel of which is used along with the flesh as medicine. It is highly astringent and contains cornin bitter, tannin, resin, and tartaric acid. The bark also has astringent as well as tonic properties and is reputed to be an effective remedy for malarial fevers. Its close North American cousin *Cornus florida,* or flowering dogwood, has similar medicinal properties.

The herb is native to China, Japan, and Korea.

MEDICINAL PART: fruit

NATURE: Energy: slightly warm
Flavor: sour
Affinity: kidneys, liver

THERAPEUTIC EFFECTS: astringent; tonic; hemostatic (TCM: tonifies kidney- and liver-energy; nourishes semen-essence)

INDICATIONS: impotence; spermatorrhea; vertigo; night sweats; profuse perspiration; lumbago; frequent and incontinent urination; blurry vision and headaches due to liver disorders; prolapse of uterus (TCM: empty kidney-energy; deficient liver-energy)

DOSAGE: decoction: 5–10 grams, in two doses, on an empty stomach

powder: pills or paste; 6–9 grams, in two or three doses, on an empty stomach

CONTRAINDICATIONS: fever; diarrhea

INCOMPATIBLES: balloon flower, *Siler divaricatum,* herbs of Menispermaceae family

REMARKS: This herb acts primarily as a yin tonic with special affinity for the kidneys and the urogenital system, which it nourishes and strengthens. Its sour, astringent properties help control involuntary ejaculation as well as urinary incontinence, and retard profuse perspiration. Recent laboratory research has isolated a quinol glycoside in the herb that acts as a urinary-tract antiseptic. Extracts of the herb also show antibacterial and antiallergenic activity.

41. DRYOPTERIS CRASSIRHIZOMA

贯众 *guan jung (guan zhong)*

OTHER NAMES: *feng wei tsao* (phoenix tail grass); *Aspidium falcatum; Nephrodium filix; Woodwardia radicans; Onoclea orientalis*

This is a common fern that grows in subtropical and temperate regions throughout the world. There are many different Latin designations because a variety of species are used interchangeably under the same name in Chinese medicine, thereby confounding translators. The lush green fronds grow to a length of 15–30 centimeters, and the starchy rhizomes are used in medicine; in ancient times the latter were also eaten as food. They contain tannin, essential oil, resin, starch, and sugar, and are mildly toxic.

MEDICINAL PART: rhizome

NATURE:
Energy: slightly cold
Flavor: bitter
Affinity: liver, stomach

THERAPEUTIC EFFECTS: anthelmintic; antidote; antipyretic; hemostatic (TCM: clears internal heat)

INDICATIONS: intestinal parasites; uterine congestion and hemorrhage after childbirth; menorrhagia; leukorrhea; inflamed abscesses due to excess heat; thyroid inflammation (TCM: internal heat)

DOSAGE: decoction: 10–12 grams, in two doses, on an empty stomach or after meals

powder: a special powder for use in controlling leukorrhea is made from this herb by peeling the dried herb, dipping it briefly in vinegar, drying it in an oven or skillet, then grinding it to a fine powder; 5 grams, in one dose, on an empty stomach (plain powder, capsules, or infusion)

CONTRAINDICATIONS: pregnancy

INCOMPATIBLES: none

42. EAGLE WOOD, *Aquilaria agallocha*
沉香 *chen hsiang (chen xiang)*

OTHER NAMES: aloes wood; agila wood; aguru

This is a deciduous tree that grows to a height of 40 meters and is reputed to have occult virtues; the fragrant wood it produces is claimed by some sources to be the aloes referred to in the Bible. After the tree has lain felled for a period of months or years, a dark aromatic resin collects in the heart of the tree, and this heavy, fragrant heartwood is used in medicine as well as incense production. The wood sinks when immersed in water, hence the Chinese name meaning "sinking incense." It has a fragrance somewhat similar to sandalwood and a pungent, bittersweet taste.

The tree is native to the Himalayan region, parts of northern India, Vietnam, Laos, Cambodia, and parts of southern China.

MEDICINAL PART: heavy resinous wood

NATURE: Energy: warm
         Flavor: bitter, pungent
         Affinity: kidneys

THERAPEUTIC EFFECTS: tonic; stimulant; diuretic; stomachic; nervine (TCM: tonifies yang-energy; harmonizes energy)

INDICATIONS: pains in chest and abdomen; angina; hypertension and nervous exhaustion, with related symptoms of frequent urination, diarrhea, and gastritis; numbness and paralysis in extremities; neurosis; fatigue

DOSAGE: powder: plain, capsules, pills, or paste; 1–3 grams, in two doses, on an empty stomach

CONTRAINDICATIONS: none

INCOMPATIBLES: none

REMARKS: This herb is reputed in TCM to be particularly effective in correcting disorders of the nervous system, including tension, exhaustion, neurosis, obsessive behavior, and so on. In monasteries and hermitages, it has long been favored as an incense because the fragrance, which carries the herb's essential energies directly into the human system via special receptors in the nasal passages, is said to calm the spirit, relax the nervous system, sink vital energy down to its base at the naval, and facilitate prolonged states of contemplation. Perhaps there is a connection between the herb's nervine properties and its popularity as a supplement to meditation.

When using this herb to treat nervous disorders, particularly neurotic and obsessive behavior, it's a good idea to keep some incense made with this herb burning in rooms occupied by the patient. When looking for this product in Chinese incense shops, simply show the clerk the Chinese characters for the herb, *chen hsiang*.

43. ECLIPTA PROSTRATA

旱蓮草 *han lien tsao (han lian cao)*

OTHER NAMES: *li tsao* (carp gut); *mo tsai* (ink vegetable); *Eclipta alba*

This is an annual herb that grows to a height of 80 centimeters, with serrated lanceolate leaves about 5 centimeters long by 10 millimeters wide, small white flowers, and winged achene fruits 3 millimeters long by 1.5 millimeters wide. When broken, the fresh plant exudes a sticky black sap, hence the nickname "ink vegetable." The plant contains nicotine.

This herb grows in damp soils in China, Japan, Taiwan, and Southeast Asia.

MEDICINAL PART: whole plant

NATURE: Energy: cold
              Flavor: sweet, sour
              Affinity: liver, kidneys

THERAPEUTIC EFFECTS: astringent; hemostatic; refrigerant to blood; blackens hair and beard (TCM: tonifies kidney-yin and liver-yin)

INDICATIONS: spermatorrhea; menorrhagia; blood in sputum or urine; premature graying of hair; dizziness and blurry vision due to liver disorders; loose teeth (TCM: deficient kidney-yin and liver-yin)

DOSAGE: decoction: 4–10 grams, in three doses, on an empty stomach or after meals

fresh juice: the freshly extracted juice of this plant can be applied directly to the scalp to promote hair growth; it also be taken internally to darken hair and beard

CONTRAINDICATIONS: none

INCOMPATIBLES: iron compounds and utensils

44. ELEUTHEROCOCCUS GRACILISTYLUS

五加皮 *wu jia pi*

OTHER NAMES: *Eleutherococcus senticosus; Acanthopanax spinosum*

This is a deciduous shrub with spiky stalks and compound leaves of five leaflets each. It has small greenish white flowers and a round black berry. The epidermis of the root is used in medicine; it is sold in brown, rolled fragments and contains resin, essential oil, starch, and a lot of vitamin A.

The herb is grown in China and Japan.

MEDICINAL PART: epidermis of root

NATURE: Energy: warm
          Flavor: pungent, bitter
          Affinity: liver, kidneys

THERAPEUTIC EFFECTS: tonic; analgesic; diuretic; stomachic; improves circulation; strengthens ligaments and bones (TCM: tonifies blood; nourishes semen-essence; tonifies kidney-energy)

INDICATIONS: rheumatism and arthritis; lumbago; cramps; impotence; damp, itching scrotum; vaginal itching (TCM: deficient kidney-energy and liver-energy)

DOSAGE: decoction: 5–10 grams, in two doses, on an empty stomach

CONTRAINDICATIONS: TCM: males with the condition of empty yin with flaring fire (see Remarks in #35 for details) should abstain from using this herb, or use it very sparingly

INCOMPATIBLE: *Scrophularia oldhami*

REMARKS: A potent herbal liquor brewed with this herb has been a popular health tonic in China for over one thousand years, and it is still produced in China and Taiwan according to the original recipe. People of all ages, male and female, take this herbal liquor for its warming, antirheumatic, and sexually tonifying properties, particularly during the cold months of winter. You'll find it for sale in the Asian section of many supermarkets and liquor shops, labeled as Wu Jia Pi Wine.

45. ELSHOLTZIA SPLENDENS

香茅 *hsiang ru (xiang ru)*

OTHER NAME: *E. cristata*

An aromatic shrub 30–45 centimeters high with small violet flowers, this plant occurs in both wild and cultivated varieties and readily grows in gardens. The entire plant is used in medicine and contains essential oil including elsholtzia ketone, furane, pinene, and terpene.

The herb is found throughout the central provinces of China, Japan, Korea, India, and Southeast Asia.

MEDICINAL PART: whole plant, including flowers

NATURE: Energy: warm
            Flavor: pungent
            Affinity: stomach, lungs

THERAPEUTIC EFFECTS: diaphoretic; carminative; stomachic; diuretic; antiemetic (TCM: expels dampness)

INDICATIONS: nausea and vomiting; bloating; summer heat and chills; damp, peeling feet (TCM: internal dampness; wind-cold injuries)

DOSAGE: decoction: 4–8 grams, in two doses, on an empty stomach

CONTRAINDICATIONS: none

INCOMPATIBLES: none

REMARKS: A decoction of this herb is a traditional Chinese remedy for halitosis (bad breath). For this purpose, it should be taken internally and used as a gargle and mouthwash.

46. ERIOCAULON SIEBOLDIANUM

谷精草 *gu jing tsao (gu jing cao)*

This is a common field weed with small leaves and tiny star-shaped flowers. It grows immediately after the harvest of grains and was therefore believed to spring spontaneously from the essential energy of the grain itself, hence the Chinese name meaning "grain essence grass." The herb is sold in dry bundles that include the flowers.

The herb grows throughout the arable regions of China and also in parts of Southeast Asia.

MEDICINAL PART: whole plant, including flowers

NATURE: Energy: warm
            Flavor: pungent
            Affinity: liver

THERAPEUTIC EFFECTS: antiphlogistic; ophthalmic; astringent; analgesic

INDICATIONS: tonsillitis; cataracts; glaucoma; headaches due to liver disorders; nosebleeds; sunstroke

DOSAGE: decoction: 3–7 grams, in three doses, on an empty stomach

eye wash: for cataracts and glaucoma, take the decoction internally, while also using it as an external eye wash

CONTRAINDICATIONS: none

INCOMPATIBLES: iron, aluminum, and other metal compounds and utensils

REMARKS: This is one of the most effective Chinese herbs for treating disorders of the eyes, such as cataracts, glaucoma, swelling, and so on. When using it to treat eye disorders, the decoction should be used internally and externally at the same time.

47. EUCOMMIA, *Eucommia ulmoides*

杜仲 *du jung*

OTHER NAME: *mu mien* (wood cotton)

This herb comes from a tree that resembles an elm, growing to heights of 5–20 meters, with oval leaves 12 centimeters long by 6 centimeters across and red flowers. The Chinese nickname refers to the delicate, silvery, silky filaments revealed when the bark is broken. It is usually sold as broken brown slabs 10–12 centimeters long, stripped of the rough outer cuticle.

The plant is native to central and southern China, where it is cultivated for the herbal trade.

MEDICINAL PART: bark

NATURE: Energy: warm
Flavor: sweet
Affinity: kidneys, liver

THERAPEUTIC EFFECTS: tonic; analgesic; sedative to fetus; lowers blood pressure; prevents miscarriage (TCM: tonifies kidney- and liver-energy; nourishes sinew and cartilage)

INDICATIONS: numbness and pain in lower back and knees; headache and dizziness due to liver disorders; chronic fatigue; impotence; restless fetus; lumbago due to pregnancy; damp, itchy scrotum; high blood pressure (TCM: deficient kidney- and liver-energy)

DOSAGE: decoction: 5–12 grams, in two doses, on an empty stomach in early morning and at bedtime

CONTRAINDICATIONS: none

INCOMPATIBLES: *Scrophularia oldhami*

REMARKS: This herb has been prized in China as a potent health tonic for over three thousand years, and in recent years it has become the focus of intensive medical research for an active principle it contains that has proven to be one of the most effective treatments for high blood pressure ever discovered. Unlike the synthetic drugs commonly used to treat high blood pressure in Western medicine, it has no negative side effects. Due to this discovery, China has strictly limited exports of this herb overseas, and consequently the price has soared in recent years. Nevertheless, for high blood pressure and associated hypertension, the efficacy of this herb justifies its cost.

In traditional medicine, this herb is regarded as one of the best remedies for the nagging pains and numbness in lower back and knees caused by lumbago. Since the herb also acts as a preventive to miscarriage and a sedative to restless fetus, it's an excellent choice for relieving the cramps and lumbago pains often experienced during pregnancy.

48. FENNEL, *Foeniculum vulgare*

茴香 *hui hsiang (hui xiang)*

OTHER NAME: *Foeniculum officinale*

An aromatic perennial herb that grows 1–2 meters high, with delicate leaflets and yellow flowers, the Chinese name *hui hsiang* (Muhammadan spice) refers to the fact that the herb first came to China from the Middle East. The fruits, usually referred to as "seeds," are medicinal, grayish brown in color, curved and beaked, with five ridges and a fragrance somewhat like anise. The stalks and the leaves of the plant were eaten as food in China. The fruits contain 3%–4% volatile oils.

The herb is native to the Middle East, North Africa, and southern Europe but is also cultivated in China.

MEDICINAL PART: fruit

NATURE: Energy: warm
Flavor: pungent
Affinity: liver, kidneys, spleen, stomach

THERAPEUTIC EFFECTS: tonic; stomachic; antitussive; expectorant; stimulates appetite (TCM: tonifies stomach-energy; balances energy)

INDICATIONS: weak digestion; dyspepsia; colic; hernia; pain and cold in abdomen; nausea and vomiting due to stomach disorders (TCM: wind injury; internal cold, especially in stomach)

DOSAGE: decoction: 3–5 grams, in three doses, on an empty stomach

powder: first toast the fennel in a dry, hot skillet until its fragrance is released, then grind to a fine powder in a mortar or food processor; take 1–5 grams daily as an infusion or in capsules; the powder can also be used in place of black pepper and chili as a table and kitchen condiment, thereby combining the herb's culinary and therapeutic functions

CONTRAINDICATIONS: excessive use is said to be harmful to the eyes

INCOMPATIBLES: none

REMARKS: Chinese pharmacopeias list "large" and "small" varieties of fennel, both of which have similar fragrance and pharmaceutical properties. It is reputed to be one of the best herbal remedies for physical weakness and lack of vitality due to insufficient or cold stomach-energy, a condition that prevents the body from assimilating sufficient nutrients and energy from food.

Like many tonic and restorative herbs, fennel increases the body's supply of available energy by enhancing the digestive system's power to digest, extract, and assimilate essential nutrients and energy from food. The modern Western approach to malnutrition and physical exhaustion caused by poor diet is to take high-potency vitamins, minerals, and other essential nutrients to compensate for what's missing in the diet, while digestive distress is treated with antacids and other chemical compounds. By contrast, the traditional Chinese way is to first improve the quality of the diet, both in terms of nutritional value as well as digestive compatibility, then to take herbs that correct digestive disorders and improve the digestive organs' capacity to extract and assimilate nutritional essence and energy from food.

49. FOXNUT, *Euryale ferox*

芡實 *chien shih (qian shi)*

OTHER NAME: *ji tou* (chicken head)

A large aquatic plant belonging to the water lily family, this herb has been cultivated, like lotus, since ancient times in China. It has large, spiny floating leaves that are green on top and purple underneath and a large violet flower that resembles a cockscomb, thus the Chinese nickname. The plant has long fleshy rhizomes that are used as food in China. The seeds, which are used in medicine, are oval, about 1 centimeter long, mottled and veined with a whitish color. They contain about 10% protein and lots of starch, and are also used for food.

The plant grows in China, Japan, and India.

MEDICINAL PART: seed

NATURE: Energy: neutral
         Flavor: sweet, sour
         Affinity: kidneys, spleen

THERAPEUTIC EFFECTS: tonic; nutrient; astringent; analgesic; regulates blood pressure (TCM: tonifies kidney- and spleen-energy)

INDICATIONS: neuralgia; neuritis; arthritis; spermatorrhea; nocturnal emissions with wet dreams; leukorrhea; impotence; premature aging (TCM: deficient kidney-energy; empty spleen-energy)

DOSAGE: decoction: 10–20 grams, in three doses, on an empty stomach

powder: plain, capsules, pills, or paste; 9–15 grams, in three doses, on an empty stomach

CONTRAINDICATIONS: none

INCOMPATIBLES: none

REMARKS: Since ancient times, this herb has been highly regarded for restoring sexual vigor and youthful energy in older men, and for retarding the common symptoms of aging.

50. GARLIC, *Allium sativum*

大蒜 *da suan*

OTHER NAMES: *Allium odorum; A. chinense; A. scorodoprasum;* Chinese chive

This plant grows to a height of 15–30 centimeters, with cylindrical stalks rising from a leaved base, long narrow leaves, and round bulbs that grow in clusters, or "heads." It has been used as food and medicine in China for at least five thousand years, although traditionally it has been a forbidden food for Buddhist monks in China, due to the presence of a volatile oil that is said to excite

sensory appetites, particularly lust. Garlic has long
been known to protect people from all sorts of parasites,
microbes, toxins, and other
noxious elements contained
in food and water, and therefore it's a very effective preventive against a wide range
of infectious agents that can
enter the body through the
digestive tract.

The garlic plant grows worldwide, in many species,
but the variety referred to here is native to China, Japan,
Tibet, Nepal, and northern India.

MEDICINAL PART: bulb

NATURE: Energy: warm
         Flavor: pungent
         Affinity: stomach, large intestine

THERAPEUTIC EFFECTS: anthelmintic; antibacterial;
antifungal; antiseptic; antidote; stomachic; tonic; eliminates accumulated mucus and phlegm; digestive, especially for meat; increases gastric, intestinal, and bronchial secretions; inhibits tumor growth; lowers blood
pressure (TCM: expels internal cold and internal dampness)

INDICATIONS: tumors and swelling; tuberculosis; hook-
worm, pinworm, and other parasites; diarrhea and dysentery; nosebleed; bacterial infections; abscesses; high
cholesterol, arteriosclerosis; high blood pressure; colds
and flu; vaginitis; *Candida* and other fungal infections;
athlete's foot (TCM: internal cold and internal damp
symptoms)

DOSAGE: fresh cloves: 3–5 per day; taken raw in food,
or in capsules

external: puree of fresh garlic cloves can be applied
to abscesses as an antiseptic and healing agent, also to
ringworm on the head; for athlete's foot, apply liberally
to infected area and wrap well with a clean, dry cloth

for 1–2 hours, then remove and wipe away excess garlic with dry cloth (but no water)

cold preventive: if you're susceptible to "catching a cold," a traditional Chinese preventive is to peel and puree ten cloves of fresh garlic, then extract the pure juice through a cloth; store the juice in a clean jar with dropper; put one drop in each nostril three times a day; this is said to be a highly effective preventive against contagious colds

CONTRAINDICATION: excessive use of garlic is said to be harmful to the eyes, cause dizziness, and scatter energy; in TCM, it is said to cause ascending fire energy

INCOMPATIBLE: honey

REMARKS: Garlic has remarkable antibacterial and antimicrobial properties, and numerous scientific studies have shown it to have a broader range of bactericidal powers than penicillin. One milligram of its major active compound, allicin, has the equivalent antibacterial power of 15 standard units of penicillin. It is also effective against many fungal infections, including *Candida*, which is responsible for most cases of vaginitis. A traditional Chinese cure for tuberculosis involves placing a thick compress of chopped raw garlic on the patient's back, covering it with a clean damp cloth, then using a laundry iron to heat the compress and force the garlic fumes through the skin into the chest cavity, where they kill the bacteria responsible for the ailment.

The therapeutic benefits of garlic have been established beyond doubt by numerous modern studies conducted throughout the world. It has been conclusively shown that allicin effectively lowers serum cholesterol by blocking its biosynthesis. Another active sulphur compound contained in garlic, methyl allyl trisulfide, helps expand constricted blood vessels, thereby preventing high blood pressure. Yet another compound called ajoene inhibits the tendency of blood cells to stick together (platelet aggregation), thereby helping to prevent stroke, heart attack, and other heart diseases caused by blood clots and restricted flow of blood.

A remarkable study on garlic in China involved eleven patients suffering from cryptococcal meningitis, which is usually fatal. All eleven patients were successfully treated and recovered after several weeks of garlic therapy. Recent independent studies in Japan and Romania have also shown garlic to be effective in protecting living organisms from the influenza virus.

51. GASTRODIA ELATA

天麻 *tien ma*

OTHER NAMES: *chih chien* (red arrow); *feng tsao* (wind grass)

This is a perennial alpine plant with a straight erect stem about 10 centimeters high, reddish in color (hence the Chinese name meaning "red arrow"), with a large central root and twelve smaller tubers about the size of eggs on the side. Traditional Taoist sources claim that the plant stirs even when the air is still, giving rise to the nickname "wind grass." The fresh tubers are used as food, either raw or steamed, while the dried tubers are used as medicine. They are sold in flat, yellowish brown pieces, shriveled and irregular in shape, about 5 centimeters long by 3 centimeters wide.

The herb is native to western and central China, Tibet, Korea, and Japan.

MEDICINAL PART: tuber

NATURE: Energy: warm
           Flavor: sweet, pungent
           Affinity: liver

THERAPEUTIC EFFECTS: sedative; anticonvulsive; stimulant to cerebral functions (TCM: sedates liver-energy; clears meridians)

INDICATIONS: nervous exhaustion; headache; neuralgia; vertigo; fainting; lumbago (TCM: ascending liver-fire)

DOSAGE: decoction: 5–10 grams, in three doses, on an empty stomach

CONTRAINDICATIONS: anemia; stroke

INCOMPATIBLES: none

REMARKS: Chinese pharmacopeias particularly extole the virtues of this herb as a remedy for headaches, vertigo, and other neuralgic cerebral afflictions caused by ascending liver-fire from inflammations of the liver.

52. GENTIAN, *Gentiana scabra*

龍胆草 *lung dan tsao (lung dan cao)*

OTHER NAMES: *Gentiana macrophylla, G. barbata*

Chinese herbals use the name *lung dan* (dragon gall) in reference to fifty-seven species of bitter herbs of the gentian family, though *G. scabra* seems to be the most commonly used in medicine. The plant, which grows in the mountain valleys of central and western China, is a perennial herb with a blue, bell-shaped flower and long, narrow leaves. The medicinal root is sold in clusters of long reddish brown rootlets attached to a short, twisted root. It contains the bitter principles gentiopicrin, gentiamarin, and gentiin and the trisaccharide gentianose.

The plant is native to China and Japan, but similar species of *Gentiana* also grow in Europe.

MEDICINAL PART: root

NATURE: Energy: very cold
Flavor: very bitter
Affinity: liver, gallbladder

THERAPEUTIC EFFECTS: antiphlogistic; antipyretic; stomachic; antirheumatic (TCM: cools liver-energy; clears internal heat)

INDICATIONS: jaundice; diarrhea due to excess heat; hot sore throat; swollen painful eyes; rheumatic pains; festering abscesses due to toxic liver; diabetes; gallbladder inflammation and stones (TCM: hot-damp symptoms)

DOSAGE: decoction: 2–5 grams, in two doses, after meals

powder: plain, capsules, or infusion; 2–3 grams, in two doses, after meals

CONTRAINDICATIONS: none

INCOMPATIBLES: *Rehmannia glutinosa*

REMARKS: Gentian has been used for thousands of years in Eastern as well as Western medicine as a bitter tonic. It stimulates all of the vital digestive organs and increases circulation within the abdominal region. It helps prevent diabetes by soothing overactive spleen- and pancreas-energy, and prevents mild cases of diabetes from getting worse. It is a reliable corrective for many chronic digestive disorders, stimulates appetite, increases bile flow, and improves the body's capacity to assimilate nutrients from food. Some studies suggest that gentian may also be helpful in controlling eating disorders such as anorexia and bulimia.

53. GINGER, DRIED, *Zingiber officinale*
乾薑 *gan jiang*

Ginger is a canelike plant that grows to a height of about 1 meter, with a sheathed base and long narrow leaves 20–30 centimeters in length that taper to a point. The fresh rhizomes occur as irregular, fleshy bulbs, yellowish green in color, and are used often in Chinese cuisine, both for flavor and for the herb's digestive properties. The dried rhizomes, which are used in herbal medicine, are hotter and more potent than the fresh. Strongly aromatic and pungent, they contain 1%–3% of a volatile oil that contains zingerone, phellandrene, camphene, cineol, borneol, and citral.

Ginger grows in the tropical zones throughout the world.

MEDICINAL PART: rhizome, dried

NATURE: Energy: warm
             Flavor: pungent
             Affinity: stomach, spleen, heart, lungs,
                       kidneys

THERAPEUTIC EFFECTS: stomachic; antiemetic; salivant; stimulant; digestive; cardiotonic; dissolves phlegm (TCM: stimulates yang-energy; warms lung-energy; warms stomach-energy)

INDICATIONS: nausea and vomiting; motion sickness; pain and cold in abdomen; cold hands and feet; weak pulse; cough with profuse phlegm; ulcers; colds with chills; high cholesterol; pancreatitis (TCM: cold spleen- and stomach-energy; cold lung-energy; deficient yang-energy; empty blood and energy)

DOSAGE: decoction: 10 grams, with brown or raw sugar to taste, in two doses, on an empty stomach

CONTRAINDICATIONS: pregnancy; high fever

INCOMPATIBLES: none

REMARKS: In TCM, fresh ginger root (also known as mother ginger) is used primarily as a remedy for colds in the lungs and stomach, and as a remedy for seafood poisoning. Note that fresh ginger is always served with raw fish and other seafood dishes in Japanese cuisine. Boiled together with the white, tendril-like rootlets of fresh scallions and some raw sugar or honey, it makes an effective remedy against colds accompanied by chills (but not fever).

When sun-dried, the root is known as *gan jiang* (dry ginger), and when that is further roasted over fire, it's called *hei jiang* (black ginger); these two varieties have similar medicinal properties.

Ginger's digestive virtues are well known throughout Asia and much of Europe. It aids digestion and assimilation, and is often added to formulas to facilitate rapid delivery of the other herbs' therapeutic benefits. It contains a digestive food enzyme called zingibain, which exceeds papain (derived from papaya) in digestive potency. Ginger also increases the concentration of the carbohydrate-digesting enzyme amylase in saliva. Further down the digestive tract, ginger improves digestion and elimination by activating peristalsis.

Recent studies show that ginger also lowers serum cholesterol and reduces platelet aggregation and this makes it a good preventive against arteriosclerosis and heart disease.

Ginger is one of the best remedies in the world for nausea, particularly motion sickness, for which some studies have shown ginger to be effective in 90% of cases tested. It works significantly better than dimenhydrinate, which is the most commonly used Western remedy for motion sickness, and has no negative side effects. When used for this purpose, take three "00"-size capsules of powdered dry ginger a few hours prior to travel, and two more every hour or two during the journey, or whenever nausea commences.

54. GINKGO KERNELS, *Ginkgo biloba*
銀杏 *ying hsing (ying xing)*

OTHER NAMES: *bai guo* (white nut); *Salisburia adiantifolia*

The ginkgo tree is the only living descendant of the Ginkgoales order which flourished as dinosaur fodder during the Mesozoic Era 150 million years ago. It's a tall, resinous tree that grows up to 35 meters, with deciduous, fan-shaped leaves and greenish white buds that bloom at night and quickly drop off, so that few people ever see the tree in flower. The fruits grow prolifically on the branches and resemble lotus seeds, with two or three longitudinal ridges and pointed tips, 1–2 centimeters long, and a smooth, hard, light-brown shell. The kernels are medicinal and are also highly favored as food in China, Korea, and Japan. They are used raw as well as cooked.

The tree is native to China and Japan but has also been transplanted to Europe and North America.

MEDICINAL PART: kernel

NATURE: Energy: neutral
         Flavor: sweet, bitter
         Affinity: kidneys, heart, lungs

THERAPEUTIC EFFECTS: astringent; sedative; antitussive; cardiotonic; digestive; anthelmintic; antidote to alcohol intoxication (TCM: tonifies primordial energy; nourishes kidney-yin; warms lung-energy)

INDICATIONS: asthma; tuberculosis; coughs; bladder infections; spermatorrhea; gonorrhea; scant frequent urination; alcohol poisoning

DOSAGE: decoction: 5–15 grams, in two doses, after meals

capsules: macerate 5–15 grams in a mortar or coffee grinder and put in capsules, in three doses, after meals

CONTRAINDICATIONS: consumption of large amounts can cause toxic reactions, such as vomiting and convulsions, while prolonged use tends to suppress appetite

INCOMPATIBLES: none

REMARKS: While traditional Chinese and other Asian medicines have used the kernels and roots of the ginkgo tree for many centuries, modern Western research has focused almost entirely on the leaf, which has been shown to have highly beneficial effects on the brain and improve a wide range of cerebral functions. In order to become therapeutically effective, however, the leaves must be rendered into a concentrated extract for medicinal use. Simple decoctions of the leaves are not sufficiently potent to deliver results.

Ginkgo leaf significantly increases circulation to the brain and can be used to treat cerebrovascular insufficiency, migraine headache, vertigo, and memory impairment. It has been shown to be an effective free-radical scavenger, with particular affinity for the central nervous system, and thus it protects brain and nerve cells from destruction by free radicals and from premature aging. It also inhibits blood-platelet aggregation, providing a strong measure of protection against stroke and coronary thrombosis. Ginkgo leaf has been shown to significantly increase the synthesis of dopamine, norepinephrine, and other vital neurotransmitters in the brain, thereby enhancing important cerebral functions such as learning, memory, alertness, information processing, and biofeedback with the endocrine system. This makes it an effective preventive and treatment for premature senility, dementia, brain damage, and a wide range of cognitive disorders.

55. GINKGO ROOT, *Ginkgo biloba*
白果根 *bai guo gen*

(See previous listing for description.)

MEDICINAL PART: root

NATURE: Energy: neutral
 Flavor: sweet
 Affinity: kidneys

THERAPEUTIC EFFECTS: tonic; astringent

INDICATIONS: spermatorrhea; nocturnal emission with wet dreams; dysmenorrhea

DOSAGE: decoction: 10–15 grams, in two doses, on an empty stomach

CONTRAINDICATIONS: none

INCOMPATIBLES: none

REMARKS: Unlike the kernels, the root of the ginkgo tree is nontoxic and can therefore be used for prolonged periods without harmful side effects. The root is thus a better choice for stubborn cases of involuntary ejaculation that require long-term therapy.

56. GINSENG, *Panax ginseng*

人参 *ren shen*

OTHER NAME: *shen tsao* (divine herb)

A perennial herb that grows to a height of 60–80 centimeters, with fleshy bifurcate roots, a straight branchless stem, and a pink flower, ginseng has long been regarded as the King of the Myriad Herbs in TCM. Formerly reserved exclusively for the emperor and his court, true ginseng was regarded as a general panacea and health tonic, as well as a potent restorative in deathbed cases. The rarest, most valuable roots are those that have grown for over one hundred years in the remote mountain wilderness of Manchuria and North Korea; these spindly specimens can sell for up to $20,000 per ounce in Hong Kong! Ginseng comes in white and red varieties, the latter being more warming and potent, and much more expensive.

The herb is native to northeast China, Manchuria, Korea, and Siberia. A related species with different pharmacological properties grows in North America and is also used in TCM.

MEDICINAL PART: root

NATURE: Energy: warm
         Flavor: sweet, slightly bitter
         Affinity: spleen, lungs

THERAPEUTIC EFFECTS: tonic; stimulant; aphrodisiac; secretagogue; enhances immune response; improves cerebral circulation and function; regulates blood pressure; regulates blood sugar (TCM: tonifies primordial energy; tonifies spleen- and lung-energy; nourishes vital fluids)

INDICATIONS: nervous exhaustion; lack of appetite; night sweats; cold extremities; recuperation after surgery, long illness, or childbirth; short-term memory loss; impotence; stroke; diabetes; hypertension; anemia; heart palpitations; adrenal deficiency; immune deficiency; high or low blood pressure; gastritis; morning sickness (TCM: deficient energy; empty lung- and spleen-energy)

DOSAGE: decoction (use ginseng cooker to steam decoct for 30–60 minutes): 5–10 grams, in one dose, on an empty stomach in the morning

acute cases: in cases of hemorrhage, stroke, heart palpitations, and other acute conditions, use 15–30 grams

liquor: steep 50–60 grams of high-grade ginseng in 1 liter of spirits for 2–4 months; take 1 ounce, one or two times daily, on an empty stomach

powder: capsules, pills, or paste; 3–6 grams, in two doses, on an empty stomach

CONTRAINDICATIONS: colds, pneumonia, and other lung infections

INCOMPATIBLES: iron and other metal compounds and utensils; amethyst; *Veratum nigrum;* opium; dairy products; tea; white turnip

REMARKS: Ginseng is no doubt the most famous herb in the entire Chinese pharmacopeia, and its reputation as a health tonic has already spread worldwide. It is also one of the herbs most widely studied by modern medical science, which not only validated most of the traditional therapeutic claims but has also discovered many more important medical properties in the herb. Ginseng is the closest thing to a cure-all that nature has to offer the human species.

Ginseng belongs to a unique class of therapeutic agents known as adaptogens. Adaptogens increase the body's resistance to all detrimental environmental influences, including stress, and automatically reestablish optimum biological homeostasis whenever vital functions are thrown off balance. Through a complex series of metabolic gymnastics, ginseng actually prevents or compensates for much of the damage to the nervous and endocrine systems normally caused by stress. It raises blood sugar when too low and lowers it when too high;

it elevates low blood pressure and reduces it when it's too high; it raises or lowers white blood cell count and generally tunes and balances all of the body's vital functions. There has been enough scientific research done on ginseng to fill a book and eliminate any doubts regarding its therapeutic value. The following list summarizes some of the major medical virtues of ginseng that have been fully validated by modern scientific studies:

1. Antitumor and anticancer properties have been shown in studies on animals, humans, and cell cultures.

2. Stimulates the immune system, including phagocytosis and production of interferon and white blood cells.

3. Stimulates almost all liver functions, including synthesis of RNA, DNA, and vital proteins.

4. Strengthens heart muscle and helps prevent myocardial infarction.

5. Regulates blood sugar levels, raising or lowering as needed.

6. Regulates blood pressure, raising or lowering as needed.

7. Regulates white blood cell count, raising or lowering as needed.

8. Regulates red blood cell count, raising or lowering as needed.

9. Regulates central nervous system response, stimulating or sedating as needed.

10. Antioxidant properties neutralize free radicals, thus preventing the cellular damage they cause.

11. Helps prevent and heal stomach ulcers.

12. Relieves fatigue, increases cerebral circulation, and enhances memory, learning, alertness, and other cognitive functions.

13. Protects adrenals from atrophy, stimulates adrenal function, and counteracts damage to adrenal-pituitary axis caused by response to acute stress.

14. Heals deformities of the cornea, especially clouding.

15. Protects tissues and blood from damage by radiation, heavy metals, air pollution, and many other toxic agents.

16. Balances male and female hormone activity.

17. Prevents alcohol intoxication when taken prior to drinking, and relieves alcohol hangover after excess consumption.

57. GOTU KOLA, *Hydrocotyle asiatica*
地钱草 *di chien tsao (di qien cao)*

OTHER NAMES: pennywort; *Centella asiatica; man tien hsing* (sky full of stars); ground ivy

This is a low-growing plant with flexible stalks that run close to the ground, like ivy, and leaves shaped like Chinese copper coins, hence the name *di chien tsao* (ground coin grass). It grows in the tropical and subtropical river valleys of central China, as well as in India, Sri Lanka, and parts of Africa. The herb contains asiaticosides and other triterpenes, and has long been reputed as a longevity tonic among Himalayan yogis and Taoist hermits.

MEDICINAL PARTS: stalk, leaves

NATURE: Energy: cool
            Flavor: sweet, bitter
            Affinity: kidney, spleen

THERAPEUTIC EFFECTS: rejuvenative; nervine; febrifuge; diuretic; alterative; builds immune system

INDICATIONS: premature aging, including hair loss; nervous disorders, including epilepsy and convulsions; chronic skin diseases; venereal diseases; memory and learning impairment; mental disorders, including neurosis and schizophrenia; recuperation after surgery or severe illness

DOSAGE: decoction: 3–5 grams, in two doses, on an empty stomach

powder: plain, capsules, pills, paste, infusion; 1–3 grams, in two or three doses, on an empty stomach

external: the powdered herb can be mixed with water or sesame oil to form a paste for application to eczema, psoriasis, festering sores, and other chronic skin conditions

CONTRAINDICATIONS: large doses can cause headache

INCOMPATIBLES: none

REMARKS: Gotu kola has long enjoyed repute among Himalayan yogis and Taoist adepts as a potent longevity herb and brain tonic. The Chinese herbalist Lee Ching-yuen, who is reported to have died in 1933 at the age of 256, recommended it above all other herbs for prolonging life, and the famous Hindu guru Nanddo Narian revealed it to be his secret elixir at the age of 107. An infusion of gotu kola with honey is recommended as a supplement to meditation practice and is said to open the crown chakra at the top of the head. The herb balances right and left hemisphere functions in the brain and improves memory and learning. It can therefore be used to treat certain mental disorders, such as neurosis and schizophrenia. Some of the traditional Asian claims for this herb have been verified in France by the biochemist Jules Lepine and by Professor Menier at the Academie Scientifique.

In addition to its remarkable nervine properties, this herb has a distinct and consistent healing influence on all of the body's solid tissues, particularly the skin and connective tissues. This effect is probably due to the presence of triterpenes, which stimulate and accelerate the natural process of cellular repair. Since it can be used both internally and externally, it is particularly effective in stimulating growth of new skin tissue when used for sores, infections, surgical incisions, traumatic wounds, and other skin afflictions.

Gotu kola is commonly used in the Ayurvedic medicine of India, primarily as a blood purifier and a specific healing agent in chronic skin diseases, including leprosy, syphilis, and psoriasis. In China, it's employed mainly by Taoist adepts as a longevity tonic. The herb's nervine, cerebral balancing, and immunotonic properties still make it a very good choice for inclusion in health and longevity tonics today.

58. GRAINS-OF-PARADISE

Amomum xanthiodes

砂仁 *sha ren*

OTHER NAME: bastard cardamom

This is an aromatic perennial with long narrow leaves and capsular fruits containing compact masses of small black seeds that closely resemble those of true cardamom, for which they are sometimes substituted. In addition to medicine, the seeds are used as a

cooking condiment, in preserves, and to flavor spirits. They are also said to hasten the dissolution and excretion of fish bones and any sort of metal object accidentally swallowed.

The plant is native to southern China and Southeast Asia.

MEDICINAL PART: seed

NATURE: Energy: warm
           Flavor: pungent
           Affinity: kidneys, spleen, stomach

THERAPEUTIC EFFECTS: digestive; stomachic; analgesic; sedative to restless fetus; carminative; decongestant; antidote to alcohol intoxication (TCM: expels internal dampness)

INDICATIONS: abdominal pain and bloating; oppression in chest; diarrhea; nausea and vomiting; indigestion; convulsions; cough with heavy phlegm (TCM: internal dampness in spleen and stomach)

DOSAGE: decoction: 4–6 grams, in three doses, on an empty stomach

    powder: can be used as a kitchen and table condiment

CONTRAINDICATIONS: none

INCOMPATIBLES: tea; white turnip

REMARKS: This herb should be used only short-term (1–7 days), as an immediate remedy for the above conditions, and terminated as soon as the condition has improved. Having no preventive or tonic properties, it is not suitable for long-term therapy.

59. GYNURA PINNATIFIDA

三七 *san chi*

OTHER NAMES: *shan chi* (mountain varnish); *jin bu huan* (gold no trade)

A perennial herb that grows about 1 meter tall, with yellow flowers and alternate leaves that grow three on one side and four on the other, this herb is reputed for its power to stop bleeding and promote the rapid healing of wounds, hence the nickname "mountain varnish." Its other name, "gold no trade," was given by China's military and martial artists, who valued it above gold due to its life-saving, healing properties. It is the main ingredient in the famous Yunnan Bai Yao powder formula, which can be applied both internally and externally to swiftly staunch heavy bleeding and promote rapid healing of tissues with minimum scarring. The medicinal root contains saponins and is sold in shriveled tapering pieces 2.5 centimeters long, grayish yellow in color; it has a taste somewhat similar to ginseng.

    The plant is cultivated as medicine in China and Japan.

MEDICINAL PART: root

NATURE: Energy: warm
         Flavor: sweet, bitter
         Affinity: liver

THERAPEUTIC EFFECTS: hemostatic; astringent; styptic; antiphlogistic (TCM: tonifies liver-energy)

INDICATIONS: all forms of hemorrhage and bleeding wounds, internal and external; bleeding ulcers; blood in sputum; cirrhosis; hepatitis; liver cancer; intestinal cancer; bloodshot eyes; bleeding gums

DOSAGE: internal: powder (plain, capsules, infusion); 2–5 grams, in two or three doses, on an empty stomach; can also be taken stirred into 1–2 ounces of wine

external: cleanse the wound, then apply the powder liberally to the bleeding area, cover with clean gauze, and hold or tape in place until clotting begins

CONTRAINDICATIONS: none

INCOMPATIBLES: none

REMARKS: When used for liver and intestinal cancer, the herb is employed as a hemostatic and styptic to staunch internal bleeding, not as a cure for cancer itself.

A few small jars of the Yunnan Bai Yao healing-powder formula that is based on this herb should be kept in every household and first-aid kit as an emergency remedy for bleeding wounds and internal hemorrhage. If applied immediately, it will often heal serious cuts and other bleeding wounds that would otherwise require stitches. During the Vietnam War, this powder was standard issue in the field kits of all North Vietnamese troops, who used it to treat their own gunshot wounds in the field. It's not expensive and is easy to use and readily available in Chinese herbal shops and even in some Asian grocery shops.

60. HARE'S EAR, *Bupleurum falcatum*
柴胡 *chai hu*

OTHER NAME: *Bupleurum chinense*

This is a perennial herb with a slender, flexible stem, small yellow flowers, and a branching root. The young white shoots are eaten as food in China, and the old dried plant is used for kindling, hence the prefix *chai* (firewood) in the Chinese name. The medicinal root is light red in color, bitter in taste, and contains furfurol and bupleurumol.

The herb grows in the northern provinces of China and in northern Europe.

MEDICINAL PART: root

NATURE: Energy: neutral
         Flavor: bitter
         Affinity: liver, pericardium, Triple Burner, gallbladder

THERAPEUTIC EFFECTS: antipyretic; analgesic; strengthens immune response (TCM: sedates liver-energy; clears internal heat)

INDICATIONS: colds with fever and sweating; malarial and blackwater fevers; amenorrhea; hepatitis, cirrhosis, and other liver disorders; prolapse of womb or rectum; cancer (TCM: liver-fire; internal heat)

DOSAGE: decoction: 3–5 grams, in two doses, on an empty stomach; for more potent effects for the above ailments, add the following herbs: 2–3 grams ginseng, 1–2 grams skullcap, 1–2 grams *Pinellia tuberifera,* and 2–3 grams *Angelica decursiva*

CONTRAINDICATIONS: none

INCOMPATIBLES: *Gleditschia chinensis*

REMARKS: This is one of the best Chinese herbs for treating serious liver disorders, such as hepatitis and cirrhosis, particularly when combined with other specific liver herbs, such as those suggested above (see Dosage section) and the liver formulas given on p. 215 and p. 216.

Recent research has shown that extracts of this herb have antibacterial activity, and a volatile oil it contains has shown antiviral effects as well. The herb has also shown some evidence of cancer- and tumor-inhibiting properties.

61. HORNY GOAT WEED

Epimedium sagittatum

淫羊藿 *yin yang huo*

OTHER NAMES: *Epimedium macranthum; Aceranthus sagittatum; hsien ling pi* (immortal spirit gall)

This perennial herb has a slender creeping root covered with fine rootlets and oval leaves that grow in clusters of three leaflets. It grows in mountain valleys throughout China, having reportedly been discovered by a curious goatherd who noticed that the herb incited his male goats to excessive copulation. It is prescribed primarily for its aphrodisiac properties.

The plant is native to China and Japan.

MEDICINAL PART: leaf

NATURE: Energy: warm
Flavor: pungent
Affinity: kidneys, liver

THERAPEUTIC EFFECTS: aphrodisiac; tonic; strengthens nerves; lowers blood pressure (TCM: tonifies kidney-yang; nourishes blood and semen-essence; expels cold-damp and wind-damp symptoms)

INDICATIONS: impotence; male and female infertility; numbness in extremities; spermatorrhea and premature ejaculation; lumbago; rheumatism; insufficient cerebral circulation (TCM: cold-damp and wind-damp symptoms; deficient kidney-yang)

DOSAGE: decoction: 6–12 grams, in two doses, on an empty stomach

powder: capsules, pills, infusion; 3–9 grams, in two or three doses, on an empty stomach

liquor: steep 60–80 grams in 1 liter of spirits for 1–3 months; take 1 ounce, twice a day, on an empty stomach; for better results, add 60–80 grams Chinese yam

CONTRAINDICATIONS: hypertension; TCM: empty yin with flaring fire (see Remarks in #35 for details)

INCOMPATIBLES: none

REMARKS: The leaves of this herb contain a glycoside and an alkaloid. Scientific studies have shown that when an extract of the leaves is administered orally to laboratory animals, the frequency of copulation increases significantly, thus lending credence to the ancient Legend of the Goat. Intravenous injection of the glycoside contained in the leaves also has been shown to increase seminal secretions in dogs. The herb is thus a direct stimulant to semen production and sexual drive in males.

Another mode of action of this herb is to dilate capillaries and other blood vessels, thereby facilitating circulation to the sexual organs as well as the brain, while also lowering blood pressure. The herb is therefore beneficial to circulation and cerebral functions, as well as sexual vitality, and is often used in Chinese medicine to correct absentmindedness, poor memory, and other symptoms of insufficient cerebral circulation.

You can strongly boost the therapeutic potency, improve the assimilation and distribution, and accelerate the overall effects of formulas for sexual-tonic herbal liquors by first steeping this herb in the spirits to be used for about 3 months, then straining out the herb and using the fortified spirits as a base to prepare your tonic liquor. To prepare 6 liters of spirits in this way, use 200–250 grams of the herb.

62. INDIAN MADDER, *Rubia cordifolia*

茜草 *chien tsao (qian cao)*

OTHER NAMES: *di hsueh* (ground blood); *hung geh* (red vine); Mandjuchaka

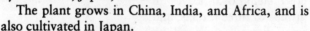

This perennial creeper grows to a length of 1 meter and has square, hollow stems that are covered in small prickles, oval leaves that grow in whorls of five, and small yellowish flowers. The medicinal root is purplish red or orange-brown in color and is used as a red dye in China, Japan, and India.

The plant grows in China, India, and Africa, and is also cultivated in Japan.

MEDICINAL PART: root

NATURE:
Energy: cold
Flavor: bitter
Affinity: liver, heart

THERAPEUTIC EFFECTS: emmenagogue; hemostatic; refrigerant; promotes circulation and purifies blood; dissolves clots and clears cholesterol; inhibits tumor growth (TCM: clears internal heat; cools blood)

INDICATIONS: amenorrhea and other menstrual disorders; uterine bleeding after childbirth and other types of internal hemorrhage; blood and liver toxicity; jaundice; hepatitis; cancer; tumors; kidney stones (TCM: hot blood and other internal-heat symptoms)

DOSAGE: decoction: 10–15 grams, in two doses, on an empty stomach

for clot-dissolving and cholesterol-clearing benefits and general blood detoxification, increase dosage to 20–25 grams

CONTRAINDICATIONS: anemia

INCOMPATIBLES: iron and other metal compounds and utensils

REMARKS: This is one of the most reliable alterative blood-purifying herbs in the Chinese pharmacopeia. It cools, detoxifies, and dissolves obstructions in the blood, particularly in the female reproductive system. Its deobstruent properties extend to tumors, kidney stones, and liver clots, all of which it helps dissolve and eliminate. It's an excellent choice for any condition that causes or is caused by blood and liver toxicity.

63. JAPANESE CATNIP

Schizonepeta tenuifolia

荊芥 *jing jie*

OTHER NAMES: *Nepeta japonica; N. tenuifolia*

A perennial with a tall erect stem, oval leaves in groups of three leaflets, and small flowers clustered on floral spikes, this herb was traditionally used in cooking as well as medicine and is reputed as a remedy for fevers and menstrual problems. It is frequently drunk as a simple infusion.

The plant is native to western and coastal China, as well as Japan.

MEDICINAL PARTS: stems, leaves, floral spikes

NATURE: Energy: warm
         Flavor: pungent
         Affinity: liver, lungs

THERAPEUTIC EFFECTS: diaphoretic; antipyretic; hemostatic; analgesic (TCM: clears internal heat; expels wind-cold)

INDICATIONS: fevers; headache; sore throat; abscesses and carbuncles; menorrhagia; uterine bleeding after childbirth; facial paralysis, loss of speech, and other stroke symptoms; stiff neck and spine (TCM: wind-cold symptoms)

DOSAGE: decoction: 3–6 grams, in two doses, on an empty stomach

powder: capsules, infusion; 2–4 grams, in two doses, on an empty stomach

CONTRAINDICATIONS: none

INCOMPATIBLES: seafood, including shellfish

64. JAPANESE HONEYSUCKLE

Lonicera japonica

金银花 *jin yin hua*

OTHER NAMES: woodbine; *ren dung* (endure winter)

This is a vinelike shrub that grows to a height of 6–9 meters, with slender, prickly branches and flowers that bloom white then turn yellow, hence the Chinese name meaning "gold and silver flower." The flowers, stem, and leaves are used in medicine and contain, respectively, inositol, saponin, and tannin. Long-term use of the flowers is said to enhance vitality and prolong life.

The plant is grown in China, Japan, Korea, and Taiwan.

MEDICINAL PARTS: flowers, stem, leaves

NATURE: Energy: cold
           Flavor: sweet
           Affinity: lungs, heart, spleen, stomach

THERAPEUTIC EFFECTS: antipyretic; refrigerant; antiphlogistic; diuretic; antidote; purifies blood (TCM: nourishes blood; clears internal heat)

INDICATIONS: inflamed and swollen sore throat; bleeding ulcers; blood in sputum and stool; infections and poisons; abscesses, skin sores, infections, and allergies; hemorrhoids; obesity (TCM: internal-heat injury)

DOSAGE: decoction: 5–10 grams, in two doses, on an empty stomach

external: an infusion of the fresh flowers is used as an external wash for abscesses, sores, and infections on the skin

CONTRAINDICATIONS: none

INCOMPATIBLES: none

REMARKS: This is another herb that should only be used for as long as it takes to relieve the symptoms for which it is being applied. If results are not obtained within 7 days, switch to a different herb with similar properties.

65. JAPANESE WAX PRIVET

Ligustrum japonicum

女貞子 *nu jen dze (nu jen zi)*

OTHER NAMES: *Ligustrum lucidum; dung ching* (winter green); *la shu* (wax tree)

An evergreen tree that grows to a height of 5 meters, with large oblong leaves 10 centimeters long by 5 centimeters wide, this plant is widely cultivated in China for the production of white wax, since the insect that produces this wax favors it as a habitat. The medicinal berries are bitter and contain syringin and invertin.

The plant is cultivated in southern China, Korea, and Japan.

MEDICINAL PART: berry

NATURE: Energy: neutral
Flavor: bitter, sweet
Affinity: kidneys, spleen

THERAPEUTIC EFFECTS: tonic; nutrient; diuretic; prevents tumor formation; builds immunity (TCM: nourishes vitality; tonifies yin; calms the Five Vital Yin Organs)

INDICATIONS: insomnia; lack of appetite; fatigue; low libido; immune deficiency (TCM: deficient yin)

DOSAGE: decoction: 5–10 grams, in two doses, on an empty stomach

CONTRAINDICATIONS: TCM: empty spleen and stomach; cold spleen and stomach

INCOMPATIBLES: none

REMARKS: The Ming dynasty master herbalist Lee Shih-chen wrote, "If one uses this herb for 10 months, the flesh will grow firm and the skin strong and supple. The elderly will find they no longer need to arise so often at night to go to the toilet, that their waist and lower back grow stronger, and their energy increases."

Recent laboratory research has revealed that the flesh of the berries has no medicinal value, but that the pharmacological principles are actually contained in the seeds within the flesh.

This is one of the herbs currently under intensive scientific scrutiny in China for its stimulant influence on the immune system. As such, it has potential applications in cancer, AIDS, and any other form of immune impairment, including that caused by chemotherapy and radiation treatment.

66. JOB'S TEARS, *Coix lacryma-jobi*

薏以仁 *yi yi ren*

OTHER NAMES: *Coix chinensis; pu ti dze* (bodhi seeds)

This is an annual grass that grows 1–2 meters tall, with a branching stem and long narrow leaves, 30 centimeters by 3 centimeters, and white globular seeds about 5 millimeters long and 4 millimeters across. The seeds resemble pearl barley, for which they are often mistaken, but they are somewhat larger and rougher. The plant was introduced to China about two thousand years ago from Southeast Asia, and it has since become one of the most highly recommended nutrient tonics in the Chinese pharmacopeia. It is usually taken as a nourishing porridge, sometimes in combination with other whole grains and often supplemented with other nutrient herbs. The seeds contain 52% starch, 7% fat, and

17% protein, including the amino acids leucine, tyrosine, lycine, glutamic acid, arginine, and histidine.

The herb is cultivated in Southeast Asia, central and western China, India, tropical Africa, and North America.

MEDICINAL PART: seed

NATURE:
Energy: slightly cold
Flavor: sweet, plain
Affinity: spleen, stomach, lungs, liver, large intestine

THERAPEUTIC EFFECTS: nutrient; diuretic; decongests lungs; antiphlogistic; antirheumatic; eliminates phlegm; refrigerant (TCM: tonifies yang-energy; eliminates dampness)

INDICATIONS: dark scanty urine; swelling and pain in joints and sinews; rheumatism; lung infections; cough with blood in sputum; dry scaly skin; hernia; stomach ulcers (TCM: internal-damp symptoms)

DOSAGE: porridge: ½ cup (20–30 grams) of seeds, soaked in pure water for 1 hour, drained, then boiled in 1 liter pure water until cooked, adding more water as needed; eat in one or two portions, either on an empty stomach, or as part of a nonmeat, nondairy meal; to increase nutrient properties, add 3–5 Chinese jujubes

powder: roast the seeds until golden brown, then grind to powder and store in an airtight container; plain, capsules, or water-paste; 6–12 grams, in two or three doses, on an empty stomach; for paste, use warm water or chicken broth.

CONTRAINDICATIONS: none

INCOMPATIBLES: none

REMARKS: In order to gain optimum therapeutic benefits from this herb, it must become part of your daily diet for a period of at least 2–3 months. Since it lends itself so well to cooking, this is quite easy. The porridge can be used as a breakfast staple, sweetened with honey and dried fruits if desired, and the seeds can also be blended with brown rice, wild rice, buckwheat, and other whole grains as a lunch and dinner dish. In between, or when cooking takes too much time, simply take the ground roast powder by the spoonful, in capsules, or as a paste.

67. JOINT FIR, *Ephedra sinica*
麻黃 *ma huang*

OTHER NAMES: ephedra; *E. vulgaris*

This is a low shrub, 30–50 centimeters tall, with short erect branches notched by nodes, or joints (hence the name). Leaves are reduced to tiny scales, and the plant bears small yellow flowers and edible red berries. The stems are used in medicine, either with the joints intact or stripped, depending on use. The joints and roots are considered to have different effects than the stems alone. They contain 1% of the alkaloid ephedrine, which is a bronchial dilator and respiratory stimulant that also stimulates the heart and cerebral cortex. Many amphetamine compounds are based on a synthetic analog of this alkaloid.

The herb is native to northern China and Mongolia, and also grows in Europe.

MEDICINAL PART: stem

NATURE: Energy: warm
Flavor: pungent, slightly bitter
Affinity: lungs, bladder

THERAPEUTIC EFFECTS: diaphoretic; dilates bronchi; stimulates respiration; diuretic; suppresses appetite (TCM: releases external heat)

INDICATIONS: bronchitis and asthma; fevers and chills; hay fever and allergies; numbness in skin and flesh; red and swollen eyes; fluid retention (edema); excess appetite; obesity (TCM: wind-cold and wind-damp symptoms)

DOSAGE: decoction: 3–10 grams, in two doses, on an empty stomach

for asthma, bronchitis, and chest colds, add 5 grams almond, 4 grams cinnamon, and 2 grams licorice

CONTRAINDICATIONS: individuals who experience chronic profuse sweating should only use the roots, which are counterdiaphoretic and will thus prevent excess loss of fluids during treatment; those with low vitality and weak constitutions may experience nocturnal sweats, insomnia, and nervousness after using ephedra

INCOMPATIBLES: magnolia; gypsum

REMARKS: In addition to stimulating respiration, pulse, and cerebral functions, ephedra also induces the body to burn white fat as a source of the calories required to sustain these enhanced vital functions. Known as thermogenesis, this effect burns unwanted white fat stored in adipose tissues of the body, without depleting supplies of essential brown fats in the vital organs, nerves, and brain. Since the herb also suppresses excess appetite if taken about an hour before mealtimes, it can be used to treat obesity. However, it should be used only for this purpose by those who are otherwise healthy and do not display any of the above contraindications.

68. JUSTICIA GENDARUSSA

秦艽 *chin jiao*

This is a low-growing plant with long twisted roots and large leaves that resemble lettuce. The plant flowers in small clusters from a central stalk and grows throughout the mountain valleys of China's southwestern provinces. The medicinal roots are

dark yellow in color, contorted, and about 20 centimeters in length. They contain the alkaloid justicine and essential oil.

MEDICINAL PART: root

NATURE: Energy: neutral
Flavor: bitter
Affinity: liver, gallbladder, stomach

THERAPEUTIC EFFECTS: antipyretic; antiphlogistic; diuretic; antidote to alcohol poisoning; antirheumatic; sedative (TCM: expels cold-damp)

INDICATIONS: rheumatism; jaundice; toothache; fever; diarrhea (TCM: cold-damp and cold-wind symptoms)

CONTRAINDICATIONS: none

INCOMPATIBLES: dairy products

69. KUDZU VINE, *Pueraria lobata*

葛根 *geh gen*

OTHER NAME: *Pachyrhizus thunbergianus*

This is a woody vine with a hairy stem, trifoliate leaflets 12–20 centimeters long, and a dense inflorescence 20–25 centimeters long with small purple flowers. The root, which is very starchy, is used both as food and medicine. A yellow cloth known as *geh bu* (vine cloth) is made from the plant fiber, highly valued in China as a summer cloth. The starch of the root is used to make a cooking condiment with properties similar to arrowroot and cornstarch.

The plant is cultivated primarily in China and Japan.

MEDICINAL PART: root

NATURE: Energy: neutral
Flavor: sweet, bitter
Affinity: spleen, stomach

THERAPEUTIC EFFECTS: antipyretic; refrigerant; diuretic; nervine; antidote to drug and alcohol poisoning; improves flesh tone (TCM: clears internal heat)

INDICATIONS: fevers, headache, and pains in neck and shoulders; dysentery; skin rashes; convulsions; alcohol and drug poisoning (TCM: wind-heat injuries)

DOSAGE: decoction: 4–10 grams, in two doses, on an empty stomach

CONTRAINDICATIONS: none

INCOMPATIBLES: none

REMARKS: Simple decoctions of kudzu vine are particularly effective in relaxing tension and relieving pain in tight, aching neck and shoulder muscles caused by exposure to wind-heat conditions, such as in summer colds and air-conditioning.

70. LEDEBOURIELLA SESELOIDES

防風 *fang feng*

OTHER NAME: *Siler divaricatum*

A perennial plant that grows 30–40 centimeters tall, with an erect stem and many branchlets, the herb resembles fennel in appearance and is often used in cooking. The medicinal roots occur in irregular branching pieces, 15 centimeters long by 1–2 centimeters in diameter, yellowish brown in color, with fragments of the stem attached to the rootstock. It is particularly effective against all sorts of wind-injury symptoms, hence the Chinese name meaning "prevent wind."

The herb is cultivated in northern China and Japan.

MEDICINAL PART: root

NATURE: Energy: warm
            Flavor: pungent, sweet
            Affinity: liver, spleen, bladder

THERAPEUTIC EFFECTS: antipyretic, analgesic; expectorant; antitussive; tonic to respiratory tract (TCM: expels all thirty-six varieties of wind)

INDICATIONS: headache and blurry vision; pain in shoulders and neck; bodily aches; bloodshot eyes (TCM: all forms of wind injury, particularly wind-damp symptoms)

DOSAGE: decoction: 8–15 grams, in two doses, on an empty stomach

CONTRAINDICATION: chronic profuse sweating

INCOMPATIBLES: ginger; aconite

REMARKS: This herb lends itself well to use in herbal cooking, particularly meat and vegetable stews. If everyone in the house has come down with similar wind-injury symptoms, such as headache and aching muscles, you can all "have your herbal medicine and eat it too" by simply cooking the herb into your family meals.

71. LEONURUS, *Leonurus sibiricus*

益母草 *yi mu tsao (yi mu cao)*

OTHER NAME: Siberian motherwort

An annual herb that grows to a height of 1 meter, with tripartite leaves and red-and-white flowers arranged in whorls around the stem joints, this plant grows near seashores and the edges of ponds and marshes. The fresh plant has a disagreeable odor, and it thus became the occupation of poor people to collect and dry it for sale to medicine shops. It is regarded as an indispensable herb for all types of female menstrual problems. The seed contains essential oil and the alkaloid leonurin.

The herb grows worldwide, particularly in northern China, Manchuria, and Siberia, India and Southeast Asia, Africa, and North America.

MEDICINAL PARTS: seeds; or entire plant except roots

NATURE: Energy: slightly cold
         Flavor: bitter, pungent
         Affinity: liver, pericardium

THERAPEUTIC EFFECTS: hemostatic; emmenagogue; diuretic; promotes circulation and clears clots; brightens eyes

INDICATIONS: uterine bleeding after childbirth; nausea during pregnancy; dysmenorrhea, irregular menses, PMS, and other menstrual disorders; female infertility; pain and swelling in breasts

DOSAGE: decoction: 10–15 grams, in two doses, on an empty stomach

CONTRAINDICATIONS: if needed for nausea and painful breasts during pregnancy, use moderately (5–10 grams daily) under supervision of TCM practitioner

INCOMPATIBLES: iron and other metal compounds and utensils

REMARKS: This herb is also known in Western herbal medicine as a reliable all-around remedy for female reproductive-system disorders, particularly those related to menstruation, pregnancy, and childbirth. Hence the common folk name "motherwort." Recent scientific research in North America has validated many of the virtues attributed to this herb in traditional medicine. Chinese women use it frequently to relieve circulatory congestion and clear residual blood clots after childbirth.

The herb grows readily in backyard gardens and is therefore easily cultivated for use at home. When using the fresh herb at home, instead of separating out the seeds, simply pick the entire plant above the ground, leaving the roots behind, dry it well in the sun, and make a daily decoction of 15 grams.

72. LICORICE, *Glycyrrhiza uralensis*

甘草 *gan tsao (gan cao)*

OTHER NAMES: *mi tsao* (honey grass); sweetwood; *Glycyrrhiza glabra; G. echinata*

Licorice is a perennial herb with an erect stem, small oblong leaves, and a long inflorescence with clusters of purple flowers. It is one of the most highly prized and frequently employed herbs in the Chinese pharmacopeia, appearing in a wide range of formulas.

Some Chinese sources refer to it respectfully as *guo lao* (venerable national treasure). It improves the taste of other herbs, harmonizes and prolongs their effects in formulas, and benefits all of the vital organs and their meridians. The medicinal root is grayish brown or dark brown on the outside, yellow on the inside, and has a sweet taste four times stronger than sugarcane. The roots are sweetest and most potent if dug before the plant bears fruit.

The plant grows plentifully throughout northern China, Mongolia, Siberia, and central Asia.

MEDICINAL PART: root

NATURE: Energy: neutral
Flavor: sweet
Affinity: all twelve organs

THERAPEUTIC EFFECTS: expectorant; demulcent to lungs and bronchi; emollient to stomach ulcers; antidote; tonic; antipyretic; laxative; sedative; antitussive; reduces cholesterol and blood sugar; inhibits tumor growth (TCM: tonifies spleen- and stomach-energy; quells heart-fire; tonifies Triple Burner and primordial energy; scatters external cold)

INDICATIONS: colds; fever; sore throat; lung and bronchial congestion; stomach ulcers; gastritis and acid indigestion; diabetes; blood and liver toxicity; gallbladder inflammation; irritability; alcohol and drug poisoning; abdominal pain; hepatitis and cirrhosis; damp, itchy scrotum and other skin rashes (TCM: empty spleen- and stomach-energy; deficient blood and energy; heart-fire)

DOSAGE: decoction: 2–8 grams, in two doses, on an empty stomach; for colds and other respiratory ailments, you can add 2–5 grams ginger root

infusion: pour 1 liter boiling water over 8–10 grams licorice root in a large teapot, cover and steep for 20 minutes; pour into another teapot, and add more boiling water to roots, up to four times. Drink warm by the cup throughout the day. For increased antidote, detoxification, and blood cooling benefits, add 4–6 grams chrysanthemum as well

sliced root: chew 10–12 slices of dried licorice root throughout the day, swallowing the juice and spitting out the pulp when spent

external wash: use the decoction three times daily for 1 week as a wash for damp, itchy scrotum and other skin rashes; let affected area soak in the herbal broth for 5 minutes, then rinse with water (but do not use soap); can also be used to cleanse and heal skin sores and rashes on dogs and cats

CONTRAINDICATIONS: none

INCOMPATIBLES: *Polygala tenuifolia; Euphorbia sieboldiana; Euphorbia pekinensis; Daphne genkwa*

REMARKS: Licorice is one of the most ancient herbal remedies in the world. Records of its use in the Ayurvedic medicine of India go back over 4,000 years, and in 1923 a large quantity of this herb was discovered in the excavation of a famous pharaoh's tomb in Egypt. Regarding its potent antidote properties, the Tang dynasty Chinese physician Sun Ssu-mo, writing 1,400 years ago in his classic health tome *Precious Recipes,* states, "The detoxifying power of licorice when it meets poisons in the human body can be compared to the melting power of a pan of boiling hot water when poured onto snow on the ground."

Licorice has been extensively researched by modern laboratory science, which has clearly validated many of the medical virtues traditionally attributed to it. Unfortunately, some unfavorable research has also been published, based entirely on studies done on fractional extracts of licorice, such as those used to make licorice candy in Europe (North American licorice candy contains very little real licorice). Like so many medicinal herbs, licorice behaves in an entirely different manner when its constituents are fractured, refined, concentrated, and applied in isolation from natural synergistic cofactors in the whole herb. Many common herbs and foods, including such apparently innocent items as lettuce, contain elements that can cause adverse toxic reactions in humans when chemically isolated and taken in concentrated doses far exceeding the natural levels found in the plant itself. Therefore, the only modern scientific research on traditional medical herbs that produces valid results is that which is conducted on whole herbs, which contain all sorts of synergistic cofactors, both known and unknown, without whose presence the herbs' active components behave very differently and do not deliver the desired therapeutic effects.

Recent research done on whole licorice root at the Green Medicine Research Laboratories in Long Island, New York, revealed that some of the herb's active components have a molecular structure very similar to hormones secreted by the adrenal cortex, known in TCM as the kidney-glands and in esoteric Tao yoga as the Gate of Life. This may explain the herb's remarkable capacity to balance and regulate so many vital functions, for secretions of the adrenal cortex play a central role in regulating the entire endocrine system, which in turn governs myriads of vital functions throughout the body. These adrenal-like constituents of licorice may also account for the herb's enhancement of overall immune response throughout the system.

Recent studies conducted on licorice in China and Japan found that the herb stimulates production of interferon, though the mechanism by which this is accomplished is not known. The finding further underlines the importance of employing the whole herb in medicine, instead of isolating only the known active compounds. The herb's interferon-producing property is what makes licorice such an effective treatment for hepatitis B and a potent inhibitor of tumor growth.

73. LIGUSTICUM WALLICHII

川芎 *chuan hsiung (chuan xiong)*

OTHER NAMES: *Conioselinum univittatum; hsiang guo* (fragrant fruit)

An umbelliferous plant similar in appearance to angelica, this herb is cultivated as medicine in southern and western China, where it also grows wild, and in Japan. The leaves are traditionally used as an anthelmintic against intestinal parasites, as well as for preparing facial cosmetics, but the part used most in medicine is the root, which is bitter and richly fragrant.

MEDICINAL PART: root

NATURE: Energy: warm
         Flavor: pungent
         Affinity: liver, gallbladder, pericardium

THERAPEUTIC EFFECTS: emmenagogue; tonic; analgesic; sedative; promotes circulation and purifies blood; lowers blood pressure (TCM: tonifies blood and essence; regulates energy)

INDICATIONS: anemia; blood toxicity; all menstrual disorders; abdominal pain after childbirth (TCM: cold-empty symptoms; wind-damp injury)

DOSAGE: decoction: 4–8 grams, in three doses, on an empty stomach

CONTRAINDICATIONS: none

INCOMPATIBLES: talc, *Coptis teeta,* astragalus, *Cornus officinalis*

REMARKS: This herb's potent blood-purifying and blood-nourishing properties are currently under study in China and Japan for potential application in the treatment of cancer, AIDS, and other serious conditions of impaired immunity in which strong blood and enhanced circulation are vital to survival and recovery of the patient.

74. LOTUS SEEDS, *Nelumbium nucifera*
蓮子 *lien dze (lien zi)*

OTHER NAMES: *Nelumbium nelumbo; N. speciosum*

This perennial aquatic herb is one of Asia's most beloved plants and has long been cultivated as food and medicine, in landscape gardening, and as a symbol of purity and spiritual cultivation in temple ponds. It has a thick edible root with much starch, large round leaves 30–50 centimeters in diameter, and a beautifully petaled blossom that blooms in various shades of pink and white. The seeds are usually sold in the dry, hard state, ivory-white with a black testa, but in season they are sold raw from the fresh pod as a culinary delicacy in Asian markets.

Lotus is cultivated throughout the tropical regions of Asia and in Australia.

MEDICINAL PART: seed

NATURE: Energy: neutral
            Flavor: sweet
            Affinity: spleen, kidneys, heart

THERAPEUTIC EFFECTS: tonic; nutrient; aphrodisiac; hemostatic; nervine (TCM: tonic to heart- and spleen-energy; nourishes semen-essence)

INDICATIONS: impotence; nocturnal emission; menor-rhagia; leukorrhea; neurasthenia; insomnia; venereal diseases; diarrhea; weak heart; pancreatitis (TCM: defi-cient heart- and kidney-energy)

DOSAGE: decoction: 6–12 grams, in three doses, on an empty stomach

powder: plain, capsules, pills, paste; 4–8 grams, in three doses, on an empty stomach

CONTRAINDICATIONS: constipation; indigestion and abdominal bloating

INCOMPATIBLES: none

REMARKS: The entire plant is used in medicine. The sta-mens are astringent and used as a remedy for spermator-rhea and premature ejaculation. The leaves, which have antipyretic and refrigerant properties, are used against symptoms of summer-heat, such as headache, respira-tory congestion, chronic thirst, and dark scanty urine. The peduncle relieves stomachaches, calms restless fetus, and controls leukorrhea, and the roots, which are often used for food, have hemostatic and astringent ef-fects.

Lotus seeds can be used to make a delicious sweet soup, which is very popular as a snack or dessert in East Asia. Simply soak a cup of lotus seeds in pure water for a few hours, drain, and boil in fresh water, adding some honey, raw sugar, palm sugar, or other natural sweet-ener.

75. MASTIC TREE, *Boswellia carterii*

乳香 *ru hsiang (ru xiang)*

OTHER NAMES: olibanum; Kunduru; *Boswellia glabra; B. thurifera*

This is a deciduous tree native to India and the Medi-terranean region, long used as a source of aromatic resin for making incense and perfume. The medicinal resin is found as an exudate beneath the bark and appears in shops as opaque, brittle, pale yellow drops, bitter and aromatic, with the typical acrid smell of tree resins. Ayurvedic practitioners of India use it mostly as an external remedy for carbuncles, and internally for gonorrhea and lung infections.

MEDICINAL PART: solidified resin

NATURE: Energy: warm
                 Flavor: pungent, bitter
                 Affinity: liver, heart, spleen

THERAPEUTIC EFFECTS:
analgesic; stimulant; emmenagogue; promotes circulation; stimulates muscle growth; astringent (TCM: activates blood and balances energy)

INDICATIONS: dysmenorrhea; amenorrhea; pains in chest and abdomen; nocturnal emissions with wet dreams; epilepsy; sluggish circulation; boils, abscesses, carbuncles (TCM: blood and energy stagnation)

DOSAGE: decoction: 3–9 grams, in two doses, on an empty stomach

   external: use the decoction as a wash for boils, abscesses, and carbuncles

   gargle: the decoction can also be used as a gargle for halitosis (bad breath)

CONTRAINDICATIONS: none

INCOMPATIBLES: none

REMARKS: An eighteenth-century Chinese herbal recommends placing a small lump of this resin in the mouth at bedtime and letting it slowly dissolve, as a remedy for nocturnal emissions with wet dreams in males.

76. MINT, *Mentha arvensis*

薄荷 *bo he*

OTHER NAMES: field mint; wild pennyroyal; peppermint

This is a perennial herb that grows 10–60 centimeters tall, with erect or running stems, a densely clustered pink inflorescence, and oval leaves with serrated edges and a downy fuzz. The plant is highly aromatic and pungent, and has long been used throughout Asia and Europe as a seasoning for food and as a refreshing herbal tea. The leaves contain volatile oils, including menthol, menthone, piperitone, and limonene.

Mint grows wild and is also cultivated throughout China, Southeast Asia, India, and Europe, with related species in North America.

MEDICINAL PARTS: leaves, tender stalks

NATURE: Energy: cool
         Flavor: pungent
         Affinity: lungs, liver

THERAPEUTIC EFFECTS: stomachic, carminative; diaphoretic; stimulant; analgesic; nervine; cooling (TCM: clears internal heat; expels wind-heat)

INDICATIONS: headaches, cough, and sore throat associated with "catching a cold"; laryngitis; sinus congestion; earache; dysmenorrhea; indigestion; flatulence (TCM: internal heat; wind-heat symptoms in head and respiratory tract)

DOSAGE: decoction: 2–4 grams, in one dose, on an empty stomach

powder: infusion; 1 gram, steeped in hot water, on an empty stomach (this is the best way to take mint; can be sweetened with some honey); for relief of sore throat, ask someone to gently blow a small amount of the finely ground powder down your throat with a straw ointment: blend a few grams of mint powder with some yellow vaseline, almond oil, lanolin, or other base, and apply it as a cooling, soothing salve to head, chest, abdomen, and other hot, painful, congested, or inflamed parts

CONTRAINDICATIONS: severe chills; nervous exhaustion

INCOMPATIBLES: none

REMARKS: Mint is a very mild, nontoxic herb and is therefore a good choice for treating children for minor digestive distress and the discomforts associated with flu and common cold. Its soothing nervine properties also help hyperactive children relax, but this benefit cannot manifest unless all "soft drinks" with high levels of sugar and caffeine are completely withdrawn from the diet.

Some varieties of mint, particularly peppermint *(Mentha piperata)* have been scientifically shown to inhibit and kill a broad range of pathogenic microbes, including influenza A, herpes simplex, mumps virus, streptococcus, staphylococcus, and *Candida albicans*. This property helps protect those who use it daily from contracting many common ailments caused by exposure to pathogens so commonly found today in food, water, air, and human contact.

77. MISHMI BITTER, *Coptis sinensis*

黃連 *huang lien*

OTHER NAME: *Coptis teeta*

A perennial herb with long trifoliate leaves, small yellowish white flowers, and a reddish brown root covered with fine rootlets, this plant is cultivated for medicine throughout China and also in parts of northern India, where it is extensively used in Ayurvedic

medicine. The root is yellowish orange on the inside, the inner pith being deeper in color, and contains the alkaloids coptisine, worenine, and berberine. In ancient China, midwives customarily fed a dose of this herb to newborn infants as a general antidote against all poisons, particularly venereal and other infections possibly contracted in the womb from the mother.

MEDICINAL PART: root

NATURE: Energy: cold
              Flavor: bitter
              Affinity: liver, heart, stomach, large
                          intestine

THERAPEUTIC EFFECTS: antipyretic; refrigerant; drying; stomachic; antidysenteric; antidote to drug and alcohol poisoning; antidote to toxins in infants and children (TCM: cools blood)

INDICATIONS: pain and oppression in chest; heart pains; red and swollen eyes; drug and alcohol poisoning; dysentery and diarrhea; abscesses; nosebleed; heatstroke; jaundice; hepatitis; gastritis (TCM: full-heat symptoms)

DOSAGE: powder: capsules of ¾-gram each; two capsules in the morning before breakfast, two capsules at bedtime

CONTRAINDICATION: TCM: empty-cold symptoms

INCOMPATIBLES: chrysanthemum; ginseng; coltsfoot; *Achyranthes bidentata;* pork; *Dictamnus albus*

REMARKS: This herb is frequently used to treat infants and children for fevers, diarrhea, swelling, pain, and other full-hot symptoms caused by consumption of contaminated food or toxic substances, or by exposure to infectious microbes.

78. MORINDA ROOT

Morindae officinalis

巴戟天 *ba ji tien*

OTHER NAME: *Polygala reinii*

This is a wintergreen shrub with small quill leaves and a sweet, medicinally warming root that has long been reputed as a strengthening sexual tonic for males. It is also recommended for bolstering willpower, lack of which is often attributed to deficient kidney-energy, which governs willpower.

The herb is relatively expensive and is cultivated in northern and central China and Japan.

MEDICINAL PART: root

NATURE: Energy: warm
           Flavor: sweet, pungent
           Affinity: kidneys

THERAPEUTIC EFFECTS: tonic; astringent; aphrodisiac; strengthens bone and sinew; increases willpower (TCM: tonifies kidney-yang; warming)

INDICATIONS: impotence; premature ejaculation; nocturnal emission; profuse urination; lumbago; weak willpower; cold and pain in lower abdomen (TCM: deficient kidney-yang)

DOSAGE: decoction: 5–9 grams, in two doses, on an empty stomach

    powder: capsule or pills; 3–6 grams, in two doses, on an empty stomach

    liquor: steep 60–70 grams in 1 liter spirits for 2–3 months; take 1 ounce, twice daily (afternoon and bedtime) on an empty stomach

CONTRAINDICATIONS: high blood pressure; constipation (TCM: empty yin with flaring fire [see Remarks page 98 for details])

INCOMPATIBLES: *Salvia miltiorhiza*

REMARKS: This herb is most effective as a male sexual tonic when taken in conjunction with other tonic herbs in properly balanced formulas, such as the tonic prescriptions found in chapter 4, "The Tried and the True." Taken alone as a decoction, powder, or liquor, it is most useful as a short-term remedy for the above indications, but for long-term tonification and restoration, formulas are always more effective. For example, to treat impotence, premature ejaculation, and other symptoms of male sexual depletion, morinda root can be combined in equal portions with dogwood tree, Chinese yam, Chinese wolfberry, and *Psoralea corylifolia,* and taken as a decoction or as pills or capsules: decoction, 5 grams of each herb, in two doses, on an empty stomach; pills or capsules, 9 grams of the combined powders, in three doses, on an empty stomach.

79. MULTIFLORA ROSE

Rosa multiflora

苞薔薇报 *bao chiang wei*

OTHER NAMES: *Rosa indica; chiang mi* (wall rose)

This is a climbing rose shrub with hooked prickles, clusters of 5–9 oblong leaflets, and small multifloral blossoms 2 centimeters wide, pink or white in color. Cultivated varieties also produce yellow, red, and purple flowers. The seeds, which have diuretic and laxative properties, contain multiflorin, kaempferol, rhamnose, quercetin, and 8% fat. The young shoots, stripped of their bark and barbs, are edible.

The plant grows wild and is also cultivated in China, Japan, and Korea.

MEDICINAL PART: root

NATURE: Energy: warm
         Flavor: sweet
         Affinity: kidneys

THERAPEUTIC EFFECTS: astringent; carminative; emmenagogue

INDICATIONS: spermatorrhea and wet dreams; frequent and profuse urination; hernia; dysmenorrhea; prolapse of uterus

Medicinal Herbs

DOSAGE: decoction: 9–18 grams, in two doses, on an empty stomach

CONTRAINDICATIONS: none

INCOMPATIBLES: none

80. NUTMEG, *Myristica fragrans*

肉荳蔻 *rou dou kou*

OTHER NAMES: *M. moschata; rou guo* (flesh nut)

Nutmeg comes from a tropical tree that grows 10–15 meters tall and produces an oblong fleshy fruit that contains pungent, highly aromatic seeds, 30 millimeters long by 24 millimeters wide, deeply grooved on one side. The seeds contain camphene, pinene, dipentene, linalol, safrole, eugenol, isoeugenol, borneol, terpineol, geraniol, and myristicin. The latter compound has narcotic effects in humans when one or two whole nutmegs are consumed, with symptoms of narcosis, delirium, and some motor stimulation that lasts 20–24 hours. The herb is not native to China and is therefore not used much as a culinary spice there.

The tree is native to the Moluccas and is also cultivated elsewhere in Southeast Asia as well as India.

MEDICINAL PART: seed

NATURE: Energy: warm
Flavor: pungent
Affinity: stomach, spleen, small intestine

THERAPEUTIC EFFECTS: stomachic; astringent; carminative; sedative in small doses; stimulant in large doses

INDICATIONS: abdominal pain and distension; intestinal gas and flatulence; nausea, especially in children; diarrhea and dysentery; poor absorption in small intestine; insomnia; premature ejaculation; urinary incontinence; pancreatitis

DOSAGE: powder: plain, capsules, pills, infusion; 250–500 milligrams, one or two times daily, on an empty stomach

culinary: for long-term use as a digestive aid, keep

some freshly ground nutmeg in the kitchen and on the table as a condiment for foods and beverages

CONTRAINDICATIONS: pregnancy; used in excess, nutmeg can cause dullness and torpor

INCOMPATIBLES: iron and other metal compounds and utensils

REMARKS: Nutmeg used to be highly prized as a cerebral stimulant in ancient Greece and Rome, when its rarity and high cost made it available only to rich and aristocratic circles. Later it became more widely known as a digestive stimulant, for which purpose it becomes most effective when the nut is ground and cooked directly in food. When utilized as a digestive cooking herb, its presence in food significantly increases absorption of nutrients in the small intestine.

81. PINELLIA TERNATA

半夏 *ban hsia (ban xia)*

OTHER NAME: *P. tuberifera*

This is a tuberous perennial herb, with light green tripartite leaves and a solitary peduncle 25–30 centimeters long. The medicinal tubers are soaked for 7 days in warm water, then dried and mixed with some ginger juice. They are sold in spherical pieces 1–2 centimeters thick, flattened on one side, yellowish white on the surface and white, dense, and amylaceous on the inside. The tubers contain essential oil, fatty oil, phytosterols, and a toxic alkaloid with sedative and antispasmodic properties similar to coniine.

The herb grows in southern and central China and Japan.

MEDICINAL PART: tuber

NATURE: Energy: warm
             Flavor: pungent
             Affinity: spleen, stomach

THERAPEUTIC EFFECTS: antiemetic; expectorant; antitussive; sedative; drying (TCM: expels dampness)

INDICATIONS: oppression in chest; nausea and vomiting; chronic cough with phlegm; dizziness; insomnia; wet dreams; leukorrhea (TCM: damp spleen-energy)

DOSAGE: decoction: 5–12 grams, in two doses on an empty stomach

    powder: capsules, pills; 4–8 grams, in two or three doses, on an empty stomach

CONTRAINDICATIONS: pregnancy; fluid deficiency symptoms such as chronic thirst, dry cough, internal heat, and stagnant blood

INCOMPATIBLES: ginger; tortoise shell; bear gall; *Fraxinus pubinervus;* lamb; seaweed; *Polygonum multiflorum; Gleditschia chinensis*

REMARKS: The toxic alkaloid in the fresh root is mostly neutralized during the preparation and drying of the herb for medicinal use. Some tea or apple cider vinegar will completely neutralize any remaining toxic residues.

82. PLANTAIN, *Plantago asiatica*

車前子 *che chien dze (che qian zi)*

OTHER NAMES: *Plantago major;* ripple grass

A perennial herb that grows 10–15 centimeters tall, the plant has broadly oval, strongly ribbed leaves that radiate from the base, with a long erect flower spike growing from the center. The seeds are mucilaginous, with a sweet taste and cooling effect. The entire  plant is widely used in native North American and traditional European herbal medicine, particularly for its diuretic and astringent properties, but in TCM mainly the seeds are used.

The plant grows prolifically by roadsides and in fields and yards throughout the world.

MEDICINAL PART: seed

NATURE: Energy: cold
            Flavor: sweet
            Affinity: liver, kidneys, lungs, small
                       intestine

THERAPEUTIC EFFECTS: diuretic; antiphlogistic; expectorant; promotes semen production; lowers blood pressure; improves vision; stimulates labor (TCM: tonifies kidney-yin)

INDICATIONS: painful urination and bladder infections; prostate inflammation; male infertility; pain and swelling in eyes; blurry or weak vision; cough with phlegm; labor difficulties (TCM: deficient kidney-yin; full-hot symptoms)

DOSAGE: decoction: 5–8 grams, in two doses, on an empty stomach

CONTRAINDICATIONS: none

INCOMPATIBLES: none

REMARKS: This herb finds its way into many tonic and aphrodisiac formulas due to its capacity to increase semen production in males. It also seems to improve female fertility and is therefore one of the preferred choices for childless couples who wish to have children. The herb lends itself well to cooking, particularly with grains and in stews, and can be added to tonic herbal liquors; therefore it can be easily incorporated into daily diet for long-term use.

83. POLYGALA TENUIFOLIA

远志 *yuan jih (yuan zhi)*

OTHER NAME: *Polygala sibirica*

This is a small shrub that grows about 25 centimeters high, with slender stems and narrow quill leaves 3 centimeters long by 2 millimeters wide, and little bell-shaped purple flowers at the stem tips. The medicinal root occurs in contorted, somewhat tubular pieces 5–6 centimeters long and 7 millimeters wide, brownish yellow in color, and contains the glycosidal saponins senegin and polygalic acid.

The plant is native to northern China, Mongolia, and Siberia.

MEDICINAL PART: epidermis of root

NATURE: Energy: warm
        Flavor: bitter, pungent
        Affinity: lungs, kidneys, heart

THERAPEUTIC EFFECTS: tonic; analgesic; expectorant; sedative; improves hearing and vision; promotes muscle growth; strengthens bone and sinew; clarifies mental faculties (TCM: tonifies heart- and kidney-energy; tonifies yang-energy; nourishes semen)

INDICATIONS: spermatorrhea and wet dreams; absent-mindedness and poor memory; weak bones; cloudy urine; dizziness and fainting; cough with heavy phlegm; insomnia; depression; mental confusion; weak will-power

DOSAGE: decoction: 5–9 grams, in two doses, on an empty stomach
    powder: plain, capsules, pills; 3–6 grams, in two doses, on an empty stomach
    liquor: 50–70 grams, steeped in 1 liter spirits for 2–3 months; take 1 ounce, twice daily, on an empty stomach

CONTRAINDICATIONS: TCM: internal fire in kidneys and/or heart; empty yin with flaring fire (see Remarks, page 98, for details)

INCOMPATIBLES: veratrum

REMARKS: This herb is reputed to improve cerebral functions such as memory, learning, and clarity, and strengthen mental powers such as will and insight. This is probably due to its highly tonifying effects on the kidneys and heart, whose energies govern many important mental faculties.

Due to the herb's strong stimulation of mucosal secretions in the throat, it combines very well with licorice as a specific expectorant remedy for smoker's cough and other forms of bronchial congestion.

84. POLYGONATUM CIRRHIFOLIUM

黄精 *huang jing*

OTHER NAMES: *Polygonatum canaliculatum; P. chinense;* deer bamboo; *shan sheng jiang* (mountain ginger)

A perennial herb that grows 6–12 centimeters tall, with thick branching rootstocks resembling ginger, leaves that look much like bamboo, and small globular berries, this plant grows in the mountains of northern and western China, and in the Himalayas. The entire plant was traditionally used for food in China, while the root, which has a sweet pleasant taste, is employed in medicine. It comes in flat pieces 3–5 centimeters long, yellow in color, and somewhat translucent and flexible.

MEDICINAL PART: root

NATURE: Energy: neutral
Flavor: sweet
Affinity: kidneys, spleen, stomach

THERAPEUTIC EFFECTS: tonic; demulcent; builds bone and sinew; retards aging; promotes semen production (TCM: tonifies kidney- and spleen-energy)

INDICATIONS: weakness and malnutrition; impotence and male infertility; arthritis; premature aging; weak bones and ligaments (TCM: deficient kidney- and spleen-energy)

DOSAGE: decoction: 5–10 grams, in two doses, on an empty stomach

culinary: the root lends a pleasant sweet flavor to stews and soups and can be included in the diet for long-term use as a rejuvenating tonic

CONTRAINDICATIONS: none

INCOMPATIBLES: none

REMARKS: This herb has a considerable reputation among Taoist adepts and Himalayan yogis as a "food of the immortals." It is recorded in a third century CE text that when the Yellow Emperor (legendary founder of China) asked his councilor which plant could be eaten to confer immortality, the reply was *huang jing* (golden essence), so named because it is said to embody the great yang principle of the sun. In a text called *Immortal Prescriptions,* it is written, "If one uses Golden Essence for only one year, the old will become young again." A famous medieval Japanese poet recorded in his diary that this herb enabled him to sire five children by three wives when he was 52–65 years old.

The herb is very mild and should be used regularly on a long-term basis in order to obtain its full benefits.

85. PSORALEA CORYLIFOLIA

補骨脂 *bu gu jih (bu gu zhi)*

This annual plant grows to a height of 90 centimeters, with roundish oval leaves that have black spots on both sides, black glands, and short, black oval pods containing the medicinal seeds, which are oval, blackish yellow, 4 millimeters long by 3 millimeters across. They contain fatty oil, an alkaloid, and psoralein.

The plant is native to India and Iran, where it is used in medicine; it is also cultivated in China.

MEDICINAL PART: seed

NATURE: Energy: warm
　　　　　Flavor: pungent, bitter
　　　　　Affinity: kidneys

THERAPEUTIC EFFECTS: aphrodisiac; tonic; stimulant; strengthens genital organs; prevents miscarriage (TCM: tonifies kidney-yang; promotes yang-energy)

INDICATIONS: impotence; spermatorrhea; lumbago; weak knees; frequent urination; leukorrhea; tendency to miscarriage (TCM: deficient kidney-yang)

DOSAGE: decoction: 4–10 grams, in two doses, on an empty stomach

powder: capsules, pills; 4–8 grams, in two doses, on an empty stomach

CONTRAINDICATIONS: fever; constipation (TCM: empty yin with flaring fire symptoms (see Remarks, page 98, for details)

INCOMPATIBLES: licorice

REMARKS: Though this herb alone is contraindicated for males with empty yin with flaring fire syndrome (that is, sexual depletion further aggravated by flaring of sexual desire), it can be used in combination with the herbs in the following formula to sedate the flaring fire caused by empty yin; it tonifies and rebalances yin- and yang-energy and thereby restores sexual potency as well as sexual equilibrium:

Psoralea corylifolia	6 grams
Chinese wolfberry	6 grams
Rehmannia glutinosa	4 grams
Schisandra chinensis	4 grams
Panax ginseng	4 grams

Decoction: in two doses, on an empty stomach

Powder: pills, capsules; 9–12 grams of the combined powder, in three doses, on an empty stomach

86. RASPBERRY, *Rubus coreanus*

覆盆子 *fu pen dze (fu pen zi)*

OTHER NAMES: *R. tokkura;* Chinese wild raspberry

This is a perennial rosaceous plant with small prickles, serrated leaves, and small red berries composed of numerous drupelets. The fresh fruits are not eaten much by the Chinese, although they are used to make jams and sweet preserves. While Western and Ayurvedic herbal medicine employs the leaves, Chinese medicine uses the unripe fruits.

The plant is native to central and western China and Europe, and a related species grows in North America.

MEDICINAL PART: unripe fruit

NATURE: Energy: slightly warm
         Flavor: sweet, sour
         Affinity: kidneys, liver

THERAPEUTIC EFFECTS: tonic; aphrodisiac; astringent; promotes semen production; improves vision (TCM: tonifies kidney- and liver-energy; stimulates yang-energy; consolidates semen)

INDICATIONS: impotence; male and female infertility; spermatorrhea; physical exhaustion; urinary incontinence, including bed-wetting in children (TCM: deficient kidney- and liver-energy)

DOSAGE: decoction: 5–10 grams, in two doses, on an empty stomach

liquor: 50–60 grams, steeped in 1 liter spirits for 1–2 months; it can also be added to any sexual tonic formula; 1 ounce, twice daily, on an empty stomach

powder: pills; 3–6 grams, in two doses with wine, on an empty stomach; long-term use of these pills is recommended for building and strengthening the male sexual organ

CONTRAINDICATIONS: none

INCOMPATIBLES: none

REMARKS: As a specific remedy for male impotence, Chinese herbals suggest toasting this herb in a hot, dry skillet, or hot oven, then grinding it to powder and taking 9 grams daily, in two doses, on an empty stomach, with a few ounces of spirits. You can also use gelatin capsules, or simply stir the powder into the spirits.

Fresh raspberry leaves can be pureed with some pure water and the juice extracted for use as an astringent wash to treat excessive watering of the eyes.

87. REHMANNIA GLUTINOSA

乾地黄 *gan di huang*

OTHER NAME: *Rehmannia chinensis*

This perennial herb has an erect stem 15–20 centimeters tall and long oval leaves covered with fine hairs; it has fluted flowers, reddish orange with purple tints, and a round capsular fruit. The root is prepared for medicine by washing it clean with water then drying it in the sun. It is sold in large, fleshy chunks, brownish yellow in color, and has a sweet moist taste. The root contains glycosides, saponins, tannin, and resins. The fresh root has similar properties to the dried but is stronger in action.

The plant grows in northern China.

MEDICINAL PART: root

NATURE:
- Energy: cold
- Flavor: sweet
- Affinity: heart, kidneys, liver, small intestine

THERAPEUTIC EFFECTS: hemostatic; antipyretic; tonic; diuretic; cooling; builds marrow; strengthens semen; promotes muscle growth; lowers blood sugar (TCM: tonifies blood and heart-energy; cools blood)

INDICATIONS: blood in sputum and urine; nosebleed; uterine bleeding; fever; damaged tendons and sprained joints; diabetes (TCM: empty-hot blood; internal-heat injury)

DOSAGE: decoction: 5–8 grams, in two doses, on an empty stomach

liquor: 60–70 grams, in 1 liter of spirits for 2–3 months; take 1 ounce, twice daily, on an empty stomach; to further enhance blood-tonifying properties, add 40–50 grams angelica root

CONTRAINDICATIONS: weak digestion

INCOMPATIBLES: *Fritillaria verticillata; Ulmus macrocarpa;* garlic and onion; iron and other metal compounds and utensils

REMARKS: This herb is used as medicine in three different stages of preparation. The strongest is the fresh root, *sheng di huang,* which is dug from the ground and then buried in dry sand prior to use. Next is *gan di huang,* or dry *Rehmannia,* which is prepared by taking the fresh root out from storage in sand, washing it well, then drying it in the sun during the wintertime. This is the form described here. The third is *shou di huang* (cooked *Rehmannia*), which is made by steaming the fresh root until cooked, then letting it dry, then steaming and drying it again several times. This latter method enhances the herb's specific blood-tonifying properties.

Rehmannia is the primary ingredient in the famous Six Flavor *Rehmannia* Tonic formula. This is one of the all-time great remedies for ailments and discomforts caused by deficient kidney-yin, such as lumbago, weak and painful knees, impotence, frequent urination, infertility, and so forth.

For nosebleeds, Chinese herbals recommend a decoction of 15 grams *Rehmannia* with 15 grams creeping lilyturf *(mai men dung),* in two doses, on an empty stomach.

88. SANDALWOOD, *Santalum album*

檀香 *tan hsiang (tan xiang)*

OTHER NAMES: *Santalum verum; jen tan* (true sandalwood)

The wood of this tree, which grows to a height of 10 meters, has long been prized throughout Asia for its highly aromatic fragrance and is widely used to make incense, perfumes, fragrant oils, and precious ritual objects. The wood is also used in medicine, occurring in brittle broken pieces, with a fibrous texture and rough furrowed surface, light yellow to reddish brown in color. It contains a volatile oil consisting of 90% alpha-santalol and beta-santalol. High doses of this oil cause irritation of the urinary tract and have been used in India and China as a treatment for gonorrhea and other venereal infections.

The tree is native to India but also grows in southern China.

MEDICINAL PART: wood

NATURE: Energy: warm
              Flavor: pungent, slightly sweet
              Affinity: spleen, lung

THERAPEUTIC EFFECTS: stomachic; carminative; antiseptic; sedative; improves appetite (TCM: balances energy; harmonizes spleen- and lung-energy)

INDICATIONS: weak digestion; loss of appetite; urethritis; cystitis; vaginitis; venereal disease; bronchitis; skin sores and infections

DOSAGE: powder: capsules; 3–6 grams, in three doses, before or after food

external: the powder can be applied to chronic sores and infections on the skin

CONTRAINDICATIONS: none

INCOMPATIBLES: none

REMARKS: Care must be taken when purchasing sandalwood, for much of the product on the market has been heavily adulterated with other woods that are first soaked in a little sandalwood oil to give them the same aroma.

In both India and China, sandalwood has traditionally been favored as an incense for meditation practice, because its aroma is said to enhance mental clarity, harmonize emotions, and "settle" vital energy in the Elixir Field *(dan tien)* just below the naval. Burning sandalwood incense in the house is a good way to obtain its therapeutic benefits for physical health as well, though not as effective as ingesting it.

89. SCHISANDRA, *Schisandra chinensis*
五味子 *wu wei dze (wu wei zi)*

This is a woody aromatic vine, with oblong alternate leaves 6 centimeters long by 3 centimeters wide, and fruits occurring as bunches of berries on a short, drooping spike. The dried berries are blackish in color, with a transparent membrane containing the two kidney-shaped seeds. The seeds contain essential oil, fatty oil, and lots of mucilage. The various parts of the dried fruit are said to encompass all of the five energies and their flavors, hence the Chinese name meaning "five flavor seeds."

The herb is native to northern China, Manchuria, and Japan.

MEDICINAL PART: dried berry

NATURE: Energy: warm
Flavor:· sour, slightly bitter, salty
Affinity: kidneys, lungs

THERAPEUTIC EFFECTS: tonic; rejuvenative; astringent; antitussive; promotes semen production; controls perspiration; antidiarrhetic; demulcent (TCM: tonifies kidney- and lung-energy)

INDICATIONS: spermatorrhea and wet dreams; frequent profuse urination; male and female infertility; profuse sweating and night sweats; chronic thirst; insomnia; headache; dizziness; neuralgia; chronic cough; asthma (TCM: empty lung-energy; deficient kidney-energy)

DOSAGE: decoction: 2–6 grams, in two doses, on an empty stomach
powder: capsules, pills; 2–4 grams, in two doses, on an empty stomach

CONTRAINDICATION: early stages of colds with cough

INCOMPATIBLES: none

REMARKS: This herb is widely used for its balanced energies and broad spectrum of therapeutic effects, attributed in TCM to the presence of all five elemental flavors and energies. A good example of this balance is the herb's combined astringent and demulcent properties, which help restore fluid balance in the human system: in cases of excess body fluid, the herb's astringent properties help dry the system; in cases of deficient fluids, its demulcent effects help moisten the system.

Schisandra has long been popular in Chinese households as an all-around sexual tonic and balanced energy rejuvenator for both men and women. It lends itself well to use in tonic longevity formulas.

90. SHINY ASPARAGUS

Asparagus lucidus

天門冬 *tien men dung*

OTHER NAMES: *Asparagus falcatus; wan sui teng* (longevity vine); Chinese asparagus

This is a creeping undershrub with numerous cylindrical branches and slender branchlets with prickly leaves. The medicinal root comes in pieces 7–8 centimeters long, fleshy and translucent, yellowish or reddish in color. It contains asparagine, starch, sugar, and mucilage. The root is sometimes preserved in sugar or honey as a sweetmeat in China.

The plant grows in southern China and Japan.

MEDICINAL PART: root

NATURE:

Energy:	very cold	
Flavor:	sweet, bitter	
Affinity:	lungs, kidneys	

THERAPEUTIC EFFECTS: tonic; nutrient; demulcent; diuretic; expectorant; relieves thirst; moistens skin and flesh (TCM: tonifies lung- and kidney-yin)

INDICATIONS: physical exhaustion; recuperation after illness or surgery; chronic thirst; cough with thick phlegm; impotence; dry skin (TCM: deficient lung- and kidney-yin)

DOSAGE: decoction: 3–6 grams, in two doses, on an empty stomach

CONTRAINDICATIONS: weak digestion; chronic diarrhea (TCM: cold stomach-energy)

INCOMPATIBLE: carp

REMARKS: This herb, which is related to the common asparagus used in Western cuisine, has been used as medicine since ancient times in China, appearing in some of the earliest herbals on record. It is gentle and slow in its action but very effective as a nutrient tonic when used consistently for prolonged periods. In the Taoist classic *Embracing the Uncarved Block,* the great herbal alchemist Ko Hung wrote of a gentleman named Tu Tze-wei, "who after using this herb for many years was able to have sexual relations with 80 wives and concubines, walk a distance of 50 [Chinese] miles a day, and attain the advanced age of 145."

Modern research has shown this herb to have some inhibiting influence on the development of cancer, as well as cardiotonic benefits and antibacterial activity.

91. SICKLE SENNA, *Cassia tora*

决明子 *jue ming dze (jue ming zi)*

OTHER NAMES: *Cassia mimosoides; C. sophora*

This annual herb grows 30–90 centimeters high and has leaves 8–12 centimeters long consisting of six obovate leaflets 3–5 centimeters long, with yellow flowers growing from the leaf axils. The plant produces a linear pod 12–14 centimeters long by 4 millimeters wide, containing about twenty-five roundish brown seeds, pointed at one end, smooth and glossy, 5 millimeters by 2 millimeters. The seeds contain emodin, a glycoside, and a phytosterol compound.

The plant grows in southern China, Southeast Asia, India, and Japan.

MEDICINAL PART: seed

NATURE: Energy: cold
         Flavor: bitter, sweet, slightly salty
         Affinity: liver, gallbladder

THERAPEUTIC EFFECTS: antipyretic; laxative; improves vision; lowers blood pressure (TCM: eliminates hot-wind; cools liver-energy)

INDICATIONS: blurry vision, heat, pain, swelling, redness, and other eye and vision problems caused by liver inflammation; chronic constipation

DOSAGE: decoction: 5–8 grams, in two doses, on an empty stomach

powder: pills, paste; 3–6 grams, in two doses, on an empty stomach

CONTRAINDICATIONS: none

INCOMPATIBLE: cannabis seeds

REMARKS: Chinese herbals suggest making a paste from the powder and some strong tea, then rubbing the paste onto the "sun" *(tai yang)* vital points on the temples, as a remedy for the eye problems listed above. The paste should be left on for several hours, or overnight, and replenished as it dries.

92. SOLOMON'S SEAL

Polygonatum officinale

玉竹 *yu ju*

OTHER NAMES: *Polygonatum vulgare*; sealwort

This is a perennial herb with an erect, angular stem, 25–50 centimeters tall, alternate oblong leaves, aromatic white flowers that grow in clusters from short peduncles, and round berries. The leaves, which along with the root are edible, resemble those of bamboo, hence the Chinese name meaning "jade bamboo." The medicinal roots come in brittle twisted pieces about 15 centimeters long, yellow or light brown in color, semitranslucent; if macerated in water, they swell three to four times in size and regain their original fleshy dimensions. The roots contain the glycosides convallarin and convallamarin; the latter stimulates appetite, increases peristalsis, slows the heart, and deepens respiration.

The plant grows in northwestern China, central Asia, and Europe.

MEDICINAL PART: root

NATURE: Energy: neutral
            Flavor: sweet
            Affinity: kidneys, spleen

THERAPEUTIC EFFECTS: tonic; nutrient; demulcent; sedative; cooling; digestive; stimulates appetite; aphrodisiac; heals broken bones (TCM: nourishes yin; tonifies energy)

INDICATIONS: impotence; spermatorrhea; frequent urination (male); lack of appetite; weak digestion; fatigue due to malnutrition; broken bones; stomach and duodenal ulcers; hypoglycemia (TCM: empty spleen- and stomach-energy)

DOSAGE: decoction: 6–10 grams, in two doses, on an empty stomach

CONTRAINDICATIONS: stomach ulcers and bloating; severe congestion

INCOMPATIBLES: none

REMARKS: This herb is also widely used in Ayurvedic medicine, primarily to restore sexual potency and promote fertility, and as a nutrient tonic for malnutrition, anemia, chronic wasting diseases, and other conditions of severe energy depletion.

In Russian folk medicine, the diluted juice of the fresh root has long been used externally to diminish freckles and other skin discolorations. A purified extract or tincture of the dried herb is even more effective for this purpose. Recent clinical studies conducted at the Academy of Sciences in Russia has shown that a decoction of the dried root is also quite effective in treating stomach and duodenal ulcers.

93. SZECHUAN PEPPER

Zanthoxylum piperitum

川 椒 *chuan jiao*

OTHER NAMES: Japanese prickly ash; *nan jiao* (southern pepper)

A small deciduous tree that grows 1.5–2 meters tall, with dark brown spiny bark and hard shiny leaves, this herb is much cultivated as a pungent culinary seasoning in Szechuan. The fruits, which appear as clusters of carpels in the axils of the twigs and leaves, are purplish red in color and have two valves, each containing a shiny black seed, known as *jiao mu* (pepper eyes). The carpels and seeds contain 2%–4% essential oil consisting of phellandrene, limonene, citronellol, geraniol, and sanshol. Dishes seasoned with ground roasted Szechuan pepper are called *ma-la* (numbing-hot).

The herb is grown in western China and Japan.

MEDICINAL PART: fruit (carpels and seeds)

NATURE: Energy: hot
         Flavor: pungent, bitter
         Affinity: kidney, spleen

THERAPEUTIC EFFECTS: stomachic; diuretic; stimulant; carminative; warming (TCM: expels damp; scatters cold)

INDICATIONS: spermatorrhea and wet dreams; stagnant food in digestive tract; frequent urination; bladder infection

DOSAGE: decoction: 2–5 grams, in two doses, before or after food

culinary: carefully remove all twigs, then roast the carpels and seeds in a dry skillet or oven until fragrant; grind in a mortar or electric coffee grinder with some sea salt and use as a cooking spice and table condiment

CONTRAINDICATIONS: pregnancy (TCM: empty yin with flaring fire syndrome [see Remarks, page 98])

INCOMPATIBLES: coltsfoot; *Siler divaricatum;* aconite; cannabis seeds; ice water

REMARKS: The carpels are considered to be mildly dele-terious in large doses or with prolonged use, which is why pregnant women are advised to avoid them. When used for diuretic purposes, the carpels can be discarded, since most of the diuretic properties are in the seeds. When used as a table condiment, however, the carpels should be retained, because they contain most of the ar-omatic elements. When used as a culinary condiment, the quantities consumed are not sufficient to cause any undesirable side effects.

94. TEASEL, *Dipsacus asper*

续继 *hsu duan (xu duan)*

OTHER NAMES: *Dipsacus japonicus; jie gu* (mend bones)

This is a perennial plant with spade-shaped leaves rising on long stalks from the base, with a floral spike growing up from the center. The medicinal roots are very hard, dark brown, and wrinkled, brownish white on the inside, and contain essential oil and the alka-loid lamine. The herb is said to promote the healing of broken bones, hence the nickname.

The plant grows in the provinces of central China and Japan.

MEDICINAL PART: root

NATURE: Energy: slightly warm
          Flavor: bitter, pungent
          Affinity: kidneys, liver

THERAPEUTIC EFFECTS: tonic; hemostatic; analgesic; promotes muscle growth; promotes healing of fractured bones (TCM: tonifies liver- and kidney-energy; nour-ishes sinew and bone)

INDICATIONS: dysmennorrhea; menorrhagia; uterine bleeding during pregnancy and after childbirth; breast tumors; spermatorrhea; frequent urination; cold hands and feet; broken bones; tendon and ligament injuries; lumbago (TCM: deficient liver- and kidney-energy)

DOSAGE: decoction: 6–12 grams, in two doses, on an empty stomach

powder: plain, capsules; 4–8 grams, in two or three doses, on an empty stomach

CONTRAINDICATIONS: none

INCOMPATIBLES: none

REMARKS: Chinese herbals particularly recommend this herb as a remedy for all female menstrual disorders, as well as any other sort of uterine bleeding, including during pregnancy. The herb's hemostatic and blood-tonifying benefits in such cases can be enhanced by adding an equal portion of *Rehmannia*.

95. THISTLE TYPE

Atractylodes chinensis
蒼朮 *tsang shu (cang zhu)*

OTHER NAMES: *Atractylodes lancea; A. lyrata; A. ovata; shan jing dze* (mountain essence)

A perennial plant with an erect stem that grows 30–60 centimeters tall, alternate cauline leaves with 3–5 lobes and corymb floral heads, this herb has long been an important ingredient in some of China's most renowned longevity elixirs. The medicinal root occurs in furrowed, finger-shaped pieces 7 centimeters long by 2 centimeters wide, reddish brown, and contains essential oil comprising atractylon and atractylol.

The herb is native to the provinces of northern China, Manchuria, Korea, and Japan.

MEDICINAL PART: root

NATURE: Energy: warm
           Flavor: bitter
           Affinity: spleen, stomach

THERAPEUTIC EFFECTS: stomachic; antiemetic; antidiarrhetic; drying (TCM: expels all types of dampness)

INDICATIONS: diarrhea and dysentery; vomiting and nausea; pain and pressure in chest and abdomen; gastroenteritis; leukorrhea; pain and swelling in muscles and joints; bloating; profuse sweating (TCM: damp spleen- and stomach-energy; damp injuries)

DOSAGE: decoction: 5–10 grams, in two doses, on an empty stomach

    powder: capsules, pills, paste; 4–8 grams, in two or three doses, on an empty stomach

CONTRAINDICATION: dehydration

INCOMPATIBLES: none

96. THUJA ORIENTALIS

柏子仁 *bo dze ren (bo zi ren)*

OTHER NAMES: *Biota orientalis; B. chinensis*

This plant is a pyramid-shaped conifer, with small scaly leaves compressed onto branching stems. The wood is often used in making traditional Chinese furniture, while the tree itself is frequently dwarfed and shaped into all sorts of exotic forms by Chinese and Japanese landscape gardeners. The kernels of the fruits, which are highly nourishing, are used in medicine and have a pleasant sweet taste. The leaves, also used in medicine, are astringent and antipyretic, with a bittersweet flavor.

The plant is native to China, Japan, and India.

MEDICINAL PART: seed

NATURE: Energy: neutral
           Flavor: sweet, pungent
           Affinity: heart, spleen, liver

THERAPEUTIC EFFECTS: tonic; nutrient; sedative; emollient to large intestine; promotes semen production

(TCM: tonifies heart-energy; assists spleen; nourishes liver)

INDICATIONS: insomnia; neurasthenia; heart palpitations; spermatorrhea; profuse sweating; constipation; physical weakness and malnutrition; male infertility

DOSAGE: decoction: 5–10 grams, in two doses, on an empty stomach

CONTRAINDICATIONS: Be careful not to buy or use rancid seeds: if the seeds show an oily film on the surface and/or smell rancid, do not buy or use them. Rancidity ruins the seeds' medicinal and nutritional value and causes digestive problems.

INCOMPATIBLE: chrysanthemum

REMARKS: The two-thousand-year-old *Shen Nung's Herbal Classic* states, "Thuja seeds eliminate rheumatic dampness and calm the five vital yin organs. Prolonged use improves complexion, sharpens hearing, and brightens the eyes. It prevents physical fatigue and prolongs life."

More recent Chinese herbals suggest steeping the fresh leaves in a 60% alcohol solution for 7 days and using the resulting extract to promote hair growth by rubbing it on balding areas three times daily.

97. TIBETAN SAFFRON, *Crocus sativus*

藏红花 *dzang hung hua*

OTHER NAME: *fan hung hua* (foreign saffron)

This herb was brought to China along with safflower and other foreign herbs from Persia and India many centuries ago, hence the name "foreign or Tibetan saffron." The latter name refers to a relatively rare and expensive variety grown in Tibet and favored in Chinese medicine. The herb is often confused with safflower, which is less expensive and can sometimes be substituted for saffron. The flowers are used in medicine, particularly the stigmas, which are also used to flavor and color the famous saffron rice dishes of India and the Middle East.

The herb is cultivated in the Middle East, India, and Tibet.

MEDICINAL PART: flower

NATURE: Energy: slightly cool
            Flavor: pungent, bitter, sweet
            Affinity: liver, heart

THERAPEUTIC EFFECTS: emmenagogue; alterative; stimulant; aphrodisiac; antispasmodic; promotes circulation

INDICATIONS: all menstrual disorders; menopause; miscarriage or abortion; circulatory disorders; hypertension; rapid pulse; heart palpitations; anemia; muscle spasms

DOSAGE: infusion: 2 grams, in two 1-gram doses, morning and evening, on an empty stomach; steep the saffron in hot water in a lidded cup or teapot; do not boil

CONTRAINDICATION: pregnancy (the herb can promote miscarriage)

INCOMPATIBLES: none

REMARKS: This is one of the most effective remedies for female menstrual and other reproductive system disorders, including frigidity and loss of libido. It's one of the few herbs whose aphrodisiac properties apply primarily to women. It is particularly recommended as a blood restorative after miscarriage or abortion, and was similarly used in ancient Egypt and India. Due to its potent benefits to blood circulation, Chinese herbals also recommend it as a remedy for depression and moodiness caused by stagnant blood and sluggish circulation.

98. TIGER THISTLE, *Cirsium japonicum*
大薊花 *da ji hua*

OTHER NAMES: *Cnicus spicatus; Cnicus japonicus; ma ji* (horse thistle)

This perennial herb grows 40–50 centimeters tall and has long, spiny basal leaves 20–40 centimeters long, with numerous red or white flowers growing from spiny heads. The entire plant is used in medicine and contains essential oil, a glycoside, and a bitter compound.

The plant grows in many parts of China, as well as in Japan and Vietnam.

MEDICINAL PART: whole plant

NATURE: Energy: cold
           Flavor: sweet
           Affinity: liver, spleen

THERAPEUTIC EFFECTS: hemostatic; calms restless fetus; refrigerant to blood; lowers blood pressure

INDICATIONS: blood in sputum, vomit, or urine; nosebleeds; tuberculosis; internal hemorrhage; colitis; menorrhagia; high blood pressure; burns; morning sickness; sprains

DOSAGE: decoction: 5–10 grams, in two doses, on an empty stomach; use as an external wash for burns

CONTRAINDICATION: This herb should be used only until symptoms disappear, not long-term. If the herb does not relieve symptoms after 1–2 weeks, switch to a different herb or formula.

INCOMPATIBLES: none

99. TREE PEONY, *Paeonia moutan*

牡丹皮 *mu dan pi*

OTHER NAMES: *Paeonia suffruticosa; hua wang* (king of flowers); *bai liang jin* (a hundred ounces of gold)

This is a many-branched perennial shrub about 1 meter tall, with long petiolate leaves and large, lush flowers 10–30 centimeters wide. It has been cultivated since ancient times in China and is highly prized for its decorative beauty, as reflected in the nicknames the Chinese have given it. The skin of the root is used medicinally, occurring in cylindrical quills 10–12 centimeters long, brown on the outside and purplish inside, with a bittersweet taste. It contains the ketone paeonol, some glycosides, and benzoic acid.

The plant is widely cultivated throughout China.

MEDICINAL PART: skin of root

NATURE: Energy: slightly cold
Flavor: sweet, pungent, bitter
Affinity: liver, kidneys, heart

THERAPEUTIC EFFECTS: antipyretic; emmenagogue; diuretic; antiseptic; refrigerant; antispasmodic; promotes circulation and prevents clots (TCM: cools blood)

INDICATIONS: fevers; headache; amenorrhea; dysmenorrhea; nosebleeds and blood in sputum; intestinal infections; septic wounds; muscle spasms; hay fever (TCM: internal-heat symptoms)

DOSAGE: decoction: 5–10 grams, in two doses, on an empty stomach

CONTRAINDICATIONS: none

INCOMPATIBLES: *Fritillaria verticillata; Cuscuta japonica; Rheum officinale;* garlic

100. TRIBULUS TERRESTRIS

蒺藜子 *ji li dze (ji li zi)*

OTHER NAME: caltrop

This is an annual herb that grows 10–50 centimeters tall, with opposite leaves consisting of 5–8 pairs of elliptical leaflets 1 centimeter long by 6 millimeters wide, with small yellow flowers growing from short peduncles and hard spiny capsules with 3 hulls containing seeds. The fruits contain linoleic acid, essential oil, tannin, phylloerythrin, a glycoside, phlobaphenes, and peroxidase.

The plant grows in China and Japan.

MEDICINAL PART: fruit

NATURE:
Energy:	warm
Flavor:	bitter
Affinity:	liver, kidneys

THERAPEUTIC EFFECTS: tonic; nutrient; galactagogue; diuretic; alterative; promotes semen production; purifies blood; strengthens bone and sinew; improves vision; facilitates labor (TCM: tonifies liver-energy; expels liver-wind; tonifies kidney-yang)

INDICATIONS: spermatorrhea; premature ejaculation; impotence; male infertility; frequent profuse urination; lumbago; tinnitus; insufficient lactation; blurry vision; anemia; malnutrition; labor difficulties (TCM: deficient kidney-yang; deficient liver-energy)

DOSAGE: decoction: 5–10 grams, in three doses, on an empty stomach; the capsule of this herb is hard and spiny and must be broken open in a mortar prior to boiling

CONTRAINDICATIONS: none

INCOMPATIBLES: none

REMARKS: Chinese herbals particularly recommend this herb for removing impurities from the blood, and for tonifying the liver, which is responsible for filtering and replenishing blood. The herb is also used sometimes to facilitate labor contractions during difficult childbirth.

101. TRIFOLIATE ORANGE

Poncirus trifoliata

枳實枳壳 *jih shih (zhi shi)*

OTHER NAMES: *Citrus trifoliata; Aegle sepiaria; jih ke* (citrus shell)

This deciduous, glabrous tree grows up to 6 meters tall, with alternate trifoliate leaves, the central leaflet larger than the others, and white flowers 5 centimeters wide. The fruit is a highly acid, inedible berry, yellowish green in color, 2–3 centimeters in diameter, and covered with a fine fuzz. The unripe fruits are medicinal and are prepared by cutting them in half and drying them. They are flat on the cut side, round on the other, with the rind forming about half the thickness of the fruit. Bitter and highly aromatic, they contain essential oil consisting of limonene, linalol, linalyl acetate, and methyl anthranilate.

The plant is indigenous to China and Japan.

MEDICINAL PART: unripe fruit

NATURE: Energy: slightly cold
          Flavor: bitter
          Affinity: spleen, stomach

THERAPEUTIC EFFECTS: stomachic; diuretic; antidiarrhetic; carminative; expectorant (TCM: tonifies spleen-energy; eliminates wind-damp symptoms)

INDICATIONS: undigested food in intestinal tract; indigestion; oppression in chest and solar plexus; abdominal bloating and pain; diarrhea; hemorrhoids; gallbladder inflammation

DOSAGE: decoction: 4–8 grams, in three doses, on an empty stomach

CONTRAINDICATIONS: weak physical constitution and low vitality

INCOMPATIBLES: none

REMARKS: Some herbals distinguish between *jih shih* (kernel) and *jih ke* (shell, or rind), while others use the terms interchangeably. The herb referred to here is the whole dried unripe fruit, which includes kernels, flesh, and rind. It helps remedy sluggish digestion by giving a strong boost to spleen and stomach functions. Undigested food, particularly putrefactive animal proteins, accumulate in the intestinal tract when the stomach and pancreas fail to secrete sufficient supplies of protein-digesting enzymes into the stomach and duodenum. Since the pancreas is governed by spleen-energy, this herb increases pancreatic enzyme secretions by stimulating the spleen.

More recent research has also shown this herb to be effective in correcting flaccid, distended stomach and prolapse of the rectum and womb.

102. TUCKAHOE, *Porio cocos*

茯苓 *fu ling*

OTHER NAMES: *Pachyma cocos*; Virginia truffle; Indian bread; China root

This is an underground fungus that grows on the roots of various conifers, especially *Pinus sinensis, P. longifolis,* and *Cunninghamia*. The Chinese use it as both food and medicine. It occurs in large tuberous bodies, with a corrugated reddish brown skin, and a

hard starchy interior varying in color from pure white to light tan. Research indicates that these tubers are actually part of the ligneous tissue of the conifer roots themselves, altered by the presence of a particular fungus.

The herb occurs worldwide, wherever the species of conifer it favors grows.

MEDICINAL PART: tuberous fungal body

NATURE: Energy: neutral
             Flavor: sweet
             Affinity: heart, kidneys, lungs, spleen, stomach

THERAPEUTIC EFFECTS: sedative; stomachic; diuretic; nervine; relieves thirst; calms fetus (TCM: tonifies spleen- and kidney-energy; sedates heart-energy and calms spirit)

INDICATIONS: hypertension; heart palpitations; scant urination; indigestion and lack of appetite; insomnia; excess fluid in stomach; spermatorrhea

DOSAGE: decoction: 8–15 grams, in two doses, on an empty stomach

     powder: plain, capsules, pills; 5–10 grams, in two doses, on an empty stomach

CONTRAINDICATIONS: none

INCOMPATIBLES: vinegar and any food prepared with vinegar; *Ampelopsis serjanaefolia; Sanguisorba officinalis; Justicia gendarussa;* tortoise shell; bear gall

REMARKS: This is one of the primary and most reliable yin tonics and diuretics in the Chinese pharmacopeia. It strengthens bladder and kidneys, enhances fluid metabolism and secretions, and regulates fluid balance throughout the system. In Chinese medicine, the nervous system is governed largely by the Water energy of the kidneys, and in fact modern studies have shown this kidney tonic to have excellent nervine properties as well. A compound that inhibits cancer has also been isolated from this herb and is currently under intensive study as an anticancer agent.

The smaller and younger varieties of this herb, known as *fu shen,* are regarded as having superior sedative properties, particularly for the heart and nervous system. The herb is safe for use by children and can therefore be used to treat hypertension and other nervous disorders during childhood. This and licorice are the two most widely used tonic herbs in Chinese medicine for treating weak and nervous children.

103. WEEPING GOLDEN BELL

Forsythia suspensa

連翹 *lien chiao (lian qiao)*

OTHER NAME: *Syringa suspensa*

This is a shrub that grows about 3 meters tall, with cylindrical branches and hollow stems, golden yellow flowers growing in axiliary clusters of 1–3, and fruits occurring as ovoid capsules with valves containing brown seeds. The valves are used in medicine, appearing as small, boat-shaped bodies 1–2 centimeters long, with a longitudinal partition. The herb contains saponins and the glycoside phillyrin, which has antipyretic properties. It is one of the main ingredients in the famous Chinese patent formula for colds, *Yin Chiao Pien* (Lonicera-Forsythia Tablets).

The herb grows in northern China and Japan.

MEDICINAL PART: fruit

NATURE:
- Energy: slightly cold
- Flavor: bitter
- Affinity: heart, gallbladder

THERAPEUTIC EFFECTS: antipyretic; antiphlogistic; antidote; diuretic; analgesic (TCM: tonifies heart-energy; clears internal heat)

INDICATIONS: fevers; allergies; colds with fever and heavy cough; abscesses and festering skin sores due to allergic reactions and internal toxins; thirst; heat rash; swelling and inflammation of lymph glands; breast tumors (TCM: internal- and external-heat injury)

DOSAGE: decoction: 3–5 grams, in one dose, on an empty stomach; use once daily for 7–14 days, or until symptoms subside; if symptoms persist, try a different herb or formula; *Lonicera japonica* (Japanese honeysuckle) has similar properties and can be used as an alternative, or in combination with *Forsythia* if it alone does not deliver results

CONTRAINDICATIONS: none

INCOMPATIBLES: none

104. WHITE PEONY, *Paeonia lactiflora*

白芍 *bai shao*

OTHER NAMES: *Paeonia albiflora; P. officinale; shao yao* (ladle medicine); Chinese peony

This is a perennial herb, with a simple erect stem, 60–90 centimeters tall, alternate compound leaves, and large solitary flowers, white or pink, growing from long, stout peduncles. The medicinal roots occur in hard heavy pieces, 20 centimeters long by 12 millimeters thick, reddish brown on the surface with a pinkish white semitranslucent interior. The root contains asparagine and benzoic acid. It is particularly employed in female ailments related to menses, pregnancy, and childbirth.

The plant is much cultivated in China and Japan, and also grows in Manchuria and Siberia.

MEDICINAL PART: root

NATURE: Energy: slightly cold
             Flavor: bitter, sour
             Affinity: liver

THERAPEUTIC EFFECTS: antipyretic, emmenagogue; hemostatic; antiseptic (TCM: tonifies blood and liver-energy)

INDICATIONS: all menstrual disorders; lower abdominal pain due to intestinal infections; heat rash; poor circulation; gallbladder inflammation (TCM: deficient blood and liver-energy)

DOSAGE: decoction: 5–10 grams, in three doses, on an empty stomach

CONTRAINDICATIONS: Women should not use this herb singly during pregnancy, nor during the first two months after childbirth, but it may be used as part of compound formulas.

INCOMPATIBLES: *Dendrobium nobile; Cirsium japonicum; Veratrum;* tortoise shell

REMARKS: According to Chinese herbals, the plant with the white blossom has stronger blood-tonifying properties, while the red variety is more hemostatic and beneficial to blood circulation. When liver inflammation (liver-fire) is present, the root from the red type is indicated. Dosages for both varieties are the same.

105. WILD CHINESE JUJUBE

Ziziphus jujuba

酸枣仁 *suan dzao ren (suan zao ren)*

OTHER NAMES: *Rhamnus soporifer; shan dzao* (mountain jujube)

    This deciduous shrub grows 10 meters high and is the wild form of *Ziziphus vulgaris* (herb #22, page 78). Unlike the cultivated variety, it has thorny spines. The fruit is a fleshy oblong drupe about 2 centimeters long, very sour, with a globular pit, which is used in medicine. The fruits and skins are dried, mashed, and sold separately as *dzao rou* (jujube flesh) and *dzao pi* (jujube skin), respectively; they have tonic and stomachic properties.

The plant grows in China, India, Malaysia, Afghanistan, and Japan.

MEDICINAL PART: seed (kernel of the pit)

NATURE: Energy: neutral
Flavor: sweet, sour
Affinity: heart, liver, spleen, gallbladder

THERAPEUTIC EFFECTS: sedative; tonic; nutrient; nervine; strengthens bone and sinew; reduces perspiration (TCM: tonifies liver-, gallbladder-, and heart-energy)

INDICATIONS: insomnia; neurasthenia; heart palpitations; hypertension; profuse perspiration; chronic thirst; malnutrition (TCM: empty liver- and gallbladder-energy)

DOSAGE: decoction: 6–12 grams, in two doses, on an empty stomach

CONTRAINDICATIONS: none

INCOMPATIBLES: *Cocculus japonicus;* herbs of Menispermaceae family

REMARKS: This is one of the most popular herbs for insomnia, hypertension, and other nervous disorders. Nontoxic and nutritious, it can be used long-term, and regular use is said to brighten complexion.

106. WILD CHINESE VIOLET

Viola yesoensis

紫花地丁 *dze hua di ding (zi hua di ding)*

OTHER NAMES: *Viola patrinii; Fumaria officinalis*

This is a perennial plant with narrow oblong leaves and solitary violet flowers growing from the axils, the fruit an oblong three-celled capsule with numerous seeds. The entire plant is used in medicine, the flowers containing both saturated and unsaturated acids

and the rest of the plant being highly mucilaginous and emollient. The fresh root can be pulverized and applied as a poultice to abscesses.

The herb grows in China, Japan, Southeast Asia, and India.

MEDICINAL PART: whole plant

NATURE: Energy: cold
           Flavor: bitter, pungent
           Affinity: heart, liver

THERAPEUTIC EFFECTS: antidote; antiphlogistic; antipyretic

INDICATIONS: abscesses; boils; carbuncles; all skin infections and sores; snakebites

DOSAGE: decoction: 5–10 grams, in two doses, on an empty stomach

external: mashed root can be applied to abscesses and other skin sores; juice of the whole fresh plant can be applied as antidote to poisonous snakebites

CONTRAINDICATIONS: none

INCOMPATIBLES: iron compounds and utensils

REMARKS: This herb is prescribed exclusively for the types of skin ailments listed above, both internally as a decoction and externally as a wash or poultice. It should not be used for any other purposes.

107. WINTER WORM–SUMMER GRASS, *Cordyceps sinensis*

冬虫夏草 *dung chiung-hsia tsao*

(dong chiung-xia cao)

Chinese herbals describe this herb as a fungal parasite that grows on the pupa of a particular species of caterpillar found in southern Tibet and the far western regions of Szechuan. Due probably to movements of the pupa, this fungus is said to be an insect in

winter and a plant in summer, so early observers named it winter worm–summer grass. It is prized as a male sexual elixir and often appears in tonic formulas, particularly herbal liquors. It is comparable in cost to good ginseng, and like many tonic herbs, it can be cooked and consumed together with tonic foods. Traditional sources suggest stewing a male duck with this herb stuffed into its cavities.

MEDICINAL PART: fungal body

NATURE: Energy: warm
              Flavor: sweet
              Affinity: kidneys, lungs

THERAPEUTIC EFFECTS: tonic; restorative; antitussive; expectorant; stimulant; builds immunity; prevents premature aging (TCM: tonifies kidney-yang; tonifies lung-energy)

INDICATIONS: impotence; spermatorrhea; lumbago; profuse sweating and night sweats; recuperation from surgery or long illness; physical and nervous exhaustion; fatigue; anemia; immune deficiency (TCM: deficient kidney-yang; deficient energy)

DOSAGE: decoction: 5–9 grams, in three doses, on an empty stomach

    powder: paste; 3–6 grams, in three doses, on an empty stomach

    liquor: 40–60 grams, steeped in 1 liter spirits for 1–3 months; take 1 ounce twice daily on an empty stomach; can also be added to male tonic formulas

    culinary: for impotence, spermatorrhea, and anemia, stew 15–30 grams of the herb with one fresh duck or chicken, for 2–3 hours, with a few cups rice wine or sherry, water, and some scallions and ginger; for extra tonic benefit, add 5–10 grams ginseng

CONTRAINDICATIONS: early stages of colds, flu, or other contagious ailment

INCOMPATIBLES: none

REMARKS: The great Ming dynasty herbologist Lee Shih-chen praised this herb as being equivalent to ginseng as a general invigorating tonic to all of the body's vital energy systems. It is particularly effective in restoring vitality after a long illness, surgery, childbirth, and other conditions of energy depletion and physical exhaustion. It has also been shown to stimulate bone marrow, thereby enhancing human immune response.

Most Chinese herbals state that cooking this herb with chicken or duck, particularly a drake, is by far the best way to extract and assimilate its full medicinal benefits. Patent herbal preparations of *Cordyceps* in essence of chicken or duck are now widely available on the market, and this is a very convenient and effective way of taking this herb as a regular daily health tonic.

108. YELLOW STARWORT

Inula britannica

旋覆花 *hsuan fu hua (xuan fu hua)*

OTHER NAMES: *Inula chinensis;* elecampane; *jin chien hua* (gold coin flower)

A perennial herb with simple erect stem 30–80 centimeters high and narrowly lanceolate leaves 4–5 centimeters long by 4–8 millimeters wide, this plant grows solitary yellow flowers that look somewhat like daisies. The flowers contain inulin and flavone.

The plant grows in northern China, Japan, Manchuria, Siberia, and some parts of Europe.

MEDICINAL PART: flower

NATURE:
	Energy:	slightly warm
	Flavor:	salty, bitter, pungent
	Affinity:	lungs, spleen, stomach, large intestine

THERAPEUTIC EFFECTS: stomachic; expectorant; antitussive; antiemetic; analgesic; carminative

INDICATIONS: nausea and vomiting; cough with heavy phlegm; fluid retention and bloating in large intestine; headache; intestinal gas (TCM: internal-damp symptoms)

DOSAGE: decoction: 3–6 grams, in two doses, on an empty stomach; it's a good idea to wrap the herb in a gauze-cloth pouch to prevent irritating fibers from entering the broth

CONTRAINDICATION: loose bowels due to empty large intestine–energy

INCOMPATIBLES: none

REMARKS: For traumatic injuries involving serious damage to ligaments and tendons, Chinese herbals suggest pulverizing the root of this herb with a bit of pure water to extract its juice, and applying the extract directly to the injured area, three times daily, for 15 days.

4

THE TRIED
AND THE TRUE

36 Healing Herbal Formulas

Among the herbal formulas presented below, some are classics culled directly from traditional Chinese herbals, while others are variations of classical prescriptions formulated by contemporary practitioners to suit the particular requirements of contemporary conditions. A few of them are traditional formulas that we have adjusted on the basis of our own experience.

The 36 internal healing formulas are arranged according to the following functional categories: respiratory system; digestive system; nervous system; bladder/urinary system; metabolic system; cardiovascular system; female reproductive system; male reproductive system. Each category is further divided into subheadings based on the general condition for which the formulas are recommended, such as hepatitis, headache, impotence, and so forth. The whole body tonics, which are essentially preventive formulas, are listed separately, with additional categories for herbal broths, washes, ointments, poultices, porridges, and pillows.

We have not included a separate category for the immune system, because many of the healing formulas from the different categories listed also have immunotonic properties, as do most of the tonic formulas. Readers with various forms of immune deficiency should look through all the formulas in this chapter, noting those with immunotonic properties, and select the formulas that most closely match their specific symptoms.

Each formula is identified by its English and Chinese names, followed by a brief introduction regarding the formula's origins and development, its particular properties and applications, and other information of interest. Next we note the specific symptomatic indications for which the formula is most effective, followed by a list of the ingredients and proportions for a single day's use, with guidelines on preparation and dosage. Under the Remarks section, we provide additional information regarding contraindications and incompatibles, dietary advice, equivalent patent preparations that can be substituted for the formula, and some other useful suggestions.

Traditionally, most Chinese formulas were compounded by a method known as the Four Responsible Roles, based on the role each ingredient plays in the formula. The four roles are called King, Minister, Assistant, and Servant. The King is the principal active herb in the formula, selected for its known therapeutic benefits for specific ailments. This herb is always the most potent ingredient in the formula, and occasionally there are two of them.

The Minister's role is to assist and reinforce the King. It has similar properties to the primary herb, providing complementary therapeutic benefits and giving the formula broader efficacy. The Assistant is usually added to counteract any potential negative side effects of the King and Minister herbs, and to neutralize any toxic compounds in either of the primary ingredients. In complex formulas, there are usually several Assistants to insure that only the desired therapeutic effects of the King and Minister are activated, while unwanted or unnecessary secondary effects are kept dormant.

The role of the Servant is to harmonize the actions of all the other ingredients and to promote their rapid absorption into the bloodstream, organs, and related energy meridians. Sometimes Servants are included to provide swift symptomatic relief of pain and discomfort, while the King and Minister gradually go to work correcting the root cause of the problem. One of the most reliable and effective Servants in the entire Chinese pharmacopeia is licorice root, which enters all twelve meridians, harmonizes and prolongs the effects of all other herbs in the formula, enhances absorption, balances metabolism, and greatly enhances the flavor of any formula. As the Great Detoxifier, it also helps rid the body of any residual toxins that might otherwise interfere with the benefits of the formula.

In selecting these tried-and-true formulas from the vast collection of remedies compiled in traditional Chinese herbals, we have tried to address our selection to some of the most common health problems experienced by men and women throughout the world today. The formulas are backed by many centuries of continuous clinical experience and have proven effective in popular practice, past and present, but in order to derive their therapeutic benefits, they must be used in careful compliance with the dietary and other guidelines that go with them. They can be safely used at home for the common ailments indicated, especially in the early stages, when "a stitch in time saves nine" and herbal cures are most effective. Any serious illness or acute condition, however, should always be diagnosed by and treated under the supervision of a qualified health professional.

HERBAL FORMULAS

RESPIRATORY SYSTEM

This category includes remedies for ailments of the upper and lower respiratory tract, including the lungs, bronchial tubes, throat, tonsils, nose, sinuses, and eustachian tubes. In the traditional Chinese system, ear ailments such as infections and eye problems such as glaucoma and cataracts are included in the section on the upper respiratory tract because they are located in the head, in close proximity to the breathing apparatus.

Colds and Flu (A)

1. PUERARIA DECOCTION

葛根湯

geh gen tang

This formula comes from the famous medical treatise *Shang Han Lun (Discussion of Fevers and Colds)*, composed around 200 BCE by the celebrated physician Dr. Chang Chung-ching, who included 113 prescriptions based on 100 herbs in this classical medical text. His formulas are so reliable that they are still used today, precisely as he composed them. This particular prescription is used for contagious colds and flu in patients with strong or average constitutions, but not for weak, infirm, or elderly patients. When applied to the following indications, this formula usually relieves symptoms of excess heat and bodily aches within 1 hour of ingestion.

INDICATIONS: contagious colds and flu, with symptoms of headache, aching shoulder and upper arm muscles, nervous discomfort, fever and body heat *without* sweating, intense aversion to cold temperatures, and stiffness in the neck and upper spine

INGREDIENTS:		
	Kudzu vine *(Pueraria)*	4 grams
	Joint fir	3 grams
	Cinnamon	2 grams
	Licorice	2 grams
	White peony	2 grams
	Chinese jujube	3 grams
	Fresh ginger root	3 grams

PREPARATION AND DOSAGE: decoction: two doses, on an empty stomach; powder: infusion, 3 grams in hot water, two or three times daily, on an empty stomach

REMARKS: When using this formula for colds and flu, avoid eating oily and deep-fried foods, pungent seasonings such as chili and black pepper, seafoods, and hard, dry foods, such as toast, nuts, and dry cereals. Instead, one should consume porridges, gruels, and hot soups, as well as fresh juices.

Patent herbal equivalents for this formula include *Yin Chiao Chieh Tu Pien* (Lonicera and Forsythia Tablets) and *Ling Yang Shang Feng Ling* (Antelope Horn Wind Injury Remedy), which are available in most Chinese herbal pharmacies, or can be ordered from suppliers of Chinese patent remedies.

Colds and Flu (B)

2. EPHEDRA DECOCTION

禰黃湯

ma huang tang

This classic formula comes from Dr. Chang Chung-ching's *Discussion of Fevers and Colds,* which remains a primary source of remedies for this sort of condition. This prescription is meant to be used for colds and flus of the "hot" type: the patient at first feels physically cold, a sensation that continues for a while even after putting on extra clothes or blankets but later transforms into a feeling of continuous and oppressive heat, accompanied by headaches and a "floating" pulse that can be seen and felt pulsating in the veins of the wrists, arm hollows, ankles, and neck.

INDICATIONS: contagious colds and flu, with symptoms of high fever but *no* sweating, headache, extreme thirst, and pains in the waist, knees, and other major joints of the body

INGREDIENTS:

Joint fir *(Ephedra)*	5 grams
Almond	5 grams
Cinnamon	4 grams
Licorice	1.5 grams

PREPARATION AND DOSAGE: decoction: two doses, on an empty stomach

REMARKS: The same dietary guidelines apply as above. After taking each dose of this formula, one should lie down quietly and let the body perspire. Shortly thereafter, the patient will begin to urinate profusely, and this will quickly reduce the fever and eliminate oppressive body heat.

The only effective patent herbal substitute for this formula is *Yin Chiao Chieh Tu Pien* (Lonicera and Forsythia Tablets).

Colds and Flu (C)

3. EPHEDRA, ASARUM, ACONITUM DECOCTION

麻黄附子細辛湯

ma huang, fu dze, hsi hsin tang

Like most Chinese remedies for colds and flu, this formula is also taken from the classical third century BCE treatise *Shang Han Lun (Discussion of Fevers and Colds)*. It is specifically formulated for colds and flu of the "cold" type: the patient feels very cold and his or her complexion becomes quite pale; although there is fever, the facial complexion remains pale, not red, and the patient continues to feel physically cold, even when wrapped in blankets and heavy clothing. This formula is particularly appropriate for patients with weak constitutions, and for the elderly and infirm.

INDICATIONS: contagious colds and flu, with fever accompanied by continuous cold sensations, with or without sweating; cough and sore throat, weak pulse, headache, and bodily aches.

INGREDIENTS:

Joint fir *(Ephedra)*	4 grams
Asarum sieboldi	3 grams
Aconitum fischeri	0.5 gram

PREPARATION AND DOSAGE: decoction: two doses, on an empty stomach

REMARKS: Follow the same dietary guidelines given in Formula #1. The patient should remain warmly clothed, avoid exposure to wind, and get plenty of rest, but may practice internal-energy meditation and breathing exercises as his or her energy permits.

The patent herbal cough syrup known as *Chuan Bei Pi Pa Lu* (Fritillaria and Eriobotrya Syrup) can be used in conjunction with this formula to relieve symptoms of cough and sore throat, although it will not remedy other symptoms of this condition. The syrup should be taken 2–3 hours apart from the decoction, on an empty stomach, and can also be used during the night to relieve persistent coughing.

Tonsillitis

4. ISATIS DECOCTION

菘藍湯

sung lan tang

This remedy was adapted from traditional formulas by herbal scientists at the Jiang Su Medical Institute in China, as a cure for tonsillitis and other throat infections associated with contagious colds and fevers. While classical formulas for this condition require a minimum of 10–15 days to take effect, this formula is designed to deliver results in 4–5 days. It was developed specifically to combat the highly virulent pathogens associated with contagious respiratory infections today. These must be treated swiftly and effectively in order to prevent further complications.

INDICATIONS: tonsillitis and other upper respiratory tract infections and inflammations associated with contagious colds, with related symptoms of fever, sore and swollen throat, difficulty swallowing, dry mouth, and chronic thirst

INGREDIENTS:

Angelica pubescens (purple)	6 grams
Isatis tinctoria	9 grams
Dandelion	9 grams

PREPARATION AND DOSAGE: decoction: two doses, preferably on an empty stomach, or after meals if stomach does not tolerate it

REMARKS: Follow the same dietary guidelines given for cold and flu conditions above. The patient should get plenty of rest, keep warm, and protect the throat from exposure to wind. Practicing internal-energy circulation and rhythmic deep breathing enhances healing and accelerates recovery.

Asthma

5. LITTLE GREEN DRAGON DECOCTION

小青龍湯

hsiao ching lung tang

The original formula for this remedy came from the third century BCE medical treatise, *Essential Prescriptions of the Golden Chest,* by Dr. Chang Chung-ching, but some of the ingredients and proportions have been changed to suit current conditions, based on contemporary clinical experience and scientific research in China. This prescription was submitted by a graduate of China's Shantou University Medical College, who now practices in Chiang Mai, Thailand. It is formulated to deal with chronic asthma and related breathing difficulties caused by allergic reactions, respiratory sensitivity to air pollution, dust, pollen, and air-conditioning, and psychosomatic factors such as stress. This is a complex condition that requires a minimum of two weeks and sometimes up to six months of herbal therapy to correct. The drugs commonly prescribed for it in modern Western medicine provide only temporary symptomatic relief and often have unpleasant side effects.

This formula is safe and effective for children as well as adults.

INDICATIONS: asthma and related symptoms of chronic cough and extreme shortness of breath, profuse and watery phlegm, sneezing and runny nose, watering eyes, wheezing breath, gurgling abdomen

INGREDIENTS:

Joint fir	10 grams	
Psoralea corylifolia	10 grams	
Licorice	6 grams	
Asarum sieboldi	6 grams	
Cinnamon	10 grams	
Almond	10 grams	
Pinellia ternata	10 grams	
White peony	10 grams	
Schisandra	6 grams	
Horny goat weed	10 grams	
Balloon flower	10 grams	
Earthworm*	10 grams	

PREPARATION AND DOSAGE: decoction: two doses, on an empty stomach

REMARKS: During the course of therapy, patients should adopt a light, mostly vegetarian diet and avoid consumption of pungent, salty, and sweet foods. Best food choices include fresh vegetables and fruits, soups and salads. Avoid large meals, especially at night, and try to avoid situations that provoke stress or anger, which severely aggravate this condition. Meditation and deep breathing are helpful in controlling symptoms and correcting root causes of this problem.

The *Grand Compilation of Practical Chinese Health Preservation Theories and Prescriptions* (Hsueh Lin Publications, Shanghai, 1990) recommends using the patent preparation *Jin Kui Shen Chi Wan* (Golden Book Tea) in conjunction with this formula, to enhance its effects and provide additional symptomatic relief.

---

*This animal product *(Perichaeta communissma)* has antipyretic and bronchodilator properties, but strict vegetarians can omit it from the formula without adding substitutes because some of the other herbs have similar properties.

Middle Ear Infections

6. MAJOR BUPLEURUM (HARE'S EAR) DECOCTION

大柴胡湯

da chai hu tang

This is one of the primary classic formulas traditionally used for infections and inflammations of the liver and gallbladder, high blood pressure, and other conditions involving internal heat. It is also prescribed for chronic infections and inflammations of the middle ear, which can be caused by persistent colds or sinus infections, abrupt changes in air pressure such as air travel or scuba diving, and adverse drug reactions. If this condition is not corrected, it can lead to chronic tinnitus (ringing in the ears) and deafness.

INDICATIONS: ear infections, with related symptoms of headache, dizziness, pain, ringing ears, and secretion of water or pus.

INGREDIENTS:

Hare's ear *(Bupleurum)*	6 grams
Pinellia ternata	3 grams
Scutellaria macrantha	3 grams
White peony	3 grams
Chinese jujube	3 grams
Trifoliate orange	2 grams
Ginger (fresh)	4 grams
Rhubarb	1 gram

PREPARATION AND DOSAGE: decoction: two doses, on an empty stomach

REMARKS: People with chronic ear infections should avoid swimming and try not to let water into the ear during showers and baths. If itching or discomfort occurs, do not stick fingers or other objects into the ear; instead, use thumb and index finger to massage and pull on the earlobes, which provides some relief to the inner ear. Also avoid alcohol, coffee, and tobacco, which can aggravate ear infections.

This formula can also be used for other internal-heat ailments, particularly liver and gallbladder infections, as well as for withdrawal symptoms from alcohol and drug abuse.

DIGESTIVE SYSTEM
This category includes ailments of the stomach, spleen, liver, gallbladder, and bowels, such as ulcers, constipation, diarrhea, cirrhosis, and other problems associated with the digestive system and its various organs.

Gastroptosis (Sagging Stomach)

7. GINSENG DECOCTION

人参湯

ren sheng tang

This is a classical formula that appears in many traditional Chinese herbals, and today it is still used in its original format. Gastroptosis is an abnormal sagging of the stomach into the lower abdomen, characterized by a loose, flaccid stomach wall that fails to respond with normal peristalis when food enters the stomach. Ingested food lies stagnant in the unresponsive stomach, resulting in putrefaction, fermentation, gas, burping, nausea, bloating, and other digestive distress. Ginseng is used here as a gastric stimulator, warming the stomach, activating the cells of the stomach wall, increasing gastric secretions, and restoring normal digestive functions in the stomach.

INDICATIONS: Gastroptosis, with symptoms of bloating in the upper stomach, heartburn, deep belching, stomach pain, nausea, loss of appetite, indigestion, regurgitation, and constipation

INGREDIENTS:

	Ginseng	3 grams
	Licorice	3 grams
	Atractylis ovata	3 grams
	Ginger (dry)	3 grams

PREPARATION AND DOSAGE: decoction: two doses, on an empty stomach

REMARKS: People with this condition should avoid pungent and sour foods, as well as hard, dry, and excessively oily foods. Raw foods should also be eliminated from the diet until the condition is corrected. Instead, porridges and gruels made from whole grains are dietary staples for this condition. Chinese herbals specifically recommend boiling 30 grams of astragalus in 2 liters of water for 1 hour, then discarding the herb and using the herbal water to prepare a brown-rice porridge.

Coffee and tea should not be consumed for at least 1 hour after taking this or any other ginseng formula.

For travel or work, you can substitute the Chinese patent formula *Shiang Sha Yang Wei Wan* (Saussurea and Amomum Stomach Nurturing Pills).

Chinese therapists also suggest doing sit-ups first thing in the morning and just before bed at night, which helps correct this condition by tightening the stomach wall and restoring normal shape to the stomach. Weak and elderly patients who are unable to do sit-ups can simply lie on their backs with a small, firm cushion under the lower spine while performing deep abdominal breathing.

Constipation (A)

8. MOISTEN BOWEL DECOCTION

潤腸湯
run chang tang

This is a classic constipation formula recorded in 1249 CE by the herbalist Lee Tung-yuan in his medical treatise *Discussion of Spleen and Stomach*. It is designed to treat constipation associated with dry bowels, blood deficiency, and insufficient bodily fluids, conditions often experienced by the elderly and postpartum women. It relieves constipation by lubricating the bowels and clearing blockages in the intestinal tract.

INDICATIONS: chronic constipation due to dry bowels, with related symptoms of dry skin and nails, dry mouth and tongue, and chronic thirst

INGREDIENTS:

Cannabis seeds (roasted)	5 grams
Peach kernels	5 grams
Angelica pubescens (purple)	3 grams
Angelica sinensis	3 grams
Rhubarb	3 grams

PREPARATION AND DOSAGE: decoction: three doses, on an empty stomach

REMARKS: This formula is contraindicated for pregnant women due to its purging effect in the lower abdomen.

Chinese herbals recommend that people with this type of constipation drink a glass of warm, slightly salted water first thing in the morning, on an empty stomach. One should also avoid pungent spicy foods, red meat, excessive emotional excitement, and all chemical laxatives, which only aggravate and prolong this condition.

China produces a patent herbal version of this formula that can be used as a convenient substitute for the decoction: *Run Chang Wan* (Moisten Bowel Pills).

Note that the *Cannabis* seeds used in this formula have been roasted and are therefore unable to germinate; hence they do not qualify as a controlled substance in North America.

Constipation (B)

9. RHUBARB AND LICORICE DECOCTION

大黄甘草湯

da huang gan tsao tang

This is a traditional Chinese formula for chronic constipation that has no apparent cause or other related symptoms. Such cases occur in weak as well as strong constitutions, the young or the elderly. This formula can be used to treat constipation when other remedies don't work.

INDICATIONS: chronic constipation; in cases of severe bowel congestion, nausea or vomiting may occur immediately after eating

INGREDIENTS:

Rhubarb	4 grams
Licorice	1 gram

PREPARATION AND DOSAGE: decoction: two doses, on an empty stomach

REMARKS: Though this formula is not as purging as the one above, pregnant women should consult a health professional before using this or any other remedy for constipation.

People with this condition should make a habit of drinking plenty of water and eating lots of food containing moisture and fiber, such as fresh fruits, vegetables, and whole-grain porridges. It also helps to sit (or preferably squat) on the toilet at regular times each day, even without the urge to defecate, in order to gradually train the bowels to move regularly.

Hemorrhoids

10. ANGELICA RESTORATIVE DECOCTION

當歸建中湯

dang gui jian jung tang

This traditional Chinese remedy for hemorrhoids comes from a compilation of classical herbal prescriptions entitled *Orthodox Applications of Chinese Herbal Medicine,* published in Taiwan in 1980. It is used for the treatment of both internal and external hemorrhoids: the former is associated with anal bleeding but usually causes no pain, while the latter can cause considerable pain but usually no bleeding. Hemorrhoids occur when the webs of small capillaries that feed the anal sphincter become clogged, causing them to form tumorous lumps that block the anal passage. Chronic constipation, prolonged periods of sitting or standing, pregnancy, and difficult defecation are often contributing factors to this condition.

INDICATIONS: internal and external hemorrhoids, with related symptoms of acute pain during and after bowel movements, rectal bleeding, and pain radiating out to the waist, hips, and lower abdomen

INGREDIENTS:

Angelica sinensis	4 grams
Cinnamon	4 grams
Ginger (fresh)	4 grams
Chinese jujube	4 grams
White peony	5 grams
Licorice	2 grams

PREPARATION AND DOSAGE: decoction: three doses, on an empty stomach

REMARKS: People with hemorrhoids should not consume alcohol, chili, black pepper, mustard, and other pungent foods and seasonings. During bowel movements, avoid using excessive pressure to evacuate the rectum, and do not sit too long on the toilet. The Western custom of reading books while sitting on the toilet waiting for the bowels to move considerably aggravates this condition, as does any other prolonged period of sitting, such as in the office or in front of the television. Pregnant women, who are particularly vulnerable to hemorrhoids, should consult a qualified health professional before using this or any other remedy for hemorrhoids. Avoid commercial suppositories sold in Western pharmacies: they provide only temporary relief and often cause constipation, which further aggravates the condition.

An effective therapeutic exercise for curing and preventing hemorrhoids is the anal sphincter lock *(mula banda)* used in Indian pranayama and Chinese *chee-gung* breathing exercises. Perform the exercise gently for five minutes at a time, several times daily, either standing, sitting, or lying down.

Purple Cloud Ointment (see Herbal Ointments, page 262) can be applied externally as a supplemental therapy. The Chinese patent herbal remedy *Jih Wan* (Hemorrhoid Pills) can be used as a substitute for this formula.

Hepatitis, Jaundice

11. BUPLEURUM AND ARTEMISIA DECOCTION

柴枡茵蔯湯

tsai hu yin chen tang

Chinese herbal medicine is renowned for its effective remedies for liver ailments, which are becoming ever more prevalent in today's polluted world. Since toxins are far more destructive to liver tissue now than in ancient times, most of the classical liver formulas have been amended to suit modern conditions, and many Chinese physicians have built their reputations on their own "secret" formulas for hepatitis, jaundice, cirrhosis, cancer, and other severe liver infections.

This formula is based on a classical prescription for hepatitis called Minor Bupleurum Decoction *(hsiao chai hu tang)*. It was adapted by Dr. Yeh Feng, a Chinese physician from Shanghai currently practicing in Bangkok, who prescribed it to the author's wife for a stubborn liver infection with jaundice, contracted during a sojourn in India. It cured her in only 7 weeks.

The formula is designed to cure serious liver infections such as hepatitis A and B in their early stages. It is therefore essential that the condition be diagnosed and treated early, before permanent damage such as cirrhosis or cancer develops. Severe cases may take 6 months or more to cure, while milder cases that are diagnosed early might be cured in 2–3 months. Patients under therapy should have their blood tested for liver functions every month in order to monitor progress.

INDICATIONS: liver infections and inflammations, including hepatitis A and B and jaundice, with related symptoms of chronic fatigue, loss of appetite, bloating, yellow eyes and palms, nausea, insomnia, constipation and/or diarrhea, enlargement of breasts in males, and painful swelling of the liver

INGREDIENTS:

White peony	24 grams
Artemisia capillaris	18 grams
Atractylodes chinensis	18 grams
Angelica sinensis	15 grams
Scutellaria macrantha	15 grams
Tuckahoe	15 grams
Hare's ear *(Bupleurum)*	15 grams
Peucedanum decursivum	15 grams
Panax quinquefolia (American ginseng)	6 grams
Licorice	6 grams

PREPARATION AND DOSAGE: decoction: two or three doses, on an empty stomach

REMARKS: This is a powerful potion with strong purging properties and often provokes rapid evacuation of the bowels. Bowel movements will generally be very fluid and contain yellowish orange bile purged from the liver and gallbladder. It's best to lie down and rest after each dose, and to avoid excessive excitement and physical exertion during the course of therapy. It's also very important to avoid anger, grief, anxiety, stress, and any other extreme emotions, which seriously aggravate liver conditions.

Diet is also important: avoid all processed junk food, spicy seasonings, refined sugar and starches, and deep-fried foods. Fresh seafood is all right as a source of protein, but avoid beef and pork. Most important of all, be sure that everything you eat and drink is clean and free of toxic additives, such as pesticides and preservatives. Eliminate alcohol, caffeine, tobacco, and other recreational drugs, all of which aggravate the liver. Dietary supplements should include 50–100 milligrams of vitamin B complex, 800–1200 international units of vitamin E, 5–10 grams of vitamin C, and 25,000 international units of beta-carotene. Wheat- and barley-grass juice, spirulina, and blue-green algae are also excellent supplements for liver problems.

Alcohol and Drug Poisoning (Liver)

12. MAJOR BUPLEURUM WITH ARTEMISIA DECOCTION

大柴胡茵蔯湯
da tsai hu yin chen tang

This is a special version of the classic *Bupleurum* Decoction liver formula, adapted specifically to treat severe toxicity of the liver due to alcohol and drug poisoning, a widespread problem throughout the world today. Drug poisoning can be caused by recreational drugs such as opiates and amphetamines as well as commonly prescribed medicinal drugs like barbiturates and antidepressants, with damage often compounded by simultaneous alcohol abuse.

This formula not only detoxifies the liver but is also designed to remedy the severe constipation that often accompanies this condition, and to relieve chronic congestion in the solar plexus and abdominal organs.

INDICATIONS: liver toxicity and "fire" (inflammation) due to alcohol and drug poisoning, with related symptoms of acute constipation, congestion of upper abdomen, tightness in chest and rib cage, loss of muscle and skin tone, and nervous tension

INGREDIENTS:		
	Hare's ear *(Bupleurum)*	6 grams
	Pinellia ternata	4 grams
	Ginger (fresh)	4 grams
	Scutellaria macrantha	3 grams
	White peony	3 grams
	Chinese jujube	3 grams
	Trifoliate orange	2 grams
	Rhubarb	2 grams

> *Artemisia capillaris*   4 grams
> *Gardenia florida*   3 grams

PREPARATION AND DOSAGE: decoction: three doses, on an empty stomach

REMARKS: The same dietary and life-style guidelines apply here as for the conditions described above in Formula #11. It should be noted that the drugs used in modern Western medicine to treat liver infections have not proven to be very effective in clinical practice, whereas traditional Chinese herbal remedies, when properly applied in strict accordance with dietary and other guidelines, usually produce positive results if the problem is treated before permanent damage is done.

Practicing "soft style" Chinese exercises such as *chee-gung*, T'ai Chi Chuan, and the Six Healing Sounds, as well as internal-energy meditations such as the Microcosmic Orbit, enhance herbal therapy and facilitate recovery.

Gastritis

13. MISHMI BITTER DISPEL TOXIC HEAT DECOCTION

黃蓮鮮毒湯
huang lien jie du tang

This is a classical Chinese prescription for the symptomatic relief and cure of chronic gastritis, taken from a collection of traditional herbal remedies compiled by Dr. Chen Tsun-ren and published in Hong Kong. Symptoms of this condition include not only the acute pains experienced immediately after eating, but also spontaneous gastric pains that can occur any time of day, often triggered by stress, anger, and other emotional extremes.

INDICATIONS: acute and chronic gastritis, with related symptoms of sharp pains and bloating after ingestion of food, deep heavy belching, nausea, spontaneous feelings of pain and pressure in the stomach, acid indigestion, heartburn, and insomnia

INGREDIENTS: Mishmi bitter   2 grams
                    Scutellaria macrantha   5 grams
                    Phellodendron amurense   2 grams
                    Gardenia florida   2 grams

PREPARATION AND DOSAGE: decoction: two doses, on an empty stomach

REMARKS: People with chronic and acute gastritis should immediately eliminate the following items from their diets: alcohol, coffee, tea, sweet soft drinks, pungent seasonings, smoked and otherwise cured or preserved foods, sour foods, ice-cold foods and beverages. Many common Western drugs, such as aspirin, antibiotics, and sulphur compounds, aggravate gastritis and should be avoided. When eating, it's important to follow the rules of food combining (trophology) and to chew food very well before swallowing. Taking digestive enzyme supplements with every meal is also helpful.

In addition to herbal therapy, acupuncture and acupressure are often quite helpful in correcting this condition, as are meditation and other deep-relaxation techniques that counteract stress.

Alternative Chinese patent herbal formulas for this condition include *Wei Yao* (Gastropathy Capsules) and *Wei Te Ling* (Special Gastric Remedy).

Peptic Ulcer

14. LAUGHTER DECOCTION

失笑湯

shih hsiao tang

The original formula for this prescription came from a Ming dynasty Chinese herbal entitled *Harmonious Medical Prescriptions*. The version given here was adapted and submitted by a mainland Chinese physician currently practicing at the Chi An Pharmacy in Chiang

Mai, Thailand. It was formulated as a specific remedy for single or multiple stomach ulcers that have not yet developed to the advanced stage in which they cause vomiting of blood. This formula is quite effective if used before ulcers reach the advanced stage.

INDICATIONS: peptic ulcers, with related symptoms of acute pain in the upper stomach, intense burning sensations, deep belching, abdominal bloating, and sour acid taste in the mouth, usually occurring within 1 hour after ingestion of food

INGREDIENTS:

Cattail	10 grams
Mastic tree	12 grams
Balsamodendron myrrha	12 grams
Salvia miltiorhiza	12 grams
Angelica sinensis	15 grams
Corydalis ambigua	10 grams
Gynura pinnatifida	6 grams

PREPARATION AND DOSAGE: decoction: two doses, on an empty stomach; powder: infusion; 4 grams in hot water three times daily, on an empty stomach

REMARKS: Ulcer patients should strictly avoid the following items in their daily diets: pungent, spicy seasonings; sour flavors; deep-fried and other oily foods; noodles and other white refined-flour foods; cold and raw foods; dairy products; coffee and alcohol. The best foods for this condition are soups (especially miso), poached foods, herbal porridges, and steamed vegetables. It's also important to avoid overeating.

A good patent herbal alternative for this condition is *Wei Te Ling* (Special Gastric Remedy).

NERVOUS SYSTEM

This category includes formulas for various ailments of the central nervous system, particularly the brain, including various types of headache, Alzheimer's disease, and neuralgia.

Headache (A)

15. EUODIA DECOCTION

吳茱萸湯

wu ju yu tang

This is a well-known classic formula for common tension headaches that appears in numerous traditional Chinese herbals. According to these herbals, such headaches are associated with anemia and are often triggered by claustrophobic conditions, particularly large crowds of people. They can also be symptoms of other chronic conditions, such as high blood pressure and menstrual problems. In most cases, however, the actual cause of the headache is difficult to trace, and many people who suffer common tension headaches are otherwise perfectly healthy. Chinese herbals highly recommend this formula not only for short-term symptomatic relief but also as a long-term cure, although stubborn cases may take 3–6 months of therapy to correct.

INDICATIONS: headache, with symptoms of acute pain, cold hands and feet, loss of appetite, nausea, tension in neck and shoulders, and/or migraine

INGREDIENTS:

Euodia rutaecarpa	3 grams
Ginseng	2 grams
Chinese jujube	4 grams
Ginger (fresh)	4 grams

PREPARATION AND DOSAGE: decoction: two doses (morning and night), on an empty stomach

REMARKS: Chinese physicians strongly discourage people from using most common Western allopathic remedies for headaches, because many of them contain caffeine as well as vasoconstrictors, providing only temporary relief of pain without eliminating root causes. Regular use of such drugs can cause damage to the nerves and cerebral capillaries. People with frequent tension and migraine headaches should avoid caffeine, alcohol, and especially tobacco, and eliminate deep-fried and other oily foods from their diets.

One of the best patent herbal formulas for headaches is called *Shiao Yao Wan* (Bupleurum Sedative Pills), which is also effective for dizziness, blurry vision, painful eyes, hay fever, and allergic reactions to food.

Headache (B)

16. CINNAMON AND GINSENG DECOCTION

桂枝人参湯
gui jir ren sheng tang

This is another popular classic formula for common tension headaches, including migraine. If Formula #15 does not work for you after using it for a week or two, then try this one.

INDICATIONS: headache, including migraine, with related symptoms of pain, nausea, congestion in chest and/or solar plexus, and profuse perspiration

INGREDIENTS:

Cinnamon	4 grams
Licorice	3 grams
Atractylis ovata	3 grams
Ginseng	2 grams
Ginger, dried	1 gram

PREPARATION AND DOSAGE: decoction: two doses (morning and night), on an empty stomach

REMARKS: According to Chinese clinical experience, this formula is effective in approximately 50% of the cases of chronic tension headache. Dietary and other advice is the same as above.

Senile Dementia (Alzheimer's)

17. SPLEEN RESTORATION DECOCTION

歸脾湯

gui pi tang

The original version of this formula comes from the thirteenth-century herbal *Prescriptions Beneficial to Life,* by Yan Yung-huo. The formula was subsequently amended by the herbalist Hsueh Chi during the sixteenth century, and his version continues to be prescribed by physicians today.

In Chinese diagnosis, senile dementia is often seen as a manifestation of functional disharmony between the spleen, which governs thought, and the heart, which houses the spirit and controls emotions. The resulting psychic confusion and emotional turmoil destabilizes the mind and gives rise to the commonly recognized mental, emotional, and behavioral patterns associated with senile dementia. This formula is designed to strengthen and stabilize spleen-energy, tonify the heart and blood, and restore functional harmony between these two vital organs, thereby correcting the psychic and emotional aberrations caused by dysfunction of their energies. It is particularly effective in restoring memory, eliminating worry and anxiety, and recovering a fundamental sense of harmony with the environment and entire cosmos.

INDICATIONS: senile dementia, including symptoms of absentmindedness, irritability, confusion, self-deprecation, insecurity, fatigue, insomnia, and loss of physical control

INGREDIENTS:		
	Astragalus	3 grams
	Ginseng	3 grams
	Atractylodes macrocephala	3 grams
	Tuckahoe	3 grams
	Wild Chinese jujube	3 grams
	Euphoria longana	3 grams

Angelica sinensis	2 grams
Polygala tenuifolia	2 grams
Chinese jujube	2 grams
Licorice	1 gram
Costus	1 gram
Ginger (fresh)	1.5 grams

PREPARATION AND DOSAGE: decoction: two doses, on an empty stomach

REMARKS: In addition to herbal therapy, Chinese physicians recommend a highly nutritious diet, appropriate forms of exercise, and a pleasant, stress-free living environment for senile-dementia patients. While cases that have already reached an advanced stage are often impossible to cure, proper therapy can certainly prevent or slow further deterioration. Today, a variety of Western "nootropic" drugs such as hydergine, piracetum, deprenyl, centrophenoxine, and others are sometimes prescribed for this condition, often with considerable success, particularly if treatment commences during the early stages. These compounds can be used in conjunction with this and other Chinese herbal formulas.

Patients who refuse to take herbal decoctions can substitute the patent remedy called *Gui Pi Wan* (Spleen Restoration Pills, also called Angelicae Longana Tea). For symptomatic relief of anxiety, insomnia, and heart palpitations, the patent formula *Ju Sha An Shen Wan* (Cinnabar Sedative Pill) can also be used. Since the latter formula contains small amounts of mercury, it should not be used for more than 2 weeks at a time.

BLADDER/URINARY SYSTEM
These two formulas are used for various types of bladder and urinary-tract infections, including those caused by pathogens contracted from external sources and those caused by excess internal dampness and/or cold.

Bladder Infections (A)

18. FIVE URINARY DRIP DECOCTION

王 淋 湯

wu lin tang

This traditional Chinese formula for bladder infections appears in different format in various herbals. We found this version in a Chinese medical manual called *Cures for Myriad Ailments with Acupuncture, Chinese Herbs, and Western Medicine,* printed in Taiwan. It can be used for bladder infections contracted from external sources (including sexual contact), internal toxicity, complications due to kidney problems, and excessive internal-cold or internal-damp conditions.

INDICATIONS: bladder infections (cystitis), with related symptoms of hot flashes, aversion to cold, headache, nausea, pain in bladder and waist, frequent and painful urination, dark yellow urine, and/or bleeding from the bladder

INGREDIENTS:

Tuckahoe	9 grams
Angelica sinensis	6 grams
White peony	6 grams
Gardenia florida	6 grams
Licorice	4 grams

PREPARATION AND DOSAGE: decoction: two doses, on an empty stomach

REMARKS: It's important to avoid pungent, spicy foods and stimulating beverages such as coffee, tea, and alcohol. The diet should consist of fresh, blandly flavored foods, preferably prepared as soups, stews, and porridges. Avoid excessively hot or cold showers and baths, and get plenty of rest.

The Chinese patent herbal remedy called *Shih Lin Tung* (Ten Urinary Drip Regulator) can be used as an alternative to this formula.

Bladder Infections (B)

19. EIGHT ORTHODOX POWDER

八正散
ba jeng san

Based on a classical formula from *A Compendium of Harmonious Remedies,* this adapted version was submitted by the herbalist at the Chi An Pharmacy in Chiang Mai, Thailand. It can be used for the same types of bladder and urinary-tract infections described above and is particularly effective for cases due to internal-heat and internal-damp conditions.

INDICATIONS: same as above

INGREDIENTS:

Plantain	10 grams
Akebia quinata	5 grams
Rhubarb	6 grams
Gardenia florida	6 grams
Magnesium silicate	12 grams
Licorice	3 grams
Dianthus sinensis	10 grams
Polygonum aviculare	10 grams
Juncus communis	1.5 grams

PREPARATION AND DOSAGE: powder: "00"-size gelatin capsules; three capsules twice a day, on an empty stomach

decoction: two doses, on an empty stomach

REMARKS: Dietary and other advice are the same as above.

METABOLIC SYSTEM

We included this category to cover three common ailments involving metabolic disorders: diabetes; obesity, and gout. These problems are caused by serious imbalances and malfunctions in the metabolism of sugars, fats, and proteins, primarily in the liver and bloodstream, usually due to excessive consumption of rich and denatured foods, such as refined sugar and starch and processed animal proteins.

Diabetes

20. BAMBOO LEAF AND GYPSUM DECOCTION

竹葉石膏湯

ju yeh shih gao tang

This is a frequently prescribed formula for diabetes listed in many Chinese herbals and included in *Cures for Myriad Ailments with Acupuncture, Chinese Herbs, and Western Medicine,* printed in Taiwan. Diabetes is a metabolic disorder caused primarily by excessive consumption of refined sugar (sucrose), resulting in a chronic depletion of insulin secretions from the pancreas. Hereditary factors, life-style habits such as alcoholism, toxins and pathogens, and obesity may also be causative or contributing factors.

INDICATIONS: diabetes, with related early-stage symptoms of profuse urination (up to 7–8 liters per day), clear watery urine, intense thirst with abundant consumption of water, strong appetite and abundant consumption of food accompanied by continuous loss of body weight, extreme fatigue, nervous sensitivity, headache, insomnia, itchy skin and skin eruptions; intermediate- and late-stage symptoms include loss of sexual drive, glaucoma, neuralgia, irregular sleeping patterns, stiff knees, painful urination (male), and vaginal itching (female)

INGREDIENTS:

Bamboo leaves		9 grams
Gypsum		15 grams
Pinellia ternata		6 grams
Adenophora tetraphylla		15 grams
Creeping lilyturf		15 grams
Dendrobium nobile		9 grams
Rehmannia glutinosa		12 grams
Licorice		3 grams
Brown rice		15 grams

PREPARATION AND DOSAGE: decoction: two doses, on an empty stomach

REMARKS: It's important to administer this decoction warm, that is, not cold or room temperature but also not too hot. According to Chinese herbals, this formula will correct diabetic conditions after 2 months of daily use. If the cure is successful, the patient should be sure to take another course of this formula for 1 month every winter, in order to prevent a recurrence and eliminate the root causes of the condition.

Diabetics must strictly avoid consumption of all sugars, refined as well as natural, and should follow other dietary advice given by their doctors or professional health advisors. They must also avoid overexertion and excessive sexual activity.

Obesity (A)

21. GYNURA DECOCTION

三七湯
san chi tang

This formula was devised and submitted by Dr. Wang Sheng-zhong, based on his studies at Shantou University Medical College in China and his own clinical experience. He says it has proven effective in virtually every type of chronic obesity he has treated.

INDICATION: obesity

INGREDIENTS:
Gynura pinnatifida	3 grams
Psoralea corylifolia	12 grams
Cassia angustifolia	10 grams
Rhubarb	10 grams

PREPARATION AND DOSAGE: decoction: two doses, on an empty stomach

REMARKS: In order to insure effective results, this decoction must be taken daily for at least 1 month, and often up to 3 months.

The Chinese patent herbal tea called *Bao Jian Mei Jian Fei Cha* (Bojenmi Chinese Tea) can be used in conjunction with, but not as a substitute for, this weight-reducing formula.

Obesity (B)

22. CHINESE CORNBIND DECOCTION

首烏湯
shou wu tang

This formula was also submitted by Dr. Wang Sheng-zhong, based on his own studies and clinical experience.

INDICATION: obesity

INGREDIENTS:

Chinese cornbind	30 grams
Angelica sinensis	30 grams
Millettia reticulata	30 grams
Tuckahoe	20 grams

PREPARATION AND DOSAGE: decoction: two doses, on an empty stomach

REMARKS: same as above

Gout

23. GREAT ORANGE PEEL DECOCTION

大橘皮湯
da ju pi tang

This is another popular traditional prescription taken from *Cures for Myriad Ailments with Acupuncture, Chinese Herbs, and Western Medicine,* printed in Taiwan. It has been amended numerous times over the centuries, according to changing dietary habits and food supplies. Gout is a condition caused by excessive uric acid in the bloodstream due to metabolic disorders, kidney dysfunction, and/or improper dietary habits. In the West it has traditionally been regarded as an ailment of the grand gourmand, due to excessive consumption of rich fatty meats and alcoholic beverages.

INDICATIONS: gout, with related symptoms of intestinal congestion, constipation, acute pain in joints (particularly in the large toe), irritability, fatigue, scant urination

INGREDIENTS:	*Citrus reticulata*	6 grams
	Costus	3 grams
	Cinnamon	3 grams
	Morus alba (seeds)	15 grams
	Clematis minor	6 grams
	Cocculus diversifolius	9 grams
	Atractylodes macrocephala	4.5 grams
	Tuckahoe	9 grams
	Alisma plantago	6 grams
	Magnesium silicate (talc)	9 grams
	Achyranthes bidentata	6 grams
	Job's tears	12 grams
	Licorice	3 grams

PREPARATION AND DOSAGE: decoction: two doses, on an empty stomach

REMARKS: This formula reduces acidosis of the blood and stimulates excretion of acid residues via the urine. During therapy, it's best to avoid all alcoholic beverages, rich fatty meats (especially organ meats), seafood, chicken and duck, all white refined-flour products (especially sweet pastries, pies, etc.), beans, and spinach. The best dietary staple for this condition is Job's Tears and Brown Rice Porridge, the recipe for which is given below under Herbal Porridges (page 266). Regular but gentle exercise and hot-spring baths are good supplemental therapies for gout.

An alternative patent herbal remedy for gout is *Du Jung Feng Shih Wan* (Eucommia Bark Wind-Damp Pills), but this is not as effective as the above formula and is strictly contraindicated during pregnancy as well as with colds and flu.

CARDIOVASCULAR SYSTEM

This category includes formulas for ailments related to malfunctions of the heart and circulatory system. As the

King of the internal organs, the heart governs the entire system by virtue of its control over blood circulation, which distributes nutrients and immune factors to every tissue in the body. It also houses the spirit and regulates emotions, so any imbalance in heart-energy also results in mental malaise and emotional turmoil that no form of psychotherapy can cure.

High Blood Pressure

24. GASTRODIA AND UNCARIA BEVERAGE

天麻鉤藤飲
tien ma gou teng yin

This is a recently revised traditional formula listed in a mainland Chinese medical text entitled *New Cures for Chronic Ailments and Symptoms*. According to traditional Chinese medicine, in order to cure high blood pressure, first the associated liver-fire must be corrected. Liver-fire overheats the blood, and via the generative relationship of liver-Wood to heart-Fire, an inflamed liver also overstimulates the heart, which further elevates blood pressure. This formula balances the liver-energy and brings flaring liver-yang back down to normal.

INDICATIONS: high blood pressure, with related symptoms of headache, dizziness, insomnia, tinnitus (ringing in the ears), heart palpitations, breathing difficulties, bloating, bloodshot eyes, and nervous tension.

INGREDIENTS:

Uncaria rhynchophylla	30 grams
Gastrodia elata	15 grams
Chrysanthemum	10 grams
Tribulus terrestris	12 grams
Loranthus yadoriki	24 grams
Prunella vulgaris	15 grams
Earthworm*	6 grams
Brown rice	15 grams

Oyster-shell powder†	30 grams
Pearl powder†	30 grams
Costus	15 grams
Eucommia	12 grams

PREPARATION AND DOSAGE: decoction: two doses, on an empty stomach

REMARKS: Those with high blood pressure are advised to avoid alcohol, tobacco, coffee and tea, stimulating spices, deep-fried and other oily foods, as well as raw and cold foods. Chinese healers strongly advise against using Western remedies for this condition, which simply lower blood pressure by chemical means without in any way curing the condition. Such drugs actually prolong the ailment by flushing materials from the bloodstream that are required to regulate blood pressure, and they also have other undesirable side effects. When such medications are stopped, the condition flares up worse than ever, leading to a lifelong drug dependence.

A good patent remedy for this condition is *Jiang Ya Wan* (Lower Blood Pressure Pills), which can be used as a substitute when it is inconvenient to prepare the above formula, such as while traveling. Neither the formula nor the patent alternative should be used during pregnancy.

Due to the potential dangers and complications of high blood pressure, we suggest that people consult a qualified health professional before using these or any other remedies for this condition.

---

*The earthworm *(Pheretima aspergillum)* is an antipyretic liver sedative that specifically lowers blood pressure. Vegetarians can omit this, since it is a minor ingredient here.

†Oyster shell and pearl *(Ostrea rivularis)* also sedate liver-fire. These parts of the oyster are regarded as minerals, not animal products, and do not violate vegetarian guidelines.

Angina Pectoris

25. TRICHOSANTHES, ALLIUM, AND PINELLIA DECOCTION

瓜蒌薤白半夏汤

gua lu, chiang bai, ban shia tang

A classic formula from Dr. Chang Chung-ching's second century BCE treatise *Discussion of Fevers and Colds*, this version was developed in China based on contemporary clinical experience. This condition is due to hardening or other abnormalities of the arteries that feed the heart muscle, resulting in irregular circulation and acute pain. Contributing factors in angina attacks include syphilis, gout, arteriosclerosis, rheumatism, and excessive use of alcohol, tobacco, and drugs.

INDICATIONS: acute pain and pressure in the heart, pale complexion, profuse cold sweat, numbness in extremities, radiating pain into left shoulder and arm; attacks usually terminate with deep belching and profuse urination, and can recur spontaneously any time.

INGREDIENTS:

Trichosanthes kirilowii	15 grams
Allium macrostemon	10 grams
Pinellia ternata	10 grams
Cattail	10 grams
Trogopterus xanthipes *	10 grams

PREPARATION AND DOSAGE: decoction: two doses, on an empty stomach

REMARKS: Chinese herbals state that this remedy must be used daily until the symptoms of angina disappear, usually 1–2 months.

The Chinese patent formula *San Chi Guan Shin Ning* (Gynura Heart Pacifier) can be used as an alternative remedy.

---

*This is an animal product taken from a species of squirrel and can be omitted by strict vegetarians.

Stroke Complications

26. TONIFY YANG ELIMINATE FIVE DECOCTION

補陽還五湯

bu yang ju wu tang

This formula comes from a nineteenth-century Chinese medical text called *Medical Errors Corrected*. Strokes are usually caused by cerebral bleeding or obstructions such as clots in the capillaries that feed the brain. This formula is designed to help correct post-stroke complications in victims who survive, such as paralysis and loss of speech.

INDICATIONS: post-stroke complications, including complete or partial paralysis, loss of speech, tremors, facial contortions, and other loss of motor controls

INGREDIENTS:	Astragalus	120 grams
	Angelica sinensis	15 grams
	Red peony*	15 grams
	Ligusticum wallichii	10 grams
	Earthworm†	10 grams
	Peach kernels	10 grams
	Tibetan saffron	10 grams

PREPARATION AND DOSAGE: decoction: two doses, on an empty stomach

REMARKS: Alcohol, tobacco, and other stimulants are prohibited in this condition. The diet should consist of light, fresh, wholesome foods, mostly vegetarian. The patient should be encouraged to move about and exercise to the extent that his or her condition permits. Therapeutic massage is also very helpful. It's important to

---

*This is a red variety of *Paeonia lactiflora*, usually referred to as white peony.

†There is no equivalent plant-derived product for this item, so strict vegetarians can simply omit it, although for such a serious condition as stroke, medical requirements should take precedence over dietary restrictions.

maintain a positive attitude and a supportive living environment, and to avoid any form of stress.

The formula should be used daily for 3 months. If loss of speech is the major complication, and if the above formula does not correct this problem, the following formula, called Unlocking Speech Elixir *(jie yu dan)*, can be tried:

INGREDIENTS:	*Gastrodia elata*	10 grams
	Scorpion *(Buthus martensi)*	6 grams
	Nandina domestica	6 grams
	Arisaema thunbergii*	6 grams
	Polygala tenuifolia	10 grams
	Acorus terrestris	10 grams
	Curcuma aromatica	10 grams
	Costus	10 grams

PREPARATION, DOSAGE, AND REMARKS: same as above

FEMALE REPRODUCTIVE SYSTEM
This category includes ailments specifically related to various aspects of the female reproductive system, particularly menstrual disorders, which are a common problem for women today. In addition, we have selected formulas for problems associated with menopause and pregnancy. Most female reproductive disorders are due to deficiencies, obstructions, toxins, and other imbalances in the blood, and to insufficient circulation in the tissues of the reproductive organs. Often these problems are associated with energy imbalance and functional impairment of the liver.

---

*The formula calls for a form of this herb that has first been soaked in the juice decocted from ox or buffalo gallstones, which increases its antispasmodic properties. This step must be done at the pharmacy by a professional herbalist.

Menstrual Disorders

27. LEONURUS EIGHT PRECIOUS DECOCTION

益母草八珍湯

yi mu tsao ba jen tang

This formula is one of the most renowned Chinese remedies for all women's menstrual disorders, including dysmenorrhea, amenorrhea, menorrhagia, scanty menstruation, and premenstrual syndrome (PMS). It is based on a blend of two of China's most ancient blood and energy tonics: Four Item Decoction *(seh wu tang)*, which tonifies blood; and Four Gentlemen Decoction *(seh jun dze tang)*, which tonifies energy. Combined to form Eight Precious Decoction by Dr. Sha Tu-mu during the fourteenth century, it was further refined during the seventeenth century by Dr. Chang Chieh-pin, who added leonurus to enhance the formula's gynecological properties.

The version given below has been further adapted by the K'an Herb Company in the United States in order to focus more on the deeper blood deficiencies associated with menstrual problems in Western women.

In addition to menstrual disorders, this formula can also be used to treat female infertility, habitual miscarriage, postpartum recovery, and general deficiencies of liver and blood.

INDICATIONS: menstrual disorders due to liver, blood, and energy deficiencies, including irregular, insufficient, absent, and excessive menstruation, with related symptoms of abdominal pain, weak limbs, discomfort in waist and lower back, fatigue, pale dry complexion, and premenstrual syndrome (PMS).

INGREDIENTS:

Angelica sinensis	10 grams
White peony	10 grams
Rehmannia glutinosa	15 grams
Ligusticum wallichii	6 grams

Ginseng	15 grams
Atractylodes macrocephala	10 grams
Tuckahoe	10 grams
Licorice	6 grams
Leonurus	6 grams
Chinese cornbind	10 grams
Chinese wolfberry	6 grams

PREPARATION AND DOSAGE: decoction: two doses, on an empty stomach

REMARKS: Most menstrual and other gynecological disorders are due to critical deficiencies in blood and energy, with blood deficiency being a particularly prevalent problem in Western women. Therefore it is important to supplement this formula with proper dietary and life-style habits. Prior to and during menstruation, women should avoid excessively pungent, spicy foods, raw and cold foods (including salads and fruits), and all processed junk foods. Raw and cold foods can easily chill the female reproductive organs, causing blood stagnation. All dairy products except butter should be strictly eliminated as well. Women with menstrual disorders should also avoid exposure to cold and damp energies, such as wind, rain, and swimming, as well as any activity or situation that causes fatigue or stress, all of which further aggravate blood and energy deficiencies.

A good patent herbal alternative for this formula is *Bai Feng Wan* (White Phoenix Pills), which can be used while traveling or at work. If PMS is a problem, the patent herbal remedy called *Shiao Yao Wan* (Bupleurum Sedative Pills) can be used for symptomatic relief for up to a week prior to the onset of menstruation, at which time it should be stopped and replaced with either the above formula or White Phoenix Pills.

Scanty Menstruation

28. HARMONIZE LIVER DECOCTION

调肝汤

tiao gan tang

A classical women's prescription for scanty, light-colored, and watery menstruation, this formula has affinity for the liver and kidneys, whose energies it boosts and balances. It is also a specific remedy for the postmenstrual discomforts often experienced by women with insufficient menstruation.

INDICATIONS: scant menstruation with light-colored, watery discharge, and related postmenstrual symptoms of chronic lower abdominal pain, pain in lower back, weak knees, dizziness, and tinnitus (ringing in the ears)

INGREDIENTS:

	Chinese yam	15 grams
	Angelica sinensis	10 grams
	White peony	10 grams
	Donkey hide glue*	10 grams
	Dogwood tree	10 grams
	Morinda root	6 grams
	Licorice	6 grams

PREPARATION AND DOSAGE: decoction: two doses, on an empty stomach

REMARKS: Traditional Chinese physicians attribute this condition to deficiencies in liver and kidney energies, which this formula is designed to correct. During herbal therapy for this condition, women should avoid strong spicy foods and seasonings, eliminate all raw and chilled foods (which can stagnate the female reproductive organs), and particularly cut out all processed junk foods and dairy products. In addition, they should avoid exposure to wind, rain, and damp conditions, and temporarily stop swimming.

---

*This product *(Equus asinus)* is an excellent blood and yin-energy tonic. Strict vegetarians can substitute *Rehmannia glutinosa*.

Menopausal Problems

29. ENHANCED ELIMINATE AND RELAX DECOCTION

加味消遙湯

jia wei shiao yao tang

This formula comes from Dr. Chang Chung-ching's second century BCE herbal classic, *Essential Prescriptions of the Golden Chest,* and is still frequently prescribed by herbal physicians today. It is designed to relieve the symptoms and correct the imbalances commonly associated with menopause, including physiological, nervous, and emotional problems.

INDICATIONS: symptoms and imbalances associated with menopause, including hormone deficiencies, nervous tension, headache, dizziness and blurry vision, nausea, excitability, insomnia, irregular appetite, and depression (including suicidal tendencies)

INGREDIENTS:		
	Angelica sinensis	3 grams
	White peony	3 grams
	Hare's ear	3 grams
	Thistle type	3 grams
	Tuckahoe	3 grams
	Mint	1 gram
	Licorice	2 grams
	Tree peony	2 grams
	Gardenia florida	2 grams
	Ginger (dried)	1 gram

PREPARATION AND DOSAGE: decoction: two doses, on an empty stomach; powder: capsules, three capsules twice a day, on an empty stomach; infusion: 3 grams in hot water twice a day, on an empty stomach

REMARKS: Modern Western remedies for menopausal problems are not very effective and often cause serious side effects, particularly when hormone replacement therapy is used. Chinese herbal remedies, however, have been shown to provide considerable and sometimes complete relief, because they correct the basic blood and energy imbalances associated with menopause.

According to TCM, the discomforts and abnormalities caused by menopause are due primarily to negligent health care during youth, not to menopause itself. Failure to maintain healthy blood and balanced energy during the years between puberty and middle age often manifests itself when the menstrual cycle stops. Young women who wish to avoid such problems later in life should therefore take preventive measures now.

Preventive for Habitual Miscarriage and Premature Birth

30. ANGELICA AND WHITE PEONY DECOCTION

當歸芍藥湯

dang gui shao yao tang

This classic formula from Dr. Chang Chung-ching's *Essential Prescriptions of the Golden Chest* is regarded by many physicians to be the foremost prescription for the prevention of miscarriage and premature birth. Its analgesic, nervine, diuretic, and blood-tonifying properties insure normal circulation, eliminate excess fluids, relieve discomfort, and calm restless fetus by preventing overheating of the blood. It can be used as a long-range preventive remedy during the early stages of pregnancy, and also as an immediate preventive measure at the first signs of an actual miscarriage.

INDICATIONS: habitual miscarriage and premature birth; also infertility and postpartum abdominal pain and bloating

INGREDIENTS:

Angelica sinensis	3 grams
Ligusticum wallichii	3 grams
White peony	4 grams
Tuckahoe	4 grams
Atractylodes macrocephala	4 grams
Alisma plantago	4 grams

PREPARATION AND DOSAGE: decoction: two doses, on an empty stomach; powder: capsules, three capsules twice a day, on an empty stomach; infusion: 3 grams in hot water twice daily, on an empty stomach

REMARKS: Chinese herbal medicine has particularly effective—and safe—remedies for the problems confronting pregnant women, including miscarriage. Properly prepared herbal remedies do not cause genetic or physical damage to the developing fetus, as chemical drugs often do. The latter should be strictly avoided during pregnancy.

Excessive physical exertion and sexual intercourse during pregnancy are regarded as major catalysts of miscarriage in women who are prone to miscarriage and should therefore be avoided during pregnancy.

The original text accompanying this formula states that it can also be used as a general remedy for many problems commonly experienced by women during pregnancy and after childbirth, including nausea, fatigue, lower back and abdominal pain, bloating, and so on.

Colds and Flu during Pregnancy

31. CINNAMON DECOCTION

桂枝湯

gui jih tang

This is another classic formula for pregnant women taken from Dr. Chang Chung-ching's *Essential Prescriptions of the Golden Chest*. It is recommended as a safe and effective remedy for colds, flu, and related symptoms experienced by women during pregnancy.

INDICATIONS: colds and flu, with related symptoms of headache, fever, profuse sweating, weakness and fatigue, and so on.

INGREDIENTS: Cinnamon   4 grams
                   (tender young stems)*
                   White peony   4 grams
                   Chinese jujube   4 grams
                   Ginger (fresh)   4 grams
                   Licorice   2 grams

PREPARATION AND DOSAGE: decoction: two doses, on an empty stomach

REMARKS: This is a popular old formula that can also be used by men and women of all ages and conditions as a general remedy for colds, headaches, neuralgia, diarrhea, and digestive problems.

Morning Sickness (Nausea)

32. TWO CURE DECOCTION

二陳湯
er chen tang

This is a traditional formula passed down for many generations in China to control vomiting, or morning sickness, in pregnant women. It can be used as an antiemetic during periods when vomiting occurs, and also helps restore appetite and normal digestion.

INDICATIONS: vomiting during pregnancy, with related symptoms of muscular aches, indigestion, loss of appetite, and fatigue

INGREDIENTS: *Pinellia ternata*   4 grams
                   Tuckahoe   4 grams
                   Citrus reticulata   4 grams
                   Licorice   4 grams
                   Ginger (fresh)   2 grams

PREPARATION AND DOSAGE: decoction: two doses, on an empty stomach

---

*This is a different part of the plant from the cinnamon bark described in herbal entry 27 (page 86). The Chinese term *gui jih* literally means "cinnamon twigs.

REMARKS: Chinese herbals suggest that pregnant women drink sour plum juice during the summer and suck on dried sour plums during the winter, as a preventive for morning sickness. They also recommend rubbing fresh ginger root on the tongue prior to meals. If constipation also occurs during periods of morning sickness, Chinese herbals suggest taking a tablespoon of honey in pure water in the morning before breakfast.

Insufficient Lactation

33. GALACTAGOGUE ELIXIR

通乳丹

tung ru dan

This is a traditional galactagogue formula that has been recently amended in China based on contemporary clinical experience. It is used to treat nursing mothers who wish to breast-feed their babies but have insufficient or no lactation due to blood, energy, and/or liver deficiencies.

INDICATIONS: insufficient lactation, with related symptoms of flaccid breasts, pale complexion, loss of appetite, fatigue, and empty feeling in breasts

INGREDIENTS:

Codonopsis dangshen	12 grams
Astragalus	10 grams
Angelica sinensis	10 grams
Creeping lilyturf	10 grams
Balloon flower	6 grams
Tetrapanax papyrifera	10 grams

PREPARATION AND DOSAGE: decoction: two doses, on an empty stomach

REMARKS: Chinese herbal galactagogue formulas such as this were traditionally boiled together with pork knuckles, and today Chinese women still prepare them this way. In Chinese medicine, pork-knuckle broth is recommended as an excellent stimulant to lactation, and its inclusion in herbal galactagogue decoctions therefore enhances the potency of such formulas. Vegetarian women can omit this ingredient, but we suggest that others try it. Diet should include plenty of soups, stews, porridges, and other watery dishes, which also help promote lactation.

Nursing mothers should not take birth control pills because they tend to suppress lactation. It is also inadvisable to use finger pressure to squeeze milk from the breasts because this can damage capillaries and other sensitive tissues.

MALE REPRODUCTIVE SYSTEM

These formulas are designed specifically for disorders of the male reproductive system, such as impotence, spermatorrhea, infertility, and prostate problems. Male sexual disorders are usually associated with imbalances and deficiencies in kidney/adrenal-energy, a condition that is often caused by excessive loss of semen due to undisciplined sexual activity. Therefore, in order for these remedies to be effective, it is essential that men exercise sexual restraint and discipline while using them.

Impotence and/or Infertility

34A. ASSIST NATURE ELIXIR

贊育丹

dzan yu dan

This is a classic male potency formula listed in *The Complete Works of Jing-Yue,* published in 1624 CE by Chang Chieh-pin. Most cases of male impotence are due to a chronic deficiency of yang (Fire) energy in the kidney/adrenal system, which in turn is usually the cumulative result of excessive and undisciplined sexual activities, chronic stress, malnutrition, and/or excessive use of alcohol, tobacco, and other drugs. While psychological inhibitions can also be contributing factors, they are usually associated with the same basic yang-energy deficiencies; therefore, when yang-energy is restored, sexual inhibitions tend to diminish.

INDICATIONS: male impotence (inability to attain or sustain erection)

INGREDIENTS:

Rehmannia glutinosa	24 grams
Atractylodes macrocephala	24 grams
Angelica sinensis	18 grams
Chinese wolfberry	18 grams
Eucommia	12 grams
Curculigo ensifolia	12 grams
Morinda root	12 grams
Dogwood tree	12 grams
Horny goat weed	12 grams
Broomrape	12 grams
Cnidium monnieri	6 grams
Allium tuberosum (seeds)	12 grams
Cinnamon	6 grams
Ginseng	3 grams
Aconitum	6 grams
Deer horn *(Cervus nippon)* *	3 grams

PREPARATION AND DOSAGE: decoction: two doses, on an empty stomach

34B. FIVE SEED DECOCTION

五子湯
wu dze tang

INDICATIONS: Infertility due to low sperm count, with related symptoms of insufficient erection and premature ejaculation

INGREDIENTS:

Chinese wolfberry	10 grams
Dodder	10 grams
Schisandra	10 grams
Raspberry	10 grams

---

*This is one of the most effective yang sexual tonics, highly recommended for impotence. Though the horn is harvested without killing the deer, strict vegans may wish to omit it.

Plantain	10 grams
Horny goat weed	10 grams
Atractylodes macrocephala	10 grams
Tuckahoe	10 grams
Citrus reticulata	10 grams
Ginseng	6 grams
Licorice	3 grams
Trigonella foenum-graecum	10 grams

PREPARATION AND DOSAGE: decoction: two doses, on an empty stomach

REMARKS: Chinese herbals recommend cessation of sexual activity during this course of herbal therapy. It is also important to avoid any sort of stress or nervous agitation, to maintain a daily program of physical exercise, and to eat wholesome, nutritious foods. Use of tobacco, alcohol, and other recreational drugs should be terminated, since they will interfere with the formula's therapeutic effects and can cause a relapse of the condition later. Frequent daily practice of the anal sphincter lock *(mula banda)* is very helpful in restoring circulation and vigor to the male sexual organs.

Predictably, Chinese patent herbal medicine offers a disproportionately large number of formulas as remedies for male impotence and infertility, and many of them are quite effective. We suggest the following products: *Kang Wei Ling* (Combat Impotence Remedy); *Nan Bao* (Male Treasure); *Ge Jie Bu Shen Wan* (Gecko Tonify Kidney Pills); *Jin Kui Shen Chi Wan* (Golden Book Tea, also known as Rehmannia 8 or Sexotan).

Spermatorrhea

35. CONDENSE SEMEN DECOCTION

秘精湯

mi jing tang

This formula appears in an herbal entitled *Prescriptions Beneficial to Life,* published in 1253 CE by Yan Yung-huo. Chinese physicians have always regarded involuntary loss of semen (spermatorrhea, nocturnal emission, and premature ejaculation) as one of the gravest threats to male health and longevity, and many Chinese herbs and formulas are used exclusively to correct this debilitating condition, which can be caused by excessive mental preoccupation with sex (including dreams and fantasies), habitual masturbation, and/or inflammation of the urogenital tract or prostate gland.

INDICATIONS: involuntary loss of semen, including nocturnal emission (with or without dreams) and premature ejaculation, with related symptoms of lumbago, chronic fatigue, headache, lethargy, insomnia, pale complexion, heart palpitations, and ennui

INGREDIENTS:		
	Dragon bones*	15 grams
	Oyster shells†	15 grams
	Schisandra	6 grams
	Tuckahoe	10 grams
	Praying Mantis‡	6 grams
	Rosa laevigana	10 grams
	Dodder	6 grams
	Allium tuberosum (seeds)	6 grams
	Foxnut	10 grams
	Kaolin	10 grams
	(hydrated aluminum silicate)	

---

*This refers to fossilized bones of reptiles and dinosaurs and is essentially a mineral

†This is the powdered shell of *Ostrea rivularis,* also a mineral product

‡This is the dried eggcase of *Paratenodera sinensis,* a highly astringent product and one of the best correctives for involuntary ejaculation and urinary incontinence

PREPARATION AND DOSAGE: decoction: two doses, on an empty stomach

REMARKS: Modern Western medicine fails to perceive the connection between frequent emission of semen and degeneration of male vitality, particularly immune response, despite abundant empirical evidence to support it. Every drop of semen that is lost is replaced at great cost to the body's reservoir of vital resources (the Chinese say, "One drop of semen costs ten drops of blood"). While problems generally do not manifest during youth (teens and twenties), after the age of thirty, excessive loss of semen can become a major cause of impotence, lumbago, chronic fatigue, immune deficiency, nervous disorders, and other problems. Besides herbal therapy, one of the best remedies for this condition is traditional Taoist sexual yoga, which trains men to engage in sexual intercourse without ejaculation, a practice that naturally controls involuntary ejaculations.

An excellent Chinese patent herbal formula for spermatorrhea is *Jin Suo Gu Jing Wan* (Golden Lock Tea), which can also be used to cultivate ejaculation control when learning Taoist sexual yoga.

Prostatitis

36. KIDNEY ENERGY DECOCTION

腎氣湯

shen chi tang

Another classic formula from *Prescriptions Beneficial to Life,* published in 1253 CE by Yan Yung-huo, this formula is prescribed as a remedy for inflammation and enlargement of the prostate gland, a common ailment among men over the age of fifty. This condition can cause considerable discomfort in the groin, interfere with urination, and lead to involuntary emission of semen.

INDICATIONS: prostatitis, with symptoms of painful swelling of the prostate gland, difficult urination, urinary incontinence, pressure in perineum, radiating pain in lower back, waist, genitals, and thighs; advanced cases may be accompanied by blood in urine, especially in alcoholics

INGREDIENTS:

Rehmannia glutinosa	20 grams
Chinese yam	10 grams
Dogwood tree	10 grams
Alisma plantago	6 grams
Tuckahoe	6 grams
Tree peony	6 grams
Cinnamon	3 grams
Achyranthes bidentata	10 grams
Plantain	10 grams
Aconitum	3 grams

PREPARATION AND DOSAGE: decoction: two doses, on an empty stomach

REMARKS: Men over the age of fifty should have their prostates checked regularly, particularly if they experience difficulties with urination. Recommended preventive measures include regular exercise, especially traditional Taoist "soft exercise" such as Ta'i Chi and *chee-gung*. Daily practice of the anal sphincter lock *(mula banda)* is particularly helpful, both as a preventive and curative measure. It's also very important to regulate sexual activity: excess sex will aggravate the condition, while complete celibacy will cause stagnation of prostate fluids. Chinese herbals suggest that men with this problem engage in sexual intercourse, with ejaculation, twice a month, in order to relieve prostate pressure. For obvious reasons, riding horses, bicycles, and motorcycles is prohibited. Diet should include plenty of fresh fruits, vegetables, and water, while eliminating pepper and other pungent spices, as well as alcohol and coffee.

China produces two patent remedies for prostate inflammation: *Chian Lieh Shian Wan* (Prostate Gland Pills) and *Jie Jie Wan* (Kai Kit Pills).

WHOLE BODY TONICS

Tonics are a unique category of Chinese herbs that are designed primarily for use by healthy individuals who wish to maintain their health, enhance their vitality, and prolong their lives. In general, tonics should not be used during periods of acute illness, although they are often employed by the elderly and those suffering from chronic energy deficiencies in order to retard the aging process and boost basic vital functions, particularly sexual vitality, immunity, and cerebral functions. Almost all Chinese tonics are classified as Superior Herbs due to their proven efficacy in maintaining health and prolonging life, and the resulting demand for such herbs has made them among the most expensive in the Chinese pharmacopeia.

Tonics have been the most popular Chinese herbs for thousands of years, and today many Chinese continue to use them on a daily basis. The favorite method of preparing tonics is to steep them in strong spirits, which extracts their full medicinal potentials and delivers them directly into the bloodstream. References to tonic herbal liquors appear in historical records of the Chou dynasty 3,100 years ago, and formulas for them are included in virtually all of the classical Chinese medical treatises. The great Ming dynasty herbalist Lee Shih-chen listed sixty-nine such formulas in his mammoth pharmacopeia *Ben Tsao Gang Mu,* which remains the primary herbal reference in Chinese medicine.

Tonics were once popular in the West as well, until the advent of allopathic medicine at the turn of the century sounded the death knell for preventive health care in Western medicine. Today, few Western doctors even know what a tonic is, much less how and when to prescribe them. One Western health professional who does know a lot about tonics is Dr. Daniel B. Mowrey, who has constructed a solid scientific basis for traditional herbal medicine. In his book *Herbal Tonic Therapies,* he defines tonics as follows:

> A tonic is any substance that balances the biochemical and physiological events that comprise body systems. . . . The consumption of tonics is a fail-safe approach to restoring balance and promoting overall health of the

> body. . . . It is a worry-free method of handling life's
> daily challenges to health and happiness.

The key word here is *balance:* according to the tenets of traditional Chinese medicine, it is imbalance in the basic vital energies of the human system that constitutes the root cause of virtually all disease and degeneration. By keeping human energies in balance and maintaining functional harmony among the various vital organ systems, tonics prevent the imbalances that cause disease and thereby promote health and prolong life. Unlike ordinary medicinal herbs, which are unidirectional (i.e., they function in only one way, regardless of circumstances), tonic herbs are bidirectional, which means that they work in whichever direction is required to restore and maintain optimum balance in the human system. Only whole plants have such bidirectional tonic powers; neither synthetic drugs nor refined fractional isolates of herbs have this capacity.

The best tonics, such as ginseng, are known in modern Western herbology as adaptogens, which means that they adapt the human system to resist adverse external conditions, such as aberrant weather, poor diet, contagious pathogens, and any stressful circumstances. Thus ginseng will either raise or lower blood pressure as well as blood sugar and restore them both to normal levels, depending on circumstances. Adaptogens are especially useful in today's stressful, toxic, fast-paced world, providing protection against cancer, immune deficiency, heart disease, and other life-threatening health problems.

Tonics work primarily by boosting the energies and improving the functions of three vital systems: immune, sexual, and cerebral. Tonic herbs have a positive influence on all three of these vital systems through a network of biofeedback mediated by hormones, neurotransmitters, and immune factors. Thus a sexual tonic will also boost immunity and enhance cerebral clarity, an immune tonic will improve sexual and cerebral functions, and so forth.

Traditional Chinese medicine classifies tonics into four types—blood, energy, yin, and yang—but since these categories are meaningful only to professional practitioners of TCM, we simply list the following tonic formulas by name and describe them in terms of their basic therapeutic actions.

T1. THE DUKE OF CHOU'S CENTENARIAN LIQUOR

周公百歲酒

jou gung bai sui jiou

This formula is purported to be the personal prescription of the Duke of Chou, who helped found the Chou dynasty in 1123 BCE. It is a classic longevity formula that enhances immune response and strengthens sexual vitality in both men and women, increasing semen production in men and boosting fertility in women. It is listed in many traditional Chinese herbals and is still prepared according to the original formula.

THERAPEUTIC ACTIONS: increases semen production; enhances immune response; increases vital energy; tonifies blood; eliminates wind-damp; strengthens kidney and adrenal functions

INGREDIENTS:		
	Polygonatum cirrhifolium	60 grams
	Astragalus	60 grams
	Rehmannia glutinosa	36 grams
	Tuckahoe	60 grams
	Cinnamon	18 grams
	Angelica sinensis	36 grams
	Codonopsis dangshen	30 grams
	Creeping lilyturf	30 grams
	Atractylodes macrocephala	30 grams
	Chinese wolfberry	30 grams
	Citrus reticulata	30 grams
	Dogwood tree	30 grams
	Ligusticum wallichii	30 grams

Ledebouriella seseloides	30 grams
Chinemys reevesii*	30 grams
Schisandra	24 grams
Angelica pubescens (purple)	24 grams

PREPARATION AND DOSAGE: Place all ingredients in a large glass or ceramic vessel and add 7 liters of vodka, rum, or brandy (the Chinese use a potent 150-proof sorghum spirit called *Kao Liang*). Cover and seal it airtight. Give the vessel a good shake once a week to mix ingredients. After 36 days, strain off half the brew (which can then be used) and replace with three fresh bottles of spirits. After 15 more days, strain off the entire batch and discard the spent herbs.

Store in clean bottles with tight corks or caps. Each bottle can be sweetened to taste with rock sugar, fructose, or honey.

One or two doses per day, 1.5 ounces per dose, taken any time of day or night, before, with, or after meals.

REMARKS: This tonic should not be used by pregnant or lactating women. Individuals with general energy and/or blood deficiency, physical weakness, or kidney deficiency, as well as those recovering from strokes or otherwise suffering from partial paralysis or numbness of the extremities can also use this tonic to restore energy and enhance vital functions.

T2. CHINESE WOLFBERRY WINE

枸杞子酒
gou ji dze jiou

This is one of the sixty-nine herbal tonic liquor formulas listed in Lee Shih-chen's great Ming dynasty herbal pharmacopeia *Ben Tsao Gang Mu*. An excellent

---

*This item is an animal product, tortoise shell. It tonifies kidney-yin, strengthens sinew, and builds bone and marrow. Vegetarians can omit it from the formula, though it is a potent yin tonic.

kidney and liver tonic that boosts male and female sexual energies, it became known in China as The Secret Wine of Harmonious Marital Relations. Wolfberry tonifies yin (Water) energy rather than yang (Fire) energy, which means that it stimulates production of hormones, blood, enzymes, and other vital fluids rather than fanning the fire of sexual desire as yang tonics do. When it comes to performance in the "flowery battlefield" of the bedroom, Water is more potent than Fire.

THERAPEUTIC ACTIONS: tonic nutrient to kidneys, nourishes liver, benefits bone marrow, brightens eyes, stimulates semen and hormone production, relieves chronic thirst, relieves lumbago and painful weak knees

INGREDIENT: Chinese wolfberry, 100 grams

PREPARATION AND DOSAGE: Place wolfberry in a clean glass or ceramic vessel and add 2 liters vodka, rum, brandy, or Chinese *Kao Liang*. Seal airtight and let steep for 36 days, giving the vessel a shake once a week. After 36 days, strain off the herbal spirits and discard the spent berries. Wolfberry has a slightly sweet flavor itself, but you can add some rock sugar, fructose, or honey to taste.

Take one or two doses of 1.5 ounces daily, preferably on an empty stomach, but with or after meals is also fine.

REMARKS: Be sure to select top-grade Chinese wolfberry—large, red, and succulent—and avoid inferior grades that have been dyed red.

As a yin tonic, this herbal liquor can be used by men and women throughout the year. The liver governs female sexual energy, while the kidneys control male sexual energy, therefore wolfberry is equally beneficial as a sexual tonic for both genders.

T3. VERMILION ELIXIR WINE

彤丹酒
tung dan jiou

The formula for this herbal liquor was created by the author's wife Chou Tung, who used our Chinese names (*tung* and *dan*) as a label. All ingredients are superior herbs, and the formula is carefully balanced to nourish blood, tonify energy, and harmonize the vital functions of all the internal organs. It provides a mild, gentle boost to both yin- and yang-energy, and is equally beneficial to men and women, without any undesirable side effects. It is a purely preventive formula, not a prescription for specific ailments, and can also be used by the weak and elderly as a general vitality tonic.

THERAPEUTIC ACTIONS: nutrient tonic to blood and energy, balances yin and yang, harmonizes vital organ functions, enhances immune response, clarifies cerebral functions, retards aging, clears obstructions to blood and energy circulation

INGREDIENTS:		
	White Korean ginseng	20 grams
	Astragalus	30 grams
	Angelica sinensis	30 grams
	Chinese cornbind	15 grams
	Atractylodes macrocephala	30 grams
	Eucommia	20 grams
	Broomrape	30 grams
	Rehmannia glutinosa	30 grams
	Chinese yam	20 grams
	Chinese wolfberry	20 grams
	Achyranthes bidentata	30 grams
	Wild Chinese jujube	20 grams
	Horny goat weed	30 grams
	Ligusticum wallichii	15 grams
	Eleutherococcus gracilistylus	30 grams
	Lotus seeds	15 grams
	Polygonatum cirrhifolium	20 grams
	Licorice	15 grams
	Tuckahoe	15 grams
	Dogwood tree	15 grams
	Chinese jujube	20 grams
	Cnidium monnieri	15 grams
	Schisandra	15 grams
	Leonurus	15 grams

| Japanese wax privet | 30 grams |
| Tibetan saffron | 10 grams |

PREPARATION AND DOSAGE: Place all ingredients in a clean glass or ceramic vessel and add 7 liters vodka, rum, brandy, or Chinese *Kao Liang*. Cover and seal it airtight, and set to steep for 45 days, shaking once a week to mix ingredients. Strain off half the brew, add 3 liters fresh spirits, and let steep another 30 days. Strain off entire remaining brew and discard spent herbs. Store in clean glass bottles with tight corks or caps, adding some rock sugar, fructose, or honey to taste to each bottle.

Take one or two doses of 1.5 ounces each daily; before, during, or after meals

REMARKS: This tonic is not suitable for obese individuals, whose systems may become overstimulated and overheated by it. Besides normal healthy people, it is particularly beneficial to weak, elderly, and underweight persons and is an excellent corrective tonic for women who experience difficulties with menopause, and for anyone with deficient immune response.

T4. GINSENG AND
REHMANNIA PILLS

人參地黃丸

ren sheng di huang wan

This formula comes from a twelfth-century Sung dynasty herbal entitled *Complete Compendium of Sacred Remedies*. The herbal essences have natural affinity for the heart, spleen, liver, and kidney organ-energy systems. This tonic, which can be used by both men and women, is a particularly beneficial corrective for male impotence.

THERAPEUTIC ACTIONS: tonifies heart and spleen, nourishes liver and kidneys, strengthens male and female sexual vitality, improves digestion and assimilation, enhances immune response.

INGREDIENTS:	Ginseng	30 grams
	Rehmannia glutinosa	30 grams
	Morinda root	30 grams
	Broomrape	30 grams
	Atractylodes macrocephala	30 grams
	Dodder	30 grams
	Chrysanthemum	30 grams
	Eleutherococcus gracilistylus	30 grams
	Dendrobium nobile	30 grams
	Thuja orientalis	30 grams

PREPARATION AND DOSAGE: Grind all ingredients to a fine powder, mix with honey, and roll into pills about the size of barley grains (or have this done at an herbal pharmacy). Take thirty pills, once a day, with some warm wine (Japanese sake is good for this purpose), on an empty stomach.

REMARKS: *Atractylodes,* which appears in many tonic formulas, is a particularly potent immune system enhancer and longevity tonic. The late Ching dynasty empress dowager Tse Hsi, who used longevity tonics throughout her long and active life as China's last "female emperor," favored this herb above all others. Today *Atractylodes* and chrysanthemum are both included in the immune system tonics being experimentally used in AIDS cases in China.

T5. KIND MOTHER DECOCTION

慈母湯
tse mu tang

This formula comes from a practical handbook of Chinese remedies called *Prescriptions from Clinical Experience* and is designed specifically as a tonic for women who experience chronic menstrual irregularities, as well as for menopause problems. However, it can also be used as a general blood and energy tonic by all women to promote health and longevity.

THERAPEUTIC ACTIONS: emmenagogue, clears blood clots and other obstructions in female reproductive system, warms the uterus, promotes circulation

INGREDIENTS:

White Korean ginseng	4.5 grams
Astragalus	4.5 grams
Rehmannia glutinosa	3.5 grams
Atractylodes macrocephala	3.5 grams
Donkey hide glue*	1.5 grams
Dogwood tree	1.5 grams
Cyperus rotundus seeds	1 gram
Licorice	1 gram
Sanguisorba officinalis	1 gram
Cimicifuga foetida	1 gram

PREPARATION AND DOSAGE: decoction: two doses, on an empty stomach

REMARKS: Women with menstrual or menopause problems should use this tonic daily for 1–3 months, or until their condition normalizes. Healthy women without any particular problems need only use it twice a month for general tonification of blood and energy.

T6. FOUR ESSENCE PILLS

四精丸
seh jing wan

A popular traditional tonic from the herbal entitled *Common Medicinal Remedies* by Chou Hsien-wang, this formula is designed as a male kidney-energy tonic and is particularly beneficial for men who experience

---

*This animal product *(Equus asinus)* tonifies blood and nourishes yin-energy and is a well-known remedy for menstrual problems. Strict vegetarians can omit it from the formula.

nocturnal emissions and other forms of involuntary ejaculation. The formula has specific affinity for the kidneys, heart, and spleen, and can be used as a general male energy tonic by all men.

THERAPEUTIC ACTIONS: tonifies kidneys, nourishes heart, strengthens spleen, all of which combine to prevent involuntary loss of semen

INGREDIENTS:		
	Broomrape	20 grams
	Spotted deer horn*	20 grams
	Tuckahoe	20 grams
	Chinese yam	20 grams

PREPARATION AND DOSAGE: Grind all ingredients to a fine powder, mix with some honey, and roll into pills about the size of barley grains (or have an herbalist do this for you). Take thirty pills, once a day, preferably with a warm decoction of Chinese jujube, which synergizes the tonic effects of the formula.

REMARKS: Nocturnal emission is often caused by deficiency and disharmony of heart and spleen energies, which this formula corrects. Another symptom of this condition is frequent urination, particularly at night. This tonic is also said to modify excessive or perverse sexual desire.

TONIC HERBAL BROTH

Chinese physicians often recommend freshly boiled chicken broth as a therapeutic tonic food for people recovering from long illness or surgery, pregnant and postpartum women, the weak and elderly, ailing children, and individuals with poor digestion. Chicken broth is a proven health tonic that is easy to assimilate and significantly increases the rate at which the body produces energy through metabolism. It is therefore an excellent source of nutritional essence and energy during periods of convalescence or general debility.

---

*This animal product *(Cervus nippon)* is one of the best male sexual tonics. Vegetarians can substitute horny goat weed.

Chicken broth can also be used as a base for preparing medicinal herbs, particularly tonics such as ginseng and astragalus. A balanced blend of food and medicine, herbal broth has been used as a health and longevity tonic for thousands of years in China. To prepare it, chop a fresh whole chicken into quarters, add a dash of sea salt and some sliced ginger root, and bring to a boil in 2 liters of pure water, using a spoon to skim off any foam that rises to the surface. Lower heat, cover, and simmer for 3–4 hours, adding a little fresh water if the volume reduces by more than half. It's essential to use fresh farm chickens that are free from synthetic hormones, antibiotics, amphetamines, and other chemical additives, which eliminates the chickens sold in most supermarkets.

Strain off the broth, skim away most of the fat that rises to the surface, and reserve about 2 cups of the broth as a base to prepare 1 day's dosage of tonic herbs. Extra broth can be kept indefinitely in the freezer, or for up to 3 days in the refrigerator. To save time later, you can boil three or four chickens at once and keep the broth frozen in individual 2-cup containers.

Add about 10 grams of sliced ginseng, astragalus, angelica, cordyceps (winter worm–summer grass), or any other tonic herb to 2 cups of fresh broth, bring to a boil, cover, then simmer over low heat for about 45 minutes. Drink warm, in either one or two doses, on an empty stomach.

For *Cordyceps,* many Chinese herbals suggest using the broth of a mature male duck.

If you wish to save the time and effort required to prepare your own herbal broth at home, or if you need a convenient alternative for work or travel, you can try some of the patent preparations of Chinese herbs in "essence of chicken" currently available on the market. Made with ginseng, angelica, or *Cordyceps,* these prepared herbal broths are excellent health tonics that can be used as daily dietary and therapeutic supplements.

HERBAL WASHES

An herbal wash is prepared by decocting a single or a combination of cleansing herbs in water for use as an external skin cleanser or vaginal douche. Herbal washes are particularly effective for fungal skin rashes, itchy skin, and vaginal yeast infections, providing relief without the toxicity of chemical creams.

W1. CNIDIUM DECOCTION

蛇床子湯

she chuang dze tang

This is a traditional woman's formula that appears in the gynecological section of many Chinese herbals. It is used as a vaginal douche and external wash to relieve itching and cure vaginitis due to parasites and yeast infections. This version of the formula was submitted by Sammy J. C. Mei, a Chinese herbalist practicing in Taiwan.

INDICATIONS: Itching and vaginal infections due to parasites, yeast, and other microbes

INGREDIENTS:		
	Cnidium monnieri	30 grams
	Phellodendron amurense	9 grams
	Melia toosendan	6 grams
	Lycium chinense	15 grams
	Alum (aluminium potassium sulfate)	15 grams

PREPARATION AND DOSAGE: Decoct the above ingredients in 6 cups of pure water, until half the liquid has evaporated. Filter it through cloth or paper, and use the herbal fluid as a vaginal douche and external wash to cleanse the entire infected area. Repeat treatment one or two times per day, until itching and irritation disappear, usually 2–4 days.

W2. CNIDIUM AND LICORICE DECOCTION

蛇床子甘草煬

she chuang dze gan tsao tang

This is a common external wash listed in many Chinese herbals. It is used mainly for relief of itching and discomfort in men with damp, itchy scrotum, but it can also be used for all types of itchy skin rashes.

INDICATIONS: damp, itchy scrotum and other itchy skin rashes

INGREDIENTS: *Cnidium monnieri*   20 grams
                   Licorice   12 grams

PREPARATION AND DOSAGE: decoct the herbs in 4 cups of water, until fluid is reduced by half; strain through cloth or paper, and use decoction as a wash for damp, itchy scrotum and other itchy rashes; for itchy scrotum, it's best to immerse the entire scrotum in a bowl of the decoction for 5 minutes; rinse with fresh water but do not use soap

REMARKS: This decoction can also be used as a wash for skin rashes and infections in pets, such as dogs and cats.

HERBAL OINTMENTS

Herbal ointments are prepared by mixing finely ground herbal powders into an oil base, such as yellow vaseline, beeswax, almond oil, and lard. They are used for external application to skin problems, wounds, burns, bruises, and other surface ailments. The most popular patent herbal ointment is Tiger Balm, an aromatic ointment produced in Singapore and sold throughout the world.

N1. PURPLE CLOUD OINTMENT

茱芸膏

dze yun gao

The original formula for this ointment was developed in Japan, based on traditional Chinese sources. The version given here was formulated by the author's wife, based upon her own research and practice. Among the changes she made was to use lard rendered from the fat of suckling pigs, rather than the ordinary lard called for in the original formula. She did this to eliminate the impurities and acidity contained in ordinary commercial lard, while still utilizing the benefits of this ingredient. Lard's own pharmacological properties harmonize the effects of the other herbs in the ointment, and it facilitates rapid absorption of the ointment into the skin. While ordinary lard is readily available in grocery shops, lard rendered from suckling pigs must be specially ordered at a butcher shop. Though lard constitutes only 1.5% of this formula, those who object to its use can substitute beeswax or almond oil, though these are less effective.

INDICATIONS: abrasions, burns, frostbite, hemorrhoids, bruises, dry scaly skin, warts, boils, insect bites, rashes, itching

INGREDIENTS:

Black sesame seed oil (pure)	1000 grams
Angelica sinensis	200 grams
Lithospermum erythrorhizon	200 grams
Beeswax	380 grams
Lard	25 grams
(preferably from suckling pigs)	

PREPARATION AND DOSAGE: Purchase the black sesame oil and the beeswax from a Chinese herbal pharmacy and have the herbalist grind the two herbs into a very fine powder. Order the rendered lard from a butcher shop, and if suckling pigs are not available, use ordinary lard, or a substitute. Heat the oil, wax, and lard in a large copper or stainless-steel pot, preferably a Chinese wok, then add the powdered herbs and stir constantly over low heat until well blended. Let cool a bit, then pour into containers while still warm and fluid and cover tightly. It can be stored indefinitely without refrigeration.

Apply to skin abrasions, bruises, boils, hemorrhoids, and so on, and rub in well, repeating as often as needed. For burns, apply a large thick layer to the entire burn, but do not rub. For serious burns, cover the ointment loosely with a piece of clean cotton gauze and tape the edges to the skin.

REMARKS: This is a particularly effective remedy for burns, and if applied immediately and often, it will prevent scarring.

HERBAL POULTICES

Herbal poultices are prepared by mixing finely powdered herbs with water to form a thick paste. The paste is then spread evenly onto a piece of cellophane or wax paper and applied directly to the injured area, and the edges are taped securely to the skin. Poultices are used primarily to heal traumatic internal injuries and inflammations of bones, joints, muscles, tendons, and nerves, sustained from external intrusions such as sprains, twists, pulls, and heavy blows. However, they should not be used on open wounds or highly sensitive skin.

P1. DR. HUANG'S INTERNAL INJURY POULTICE

黄氏内傷敷药

huang shih nei shang fu yao

The formula for this poultice was created by the late Dr. Huang Po-wen, a master of traditional Chinese medicine practicing in Taiwan, and one of the author's main medical mentors. It is one of the best herbal poultices we have ever encountered, with marvelous anti-inflammatory and tissue healing powers. It is particularly effective for healing sports injuries, such as sprained joints, pulled muscles, twisted tendons, and inflamed nerves.

INDICATIONS: traumatic injury and/or inflammation of joints, muscles, tendons, and nerves

INGREDIENTS:

Rhubarb *(Rheum officinale)*	60 grams
Scutellaria baicalensis	60 grams
Phellodendron amurense	60 grams
Trichosanthes multiflora (root)	30 grams
Mastic tree	30 grams
Commiphora myrrha (resin)	30 grams
Vitis serianaefolia	30 grams
Bletilla striata	30 grams
Angelica anomala	30 grams
Eleutherococcus gracilistylus	30 grams
Gardenia florida (kernels)	30 grams
Citrus reticulata	60 grams
Arisaema consanguineum	30 grams
Thistle type	60 grams
Clove	30 grams
(Eugenia caryophyllata)	

PREPARATION AND DOSAGE: Have all ingredients ground to a very fine powder, mix well, and store in an airtight container. To use, place 3–4 tablespoons of powder in a bowl and slowly add water while stirring with a spoon, until a paste the consistency of peanut butter is formed. Spread the paste evenly onto a piece of cellophane (not plastic) or wax paper, cut just large enough to cover the injured area. Place the paste directly on the skin over the injured area, cover the cellophane or paper with a piece of cotton gauze, and tape securely in place. Leave it on for 12–18 hours, then remove. If the skin shows no adverse reactions to the poultice, this treatment can be repeated daily for up to a week. If the skin reacts with a slight rash, then skip a day or two before applying the next poultice.

REMARKS: Treatment should be terminated if the skin shows a severe rash or other allergic reaction to the poultice. A slight rash or wrinkling of the skin is normal, in which case skip a day. If injury is accompanied by an open skin wound, wait until the wound is closed and well healed before applying the poultice to heal the internal injury.

HERBAL PORRIDGES

Nothing combines the functions of food and medicine as palatably as herbal porridge *(yao jou)*, one of the oldest and most popular creations of the Chinese kitchen clinic. Porridge, or gruel, has been a staple food item in China for thousands of years, but in the West it went out of style with the horse-and-buggy, replaced by instant oatmeal, cornflakes, and other processed fast foods that sacrifice nutrition for convenience.

Herbal porridge is made with a base of one or more whole grains, combined with one or more medicinal herbs, and boiled together in pure water or chicken broth until the grains are soft and the herbal essences have been thoroughly extracted. It makes a tasty and highly fortifying breakfast food and can also be eaten along with other dishes for lunch or dinner, or any time as a simple snack. The Chinese usually prepare a large pot for breakfast early in the morning and leave it on the stove all day, warming it up whenever someone gets hungry. However, leftovers should be discarded or fed to animals, not kept for the next day, because the porridge loses its nutritional and medicinal benefits if kept overnight.

Herbal porridge is one of the best and least expensive tonic foods money can buy, far better for health and longevity than anything on a typical Western breakfast menu. The whole grains provide protein and carbohydrates as well as B vitamins and minerals, all in highly digestible form, plus plenty of bulk fiber and moisture to facilitate bowel functions, while the herbs yield potent therapeutic essences and energies that are rapidly absorbed and metabolized along with the nutrients. Herbal porridges are particularly kind to the stomach and intestinal tract, facilitating rather than straining digestion, and they are frequently prescribed as medicinal foods for people with liver, gallbladder, and pancreas disorders, as well as gastritis, ulcers, constipation, and other digestive problems. Many digestive disorders today start at the breakfast table, where people indiscriminately dump coffee, orange juice, eggs, bacon, ham, bread, jam, cow's milk, sugared cereals, and other incompatible combinations into their stomachs, ruining their days as well as their digestive systems. Instead, try breaking your fast with an herbal porridge each morning for a few months and discover what a difference it makes to start the day on the right digestive track.

1. JOB'S TEARS AND BROWN RICE PORRIDGE

薏以仁糙米

yi yi ren dzao-mi jou

Based on a traditional Chinese recipe, this particular version comes from our own kitchen clinic, where it has replaced almost all other rice and noodle dishes. For breakfast we use extra water to make a more fluid porridge, while for dinner we cook it drier as a grain dish that goes well with other foods on the table.

INGREDIENTS: 1 cup Job's tears
                 1 cup brown rice
                 8 cups pure water (more or less)

PREPARATION: Wash and rinse the rice and Job's tears well, then soak them in 8 cups of pure water for about 2 hours, or overnight. Pour the grain, herb, and water into a large nonaluminum pot, bring to a boil, cover, then lower heat and simmer for about 1 hour, until the grain is thoroughly cooked and the fluid begins to thicken. Serves 4–6 persons.

VARIATIONS: (1) Use ½ cup brown rice and ½ cup wild rice, which is how we usually do it at home. Wild rice imparts a rich, nutty taste and higher protein content to the porridge.

(2) Use fresh chicken broth instead of water to cook the porridge. This provides a richer flavor and extra nutrition, particularly good in cold winter weather.

(3) Add 8–10 red or black Chinese jujubes. These lend a sweet flavor and additional tonic punch to the porridge, making it especially good for breakfast. Be sure to crush each jujube with pliers until the kernal inside cracks open, to release the full medicinal potential.

(4) Sweet porridge: add your own preferred combination of sweet condiments to each bowl of cooked porridge (not to the pot), such as sliced banana, chopped figs or dates, raisins, prunes, honey, or maple syrup.

(5) Salty porridge: to each individual serving bowl, add ½ teaspoon sea salt, 1 teaspoon dark Chinese sesame oil, and 1–2 tablespoons chopped fresh scallions (green onions); ladle hot porridge into bowl and stir well to blend flavors. You can also add one fresh egg yolk for extra nutrition.

2. LOTUS SEED AND BROWN RICE PORRIDGE

蓮子糙米

lien-dze dzao mi jou

Lotus seeds have cardiotonic and nervine properties, and also invigorate the sexual organs. They help remedy chronic insomnia and nervous tension, relieve excessive urination, and function as a general nutrient tonic to the entire body. Their rich flavor and chewy texture lend themselves very well to porridge.

INGREDIENTS: ¾ cup lotus seeds
                       1½ cups brown rice
                       8 cups pure water (more or less)

PREPARATION: Same as above

VARIATIONS: Same as above; for sweet lotus-seed porridge, you can add some honey, raw sugar, or maple syrup directly to the boiling porridge

3. PLANTAIN SEED AND BROWN RICE PORRIDGE

辛甬子楬米

che chien dze dzao mi jou

This herbal porridge is an excellent sexual tonic for both men and women, promoting fertility and increasing sexual secretions. It also reduces prostate inflammation in men, helps cure bladder and urinary-tract infections, and lowers blood pressure.

INGREDIENTS: 30 grams plantain seeds
                       1½ cups brown rice
                       8 cups pure water (more or less)

PREPARATION: Soak the rice in 5 cups of the water; in a separate pot, boil the plantain seeds in 3 cups of water until the fluid is reduced by half; discard the seeds, add the herbal water to the 5 cups of water, and boil the rice until porridge is cooked.

VARIATIONS: Prepare salty porridge as suggested above. For sweet porridge, use only 1–2 teaspoons of raw or brown sugar, nothing else.

4. GINGER, JUJUBE, AND BROWN RICE PORRIDGE

生薑火枣楬米

sheng jiang da dzao dzao mi jou

This recipe is particularly good for those with weak digestive systems, stomach ailments, nausea, and poor appetite. Ginger warms the stomach, stimulates the spleen, and improves digestion, while jujube improves kidney function, stimulates metabolism, and improves appetite.

INGREDIENTS: 5 grams ginger (dried or fresh)
6 Chinese jujubes, crushed
1½ cups brown rice
8 cups pure water (more or less)

PREPARATION: Soak the rice in the water for 2–3 hours or overnight; bring the rice to a boil, then add the ginger and jujubes.

VARIATIONS: As above; for colds and flu, omit the jujubes and add the white fleshy portion of six fresh scallions.

HERBAL PILLOWS

Herbal pillows are one of the most ancient and effective forms of aromatherapy in the world. Though not yet well known in the West, the Chinese have been sleeping on aromatic herbal pillows for thousands of years. Utilizing body heat from the head, these pillows release the essential energies and flavors contained in medicinal herbs and transmit their therapeutic benefits during sleep, thereby enabling people to use dormant sleeping hours for practical health purposes.

Activated by heat from the head, the aromatic energies of the herbs in the pillow waft up throughout the night and enter the system through the nose and sinuses, where special olfactory receptors pick them up and transmit them directly into the vital energy channels, which then carry them to the organs and glands for which they have affinity. These volatile herbal energies also seep into the system directly through sensitive vital energy points on the head and neck, which are pressed against the pillow during sleep, and link the brain to the rest of the body.

METHOD: Select the herb or combination of herbs required for your condition and stuff them whole into a clean cotton pillowcase about 15 inches long by 10 inches wide (38 × 25 centimeters), or smaller if you prefer. The pillow should be no larger than this, otherwise the herbs will bunch up and separate at night. Add enough herbs to make the pillow firm but not too hard and tight. Sew or zip up the opening, then slip the pillow into another cotton case. Sleep on the pillow at night and also during daytime naps. If you practice meditation, you can make a separate, slightly firmer pillow with the same or different blends of herbs and sit on it during your daily practice.

It's a good idea to set the pillows out in the sun for an hour or two several times per week, particularly in damp climates, in order to keep them dry and prevent mildew, but don't leave them out too long, lest the heat dissipates their volatile aromatic energies. Herbal pillows can be used for three months up to a year or more, depending on the herbs inside and how often you use them. When they're no longer aromatic, it's time to change the herbs.

HP1. TEA PILLOW

茶枕
cha jen

Tea pillows should be made only with Chinese oolong tea—not with black or green teas—preferably top-grade High Mountain Oolong from Taiwan. After drinking the tea, save the spent leaves, dry them thoroughly in the sun, and store them in a closed plastic bag until you've collected enough to make a pillow.

Oolong tea pillows, whose energies enter the heart, lung, and stomach meridians, clarify the brain, brighten the eyes, deepen sleep, and help prevent hangovers after excess consumption of alcohol. They are particularly beneficial for people with busy, stressful life-styles, permitting maximum rest even when sleeping time is short. They can be used regularly by men and women over the age of fifteen.

Tea pillows will last longer if you empty the contents every two months and set them out in the sun for an hour or two, replacing pulverized leaves with fresh ones before restuffing the pillow.

HP2. BROWN RICE PILLOW

胚芽米枕
pei ya mi jen

Brown rice pillows are recommended for children between the ages of 2 and 12 years. They facilitate sound sleep, promote normal development of the brain, and balance cerebral functions, thereby controlling hyperactivity and other behavioral disorders in children.

Select the highest quality, most aromatic brown rice available. Be careful not to overstuff the pillow, otherwise it may be too hard and inflexible for sleep. It's a good idea to empty the contents every 2 months and set them out in the sun for an hour or two to dry and prevent mildew. Replace any crushed kernels with new rice.

HP3. CHRYSANTHEMUM AND
UNCARIA PILLOW

菊花钩藤枕
ju hua gou teng jen

This pillow employs equal portions of dried chrysanthemum blossoms and *Uncaria rhynchophylla* (also known as *Nauclea sinensis*). This blend lowers blood pressure, remedies dizziness and blurry vision, and reduces painful swelling of the eyes. Its energies enter the liver channel and soothe liver inflammation. It is especially recommended as a supplemental therapy for people with high blood pressure.

After rising in the morning, cover the pillow well under a sheet in order to prevent the aromas from escaping during the day. This also impregnates the sheet with the herbs' volatile energies, which are then reabsorbed through the skin at night.

HP4. LIGUSTICUM AND ANGELICA ANOMALA PILLOW

川芎白芷枕

chuan chiung bai-jir jen

This blend of fragrant, warming herbs (mixed in equal parts) is recommended primarily as an analgesic remedy for all sorts of headaches, including migraine. It also helps relieve chronic runny nose and watery eyes and promotes blood circulation.

During the day, the pillow should be kept well covered under a sheet to prevent escape of volatile energies and to infuse the sheet with the aromatic essences of the herbs.

HP5. GYPSUM PILLOW

石膏枕

shir gao jen

Gypsum is a common medicinal mineral frequently used in Chinese medicine for its cold energy, which has antipyretic and antiphlogistic properties. Gypsum pillows are recommended as a remedy for fevers, to reduce profuse sweating, and for the relief of excessive summer heat. For the latter purpose, you can also use bamboo leaves, either in combination with gypsum or alone.

Prior to making the pillow, the gypsum should be crushed to the consistency of fine gravel, but not to powder. Herbal pharmacies will do this for you on request.

APPENDIX A

Herbal Suppliers

The Chinese herbs and patent formulas mentioned in this book are most readily available at traditional Chinese herbal pharmacies, which you'll usually find located in the Chinatown districts of major cities throughout the world. In addition, many health food shops and Asian grocery stores carry a variety of the most popular herbs and patent remedies.

If you're living in an area that has no Chinese pharmacies or any other shops that stock Chinese herbal products, try contacting one of the mail-order suppliers listed below and ask them if they stock the particular herbs and formulas you wish to purchase. You should also request that they send you their complete catalog of products and any other printed materials they have available. Most of these suppliers produce their own line of herbal remedies, and some also carry patent formulas imported from China. Often you will discover a formula made in the West that is equivalent to the Chinese patent you're looking for, but under a different name and label, and most of the herbal products produced in the United States are equal or superior in quality to those made in China.

UNITED STATES

Herbs and Formulas

Dragon River Herbal, P.O. Box 28, El Rito, NM 87530
    Tel. and Fax (505) 581-4441

Health Concerns, 2415 Mariner Sq. Drive, #3, Alameda, CA
    94501, Tel. (800) 233-9355

K'an Herb Company, 6001 Butler Lane, Scotts Valley, CA
    95066, Tel. (408) 438-9450, Fax (408) 438-9457

Kanpo Formulas, P.O. Box 60279, Sacramento, CA 95860,
Tel. (916) 487-9044

Mayway Trading Company, 780 Broadway, San Francisco,
CA 95073, Tel. (415) 788-3646

McZand Herbal, P.O. Box 5312, Santa Monica, CA 90409,
Tel. (800) 800-0405

Herbal Internal Cleansing and Fasting Products

Arise & Shine, P.O. Box 901, Mt. Shasta, CA 96067,
Tel. (916) 926-0891, Fax (916) 926-8866

Colema Boards, Inc., P.O. Box 1879, Cottonwood, CA 96022,
Tel. (916) 347-5868, Fax (916) 347-5921

UNITED KINGDOM

Acumedic Ltd., 101 Camden High Street, London, Tel. (071)
388-6704

East West Herbs Ltd., Langston Priory Mews, Kingham,
Oxfordshire OX7 6UP, Tel. (0608) 658-862

Retail Shop and Clinic, 3 Neals Yard, London WC2H 9DP,
Tel. (071) 379-1312

Maiway (UK) Ltd., 40 Sapcote Trading Square, Dudden Hill
Lane, London NW10, Tel. (081) 459-1727

AUSTRALIA

Cathay, P.O. Box 878, Haymarket, NSW 2000, Tel. (02) 212-
5151, Fax (02) 212-7944

Chinaherb, 29A Albion Street, Surry Hills, NSW 2010, Tel.
(02) 281-2122, Fax (02) 281-9040

Green Medicine Company, P.O. Box 328, Armadale, Vic.
3143, Tel. (01) 800-643-320 (toll free)

APPENDIX B

Herbal Schools

Today there are many schools and institutes in the West that offer certified programs of study in various branches of traditional Chinese medicine, including herbology, acupuncture, nutrition, therapeutic massage, and other courses. The schools listed below offer particularly good programs specializing in the herbal branch of traditional Chinese medicine:

UNITED STATES

American College of Traditional Chinese Medicine, 455 Arkansas Street, San Francisco, CA 94107, Tel. (415) 282-7600

Colorado School of Traditional Chinese Medicine, 1441 York Street, #202, Denver, CO 80206, Tel. (303) 329-6355

New England School of Acupuncture, 30 Common Street, Watertown, MA 02172, Tel. (617) 926-1788

Northwest Institute of Acupuncture, 1307 North 45th Street, #300, Seattle, WA 98103, Tel. (206) 633-2419

Pacific College of Oriental Medicine, 702 W. Washington, San Diego, CA 92103, Tel. (619) 574-6909

Pacific Institute of Oriental Medicine, 915 Broadway, 3rd Floor, New York, NY 10010, Tel. (212) 982-3456

UNITED KINGDOM

The London Academy of Oriental Medicine, 7 Newcourt Street, London NW87AA, Tel. (071) 722-5797

London School of Acupuncture and Traditional Chinese Medicine, 36-37 Featherstone Street, London EC1Y 8QX, Tel. (071) 490-0513

Northern College of Acpuncture, 124 Acomb Road, York
    YO2 4EY, Tel. (0904) 785-120

School of Chinese Herbal Medicine, Administrative Office,
    Midsummer Cottage Clinic, Nether Westcote, Kingham,
    Oxon OX7 6SD, Tel. (0993) 830-957

*For additional information regarding Chinese herbal medicine
in England, you can contact one of the following registers:*

International Register of Oriental Medicine (UK), Green
    Hedges House, Green Hedges Avenue, East Grinstead, West
    Sussex RH19 1DZ

Register of Chinese Herbal Medicine, P.O. Box 400, Wembley,
    Middlesex HA9 9NZ

Register of Traditional Chinese Medicine, 19, Trinity Road,
    London N2 8JJ

AUSTRALIA

There are basically three ways to get a comprehensive educa-
tion in traditional Chinese medicine in Australia: government-
funded university programs; private colleges; and correspondence courses. The best programs currently available are listed
below:

Government-Funded Courses

The first two universities listed below currently offer
courses in acupuncture only, to the Bachelor level, and soon
plan to offer a postgraduate Master's Degree program in Chinese herbal medicine as well. The third institution, R.M.I.T.,
offers a Master of Applied Science degree in traditional Chinese medicine.

University of Technology, Sydney, P.O. Box 123, Broadway,
    NSW 2007, Tel. (02) 330-2500, Fax (02) 281-2267

Victoria University of Technology, P.O. Box 14428, M.M.C.,
    Vic. 3000, Tel. (03) 365-2111, Fax (03) 467-2794

Royal Melbourne Institute of Technology (R.M.I.T.), Plenty
    Road, Bundoora, Vic 3038, Tel. (03) 468-2596, Fax (03)
    467-2794

Private Colleges

The private institutions listed below offer complete courses in traditional Chinese medicine, including herbology.

The Academy of Traditional Chinese Medicine, 96-98 Union Street, Northcote, Vic 3070, Tel. (03) 489-2266, Fax (03) 481-6994

Australian College of Natural Medicine, 362 Water Street, Fortitude Valley, Qld 4006, Tel. (07) 257-1883

Sydney College of Traditional Chinese Medicine, 20 St. Peters Street, St. Peters, NSW, Tel. (015) 437-788

Correspondence Courses:

Cathay (see address in Appendix A)

Chinaherb (see address in Appendix A)

Lifegate, 31 Ada Place, Ultimo, NSW 2007, Tel. (02) 660-7708

APPENDIX C

Recommended Reading

CHINESE HERBAL MEDICINE

Fratkin, Jake. *Chinese Classics: Popular Chinese Herbal Formulas*. Boulder, Colo.: Shya Publications, 1990.

Fratkin, Jake. *Chinese Herbal Patent Formulas*. Boulder, Colo.: Shya Publications, 1986.

Frawley, D. and L. Vasant. *The Yoga of Herbs*. Twin Lakes, Wisc.: Lotus Light, 1986.

Hobbs, Christopher. *Handbook for Herbal Healing: A Concise Guide to Herbal Products*. Capitola, Calif.: Botanica Press, 1990.

Hsu, H. Y. *Commonly Used Chinese Herb Formulas*. Los Angeles: Oriental Healing Arts Institute, 1980.

Hsu, H. Y. *The Way to Good Health with Chinese Herbs*. Los Angeles: Oriental Healing Arts Institute, 1982.

Mowrey, Daniel. *Herbal Tonic Therapies*. New Canaan, Conn.: Keats Publishing, 1983.

Mowrey, Daniel. *The Scientific Validation of Herbal Medicine*. New Canaan, Conn.: Keats Publishing, 1986.

Ramholz, James. *Shaolin and Taoist Herbal Training Formulas*. Chicago: Silk Road Books, 1992.

Reid, Daniel. *Chinese Herbal Medicine*. Boston: Shambhala Publications, 1986.

Teeguarden, Ron. *Chinese Tonic Herbs*. Tokyo: Japan Publications, 1984.

RELATED TOPICS (*CHEE-GUNG,* TAOIST SEXUAL
YOGA, DIET & NUTRITION, INTERNAL
CLEANSING, ETC.)

Colbin, Annemarie. *Food and Healing.* New York: Ballantine, 1986.

Igram, Cass. *Eat Right or Die Young.* Cedar Rapids, Mich.: Literary Visions, 1989.

Jensen, Bernard. *Tissue Cleansing Through Bowel Management.* Escondido, Calif.: Jensen Enterprises, 1981.

Reid, Daniel. *The Complete Book of Chinese Health and Healing: Guarding the Three Treasures.* Boston: Shambhala Publications, 1994.

Reid, Daniel. *The Tao of Health, Sex, and Longevity.* New York: Simon & Schuster, 1989.

Wile, Douglas. *Art of the Bedchamber: The Chinese Sexual Yoga Classics.* Albany: State University of New York Press, 1992.

APPENDIX D

Herbal Formula Ingredients

Listed below are the ingredients for many of the herbal formulas, whole body tonics, washes, ointments, and poultices included in chapter 4, with the Chinese characters for each. Most if not all of the ingredients listed can be ordered from mail-order supply houses using the Western names for Chinese herbs. But if you plan to do your shopping at a Chinese pharmacy, you will find the Chinese characters for the herbs helpful, if not necessary, in obtaining the ingredients you are looking for. Most Chinese pharmacists won't be familiar with the Western names, but you can just point to the Chinese characters listed below in order to obtain the proper ingredients for each formula.

HERBAL FORMULAS

1. Pueraria Decoction

Kudzu vine *(Pueraria)*	葛根	4 grams
Joint fir *(Ephedra)*	麻黃	3 grams
Cinnamon	桂枝	2 grams
Licorice	甘草	2 grams
White peony	芍葯	2 grams
Chinese jujube	大棗	3 grams
Ginger (fresh)	生薑	3 grams

2. Ephedra Decoction

Joint fir *(Ephedra)*	麻黃	5 grams
Almond	杏仁	5 grams
Cinnamon	桂枝	4 grams
Licorice	甘草	1.5 grams

3. *Ephedra, Asarum, Aconitum Decoction*

Joint fir *(Ephedra)*	麻黃	4 grams
Asarum sieboldi	細辛	3 grams
Aconitum fischeri	附子	0.5 gram

4. *Isatis Decoction*

Angelica pubescens (purple)	羌活	6 grams
Isatis tinctoria	板籃根	9 grams
Dandelion	蒲公英	9 grams

5. *Little Green Dragon Decoction*

Joint fir *(Ephedra)*	麻黃	10 grams
Psoralea corylifolia	補骨子	10 grams
Licorice	甘草	6 grams
Asarum sieboldi	細辛	6 grams
Cinnamon	桂枝	10 grams
Almond	杏仁	10 grams
Pinellia ternata	半夏	10 grams
White peony	芍藥	10 grams
Schisandra	五味子	6 grams
Horny goat weed	淫羊藿	10 grams
Balloon flower	桔梗	10 grams
Earthworm	地龍	10 grams

6. *Major Bupleurum (Hare's Ear) Decoction*

Hare's ear *(Bupleurum)*	柴胡	6 grams
Pinellia ternata	半夏	3 grams
Scutellaria macrantha	黃芩	3 grams
White peony	芍藥	3 grams
Chinese jujube	大棗	3 grams
Trifoliate orange	枳實	2 grams
Ginger (fresh)	生薑	4 grams
Rhubarb	大黃	1 gram

7. *Ginseng Decoction*

Ginseng (fresh)	人參	3 grams
Licorice	甘草	3 grams
Atractylis ovata	白朮	3 grams
Ginger (dried)	乾薑	3 grams

8. Moisten Bowel Decoction

Cannabis seeds (roasted)	麻子仁	5 grams
Peach kernels	桃仁	5 grams
Angelica pubescens (purple)	羌活	3 grams
Angelica sinensis	當歸	3 grams
Rhubarb	大黃	3 grams

9. Rhubarb And Licorice Decoction

Rhubarb	大黃	4 grams
Licorice	甘草	1 gram

10. Angelica Restorative Decoction

Angelica sinensis	當歸	4 grams
Cinnamon	桂枝	4 grams
Ginger (fresh)	生薑	4 grams
Chinese jujube	大棗	4 grams
White peony	芍藥	5 grams
Licorice	甘草	2 grams

11. Bupleurum and Artemisia Decoction

White peony	芍藥	24 grams
Artemisia capillaris	茵蔯	18 grams
Atractylodes chinensis	蒼朮	18 grams
Angelica sinensis	當歸	15 grams
Scutellaria macrantha	黃芩	15 grams
Tuckahoe	茯苓	15 grams
Hare's ear *(Bupleurum)*	柴胡	15 grams
Peucedanum decursivum	前胡	15 grams
Panax quinquefolia (American ginseng)	西洋參	6 grams
Licorice	甘草	6 grams

12. Major Bupleurum with Artemisia Decoction

Hare's ear *(Bupleurum)*	柴胡	6 grams
Pinellia ternata	半夏	4 grams
Ginger (fresh)	生薑	4 grams
Scutellaria macrantha	黃芩	3 grams
White peony	芍藥	3 grams
Chinese jujube	大棗	3 grams

Trifoliate orange	枳實	2 grams
Rhubarb	大黄	2 grams
Artemisia capillaris	茵蔯	4 grams
Gardenia florida	梔子	3 grams

13. *Mishmi Bitter Dispel Toxic Heat Decoction*

Mishmi bitter	黄蓮	2 grams
Scutellaria macrantha	黄芩	5 grams
Phellodendron amurense	黄柏	2 grams
Gardenia florida	梔子	2 grams

14. *Laughter Decoction*

Cattail	蒲黄	10 grams
Mastic tree	乳香	12 grams
Balsamodendron myrrha	沒藥	12 grams
Salvia miltiorhiza	丹參	12 grams
Angelica sinensis	當歸	15 grams
Corydalis ambigua	元胡	10 grams
Gynura pinnatifida	三七粉	6 grams

15. *Euodia Decoction*

Euodia rutaecarpa	吳茱萸	3 grams
Ginseng	人參	2 grams
Chinese jujube	大棗	4 grams
Ginger (fresh)	生薑	4 grams

16. *Cinnamon and Ginseng Decoction*

Cinnamon	桂枝	4 grams
Licorice	甘草	3 grams
Atractylis ovata	朮	3 grams
Ginseng	人參	2 grams
Ginger (dried)	乾薑	1 gram

17. *Spleen Restoration Decoction*

Astragalus	黄耆	3 grams
Ginseng	人參	3 grams
Atractylodes macrocephala	白朮	3 grams
Tuckahoe	茯苓	3 grams
Wild chinese jujube	酸棗仁	3 grams

Euphoria longana	龍眼肉	3 grams
Angelica sinensis	當歸	2 grams
Polygala tenuifolia	遠志	2 grams
Chinese jujube	大棗	2 grams
Licorice	甘草	1 gram
Costus	木香	1 gram
Ginger (fresh)	生薑	1.5 grams

18. Five Urinary Drip Decoction

Tuckahoe	茯苓	9 grams
Angelica sinensis	當歸	6 grams
White peony	赤芍	6 grams
Gardenia florida	梔子	6 grams
Licorice	甘草	4 grams

19. Eight Orthodox Powder

Plantain	車前子	10 grams
Akebia quinata	木通	5 grams
Rhubarb	炒梔子	6 grams
Gardenia florida	大黃	6 grams
Magnesium silicate	滑石	12 grams
Licorice	甘草梢	3 grams
Dianthus sinensis	瞿麥	10 grams
Polygonum aviculare	萹蓄	10 grams
Juncus communis	燈心草	1.5 grams

20. Bamboo Leaf and Gypsum Decoction

Bamboo leaves	竹葉	9 grams
Gypsum	石膏	15 grams
Pinellia ternata	半夏	6 grams
Adenophora tetraphylla	沙參	15 grams
Creeping lilyturf	麥門冬	15 grams
Dendrobium nobile	石斛	9 grams
Rehmannia glutinosa	生地黃	12 grams
Licorice	甘草	3 grams
Brown rice	粳米	15 grams

21. Gynura Decoction

Gynura pinnatifida	三七	3 grams
Psoralea corylifolia	補骨脂	12 grams

| Cassia angustifolia | 番瀉葉 | 10 grams |
| Rhubarb | 大黃 | 10 grams |

22. Chinese Cornbind Decoction

Chinese cornbind	首烏	30 grams
Angelica sinensis	當歸	30 grams
Millettia reticulata	雞血藤	30 grams
Tuckahoe	茯苓	20 grams

23. Great Orange Peel Decoction

Citrus reticulata	陳皮	6 grams
Costus	木香	3 grams
Cinnamon	桂枝	3 grams
Morus alba (seeds)	桑枝	15 grams
Clematis minor	威靈仙	6 grams
Cocculus diversifolius	防己	9 grams
Atractylodes macrocephala	白朮	4.5 grams
Tuckahoe	茯苓	9 grams
Alisma plantago	澤瀉	6 grams
Magnesium silicate (talc)	滑石	9 grams
Achyranthes bidentata	牛膝	6 grams
Job's tears	薏以仁	12 grams
Licorice	甘草	3 grams

24. Gastrodia and Uncaria Beverage

Uncaria rhynchophylla	金勾藤	30 grams
Chrysanthemum	菊花	10 grams
Tribulus terrestris	蒺藜	12 grams
Loranthus yadoriki	桑寄生	24 grams
Prunella vulgaris	夏枯草	15 grams
Earthworm	地龍	6 grams
Brown rice	槐米	15 grams
Oyster-shell powder	生牡蠣	30 grams
Pearl powder	珍珠母	30 grams
Costus	木香	15 grams
Eucommia	杜仲	12 grams

25. Trichosanthes, Allium, and Pinellia Decoction

| *Trichosanthes kirilowii* | 瓜蔞 | 15 grams |
| *Allium macrostemon* | 薤白 | 10 grams |

Pinella ternata	制半夏	10 grams
Cattail	蒲黃	10 grams
Trogopterus xanthipes	五靈脂	10 grams

26. *Tonify Yang Eliminate Five Decoction*

Astragalus	黃芪	120 grams
Angelica sinensis	當歸尾	15 grams
Red peony	赤芍	15 grams
Ligusticum wallichii	川芎	10 grams
Earthworm	地龍	10 grams
Peach kernels	桃仁	10 grams
Tibetan saffron	紅花	10 grams

The formula should be used daily for three months. If loss of speech is the major complication, and if the above formula does not correct this problem, the following formula, called "Unlocking Speech Elixir" *(jie yu dan;* 資壽解語丹*)*, may be tried:

Gastrodia elata	天麻	10 grams
Scorpion *(Buthus martensi)*	全蝎	6 grams
Nandina domestica	胆南星	6 grams
Arisaema thunbergii	天竺黃	6 grams
Polygala tenuifolia	遠志	10 grams
Acorus terrestris	菖蒲	10 grams
Curcuma aromatica	郁金	10 grams
Costus	木香	10 grams

27. *Leonurus Eight Precious Decoction*

Angelica sinensis	當歸	10 grams
White peony	白芍	10 grams
Rehmannia glutinosa	熟地黃	15 grams
Ligusticum wallichii	川芎	6 grams
Ginseng	人參	15 grams
Atractylodes macrocephala	白朮	10 grams
Tuckahoe	茯苓	10 grams
Licorice	炙甘草	6 grams
Leonurus	益母草	6 grams
Chinese cornbind	何首烏	10 grams
Chinese wolfberry	枸杞子	6 grams

28. *Harmonize Liver Decoction*

Chinese Yam	炒山葯	15 grams
Angelica sinensis	當歸	10 grams
White peony	白芍	10 grams
Donkey hide glue	阿膠	10 grams
Dogwood tree	山萸肉	10 grams
Morinda root	巴戟	6 grams
Licorice	甘草	6 grams

29. *Enhanced Eliminate and Relax Decoction*

Angelica sinensis	當歸	3 grams
White peony	芍藥	3 grams
Hare's ear	柴胡	3 grams
Thistle type	朮	3 grams
Tuckahoe	茯苓	3 grams
Mint	薄荷	1 gram
Licorice	甘草	2 grams
Tree peony	牡丹皮	2 grams
Gardenia florida	梔子	2 grams
Ginger (dried)	乾薑	1 gram

30. *Angelica and White Peony Decoction*

Angelica sinensis	當歸	3 grams
Ligusticum wallichii	川芎	3 grams
White peony	芍藥	4 grams
Tuckahoe	茯苓	4 grams
Atractylodes macrocephala	白朮	4 grams
Alisma plantago	澤鴻	4 grams

31. *Cinnamon Decoction*

Cinnamon (tender young stems)	桂枝	4 grams
White peony	芍藥	4 grams
Chinese jujube	大棗	4 grams
Ginger (fresh)	生薑	4 grams
Licorice	甘草	2 grams

32. *Two Cure Decoction*

Pinellia ternata	半夏	4 grams
Tuckahoe	茯苓	4 grams

Citrus reticulata	陳皮	4 grams
Licorice	甘草	4 grams
Ginger (fresh)	生薑	2 grams

33. *Gactagogue Elixir*

Codonopsis dangshen	黨參	12 grams
Astragalus	黃芪	10 grams
Angelica sinensis	當歸	10 grams
Creeping lilyturf	麥門冬	10 grams
Balloon flower	桔梗	6 grams
Tetrapanax papyrifera	通草	10 grams

34A. *Assist Nature Elixir*

Rehmannia glutinosa	熟地黃	24 grams
Atractylodes macrocephala	白朮	24 grams
Angelica sinensis	當歸	18 grams
Chinese wolfberry	枸杞	18 grams
Eucommia	炒杜仲	12 grams
Curculigo ensifolia	仙茅	12 grams
Morinda root	巴戟天	12 grams
Dogwood tree	山萸肉	12 grams
Horny goat weed	淫羊藿	12 grams
Broomrape	肉蓯蓉	12 grams
Cnidium monnieri	蛇床子	6 grams
Allium tuberosum (seeds)	炒薤子	12 grams
Cinnamon	肉桂	6 grams
Ginseng	人參	3 grams
Aconitum	制附子	6 grams
Deer horn *(Cervus nippon)*	鹿茸	3 grams

34B. *Five Seed Decoction*

Chinese wolfberry	枸杞子	10 grams
Dodder	菟絲子	10 grams
Schisandra	五味子	10 grams
Raspberry	覆盆子	10 grams
Plantain	車前子	10 grams
Horny goat weed	淫羊藿	10 grams
Atractylodes macrocephala	白朮	10 grams
Tuckahoe	茯苓	10 grams

Citrus reticulata	陳皮	10 grams
Ginseng	人參	6 grams
Licorice	甘草	3 grams
Trigonella foenum-graecum	胡蘆巴	10 grams

35. *Condense Semen Decoction*

Dragon Bones	煅龍骨	15 grams
Oyster shells	煅牡蠣	15 grams
Schisandra	五味子	6 grams
Tuckahoe	茯苓	10 grams
Praying mantis	桑螵蛸	6 grams
Rosa laevigana	煅白石脂	10 grams
Dodder	菟絲子	6 grams
Allium tuberosum (seeds)	韭菜子	6 grams
Foxnut	金櫻子	10 grams
Kaolin (hydrated aluminum silicate)	茨實	10 grams

36. *Kidney Energy Decoction*

Rehmannia glutinosa	熟地黃	20 grams
Chinese yam	山葯	10 grams
Dogwood tree	山萸肉	10 grams
Alisma plantago	澤瀉	6 grams
Tuckahoe	茯苓	6 grams
Tree peony	丹皮	6 grams
Cinnamon	肉桂	3 grams
Achyranthes bidentata	牛七	10 grams
Plantain	車前子	10 grams
Aconitum	制附子	3 grams

WHOLE BODY TONICS

T1. *The Duke of Chou's Centenarian Liquor*

Polygonatum cirrhifolium	黃精	60 grams
Astragalus	黃耆	60 grams
Rehmannia glutinosa	地黃	36 grams
Tuckahoe	茯苓	60 grams
Cinnamon	肉桂	18 grams
Angelica sinensis	當歸	36 grams

Codonopsis dangshen	黨參	30 grams
Creeping lilyturf	麥門冬	30 grams
Atractylodes macrocephala	白朮	30 grams
Chinese wolfberry	枸杞子	30 grams
Citrus reticulata	陳皮	30 grams
Dogwood tree	山茱萸	30 grams
Ligusticum wallichii	川芎	30 grams
Ledebouriella seseloides	防風	30 grams
Chinemys reevesii	龜板	30 grams
Schisandra	五味子	24 grams
Angelica pubescens (purple)	羌活	24 grams

T3. Vermilion Elixir Wine

White Korean ginseng	韓國參	20 grams
Astragalus	黃耆	30 grams
Angelica sinensis	當歸	30 grams
Chinese cornbind	何首烏	15 grams
Atractylodes macrocephala	白朮	30 grams
Eucommia	杜仲	20 grams
Broomrape	肉蓯蓉	30 grams
Rehmannia glutinosa	地黃	30 grams
Chinese yam	山藥	20 grams
Chinese wolfberry	枸杞	20 grams
Achyranthes bidentata	牛七	30 grams
Wild Chinese jujube	酸棗仁	20 grams
Horny goat weed	淫羊藿	30 grams
Ligusticum wallichii	川芎	15 grams
Eleutherococcus gracilistylus	五加皮	30 grams
Lotus seeds	蓮子	15 grams
Polygonatum cirrhifolium	黃精	20 grams
Licorice	甘草	15 grams
Tuckahoe	茯苓	15 grams
Dogwood tree	山茱萸	15 grams
Chinese jujube	大棗	20 grams
Cnidium monnieri	蛇床子	15 grams
Schisandra	五味子	15 grams
Leonurus	益母草	15 grams
Japanese wax privet	女貞子	30 grams
Tibetan saffron	紅花	10 grams

T4. *Ginseng and Rehmannia Pills*

Ginseng	人參	30 grams
Rehmannia glutinosa	地黃	30 grams
Morinda root	巴戟天	30 grams
Broomrape	肉蓯蓉	30 grams
Atractylodes macrocephala	白朮	30 grams
Dodder	菟絲子	30 grams
Chrysanthemum	菊花	30 grams
Eleutherococcus gracilistylus	五加皮	30 grams
Dendrobrium nobile	石斛	30 grams
Thuja orientalis	柏子仁	30 grams

T5. *Kind Mother Decoction*

White Korean ginseng	韓國參	4.5 grams
Astragalus	黃耆	4.5 grams
Rehmannia glutinosa	熟地黃	3.5 grams
Atractylodes macrocephala	白朮	3.5 grams
Donkey hide glue	阿膠	1.5 grams
Dogwood tree	山茱萸	1.5 grams
Cyperus rotundus seeds	香附子	1 gram
Licorice	甘草	1 gram
Sanguisorba officinalis	地榆	1 gram

T6. *Four Essence Pills*

Broomrape	肉蓯蓉	20 grams
Spotted deer horn	鹿茸	20 grams
Tuckahoe	茯苓	20 grams
Chinese yam	山藥	20 grams

HERBAL WASHES

W1. *Cnidium Decoction*

Cnidium monnieri	蛇床子	30 grams
Phellodendron amurense	黃柏	9 grams
Melia toosendan	苦楝子	6 grams
Lycium chinense	枸杞子	15 grams
Alum (aluminium potassium sulfate)	白礬	15 grams

W2. *Cnidium and Licorice Decoction*

Cnidium monnieri	蛇床子	20 grams
Licorice	甘草	12 grams

HERBAL OINTMENT

N1. *Purple Cloud Ointment*

Black sesame seed oil (pure)	純胡麻油	1000 grams
Angelica sinensis	當歸	200 grams
Lithospermum erythrorhizon	紫草	200 grams
Beeswax	蜂腊	380 grams
Lard	乳豬油	25 grams

HERBAL POULTICE

P1. *Dr. Huang's Internal Injury Poultice*

Rhubarb *(Rheum officinale)*	大黃	60 grams
Scutellaria baicalensis	黃芩	60 grams
Phellodendron amurense	黃柏	60 grams
Trichosanthes multiflora (root)	天花	30 grams
Mastic tree	乳香	30 grams
Commiphora myrrha (resin)	沒葯	30 grams
Vitis serianaefolia	白斂	30 grams
Bletilla striata	白芨	30 grams
Angelica anomala	白芷	30 grams
Eleutherococcus gracilistylus	五加皮	30 grams
Gardenia florida (kernels)	山枝子仁	30 grams
Citrus reticulata	陳皮	60 grams
Arisaema consanguineum	制南星	30 grams
Thistle type	蒼朮	60 grams
Clove *(Eugenia caryophyllata)*	丁香	30 grams

GLOSSARY OF
THERAPEUTIC TERMS

ALTERATIVE: restoring normal health and vital functions, particularly by cleansing and purifying the blood

ANAESTHETIC: relieves pain by suppressing sensations transmitted by the central nervous system

ANALGESIC: relieves pain, without suppressing consciousness or other vital functions

ANTHELMINTIC: destroys and expels worms and other parasites from the intestines

ANTIBIOTIC: destroys or inhibits growth of bacteria and other microbes

ANTIDIARRHETIC: controls and prevents diarrhea

ANTIDOTE: counteracts and neutralizes poisons

ANTIDYSENTERIC: controls and prevents dysentery

ANTIEMETIC: stops vomiting

ANTIPHLOGISTIC: counteracts and reduces inflammation

ANTIPYRETIC: reduces fever and dispels heat

ANTIRHEUMATIC: eliminates discomfort and reduces inflammation of rheumatism

ANTISEPTIC: inhibits activity of bacteria, particularly putrefaction

ANTISPASMODIC: relieves or prevents muscle spasms

ANTITUSSIVE: reduces coughing and relieves sore throat

APHRODISIAC: invigorates the sexual organs and increases sexual drive

AROMATIC: containing volatile oils that stimulate vital functions, particularly digestion

ASTRINGENT: contracts tissues and blood vessels to arrest bleeding and other discharges

CARDIOTONIC: strengthens tissues and enhances functions of the heart

CARMINATIVE: expels gas from intestinal tract

CATHARTIC: causes rapid evacuation of the bowels

CHOLAGOGUE: increases the flow of bile

DEMULCENT: soothes and relieves inflammations of the mucous membranes

DEOBSTRUENT: removes internal obstructions

DIAPHORETIC: causes perspiration and increases elimination of wastes through the skin

DIGESTIVE: aids digestion and assimilation

DIURETIC: increases secretions and flow of urine

ELIMINATIVE: removes digestive and other wastes from the body via colon, kidneys, lymph, and skin

EMETIC: causes vomiting

EMMENAGOGUE: stimulates and regulates menstruation

EMOLLIENT: soothes and softens irritated tissues, particularly skin

EXPECTORANT: facilitates discharge of mucus and phlegm from lungs and throat

FEBRIFUGE: abates and reduces fevers

GALACTAGOGUE: stimulates lactation

HEMOSTATIC: stops the flow of blood

IMMUNOTONIC: strengthens immune functions and increases production of immune factors such as hormones, enzymes, and white blood cells

LAXATIVE: promotes bowel movements without radical purging

LEUKORRHEA: A viscous white or yellowish discharge from the vagina caused by inflammation, infection, or congestion of the mucus membranes in the vagina or uterus.

NERVINE: relieves nervous excitement and strengthens functions of the nervous system

NUTRIENT: nourishes body and promotes growth of tissues

OPHTHALMIC: remedy for eye problems

PURGATIVE: induces radical evacuation of the bowels

REFRIGERANT: cools the body and reduces temperature

REJUVENATIVE: prevents degeneration, retards aging, and re-vitalizes the vital organs

SALIVANT: increases secretion of saliva

SECRETAGOGUE: increases secretion of vital bodily fluids

SEDATIVE: calms the body, reduces excitement, and promotes sleep

STIMULANT: increases metabolism, circulation, and other vital functions

STOMACHIC: strengthens stomach functions and facilitates digestion

STYPTIC: arrests bleeding

TONIC: strengthens vital functions, invigorates vital organs, and improves muscle and tissue tone

VASODILATOR: relaxes the blood vessels and promotes circulation

INDEX OF SYMPTOMS
AND AILMENTS

The symptoms and ailments in this index are arranged in alphabetical order, with the corresponding herbs (H) and formulas (F) listed by entry number. Under formulas (F), plain numbers refer to one of the 36 curative internal formulas, the code letter *T* refers to one of the tonics; *W* to an herbal wash, *N* to the ointment, *P* to the poultice, and *HP* to one of the herbal pillows. To avoid confusion, only standard Western medical terms are used in these listings; traditional Chinese terms such as "empty kidney-yang" are not included.

When looking for a recommended remedy for a specific problem, we suggest that you consult all of the entries listed for it; this will help insure that you select the herbs and formulas that most closely fit your requirements. Take note of each herb's full range of therapeutic properties, not just the ones you wish to utilize, and see if any of the other indications apply to your own condition. With a bit of practice, you will soon come to know how your system reacts to various types of herbs under different conditions, and you'll get to know how each herb behaves, both alone and in the company of other herbs.

GENERAL INDEX